BLESSED IS THE KINGDOM

Reflections on the Divine Liturgy of St. John Chrysostom

FR. STAVROS N. AKROTIRIANAKIS

ANCIENT FAITH PUBLISHING
CHESTERTON, INDIANA

Blessed Is the Kingdom: Reflections on the Divine Liturgy of St. John Chrysostom

Published by:
Ancient Faith Publishing
A Division of Ancient Faith Ministries
1050 Broadway, Suite 6
Chesterton, IN 46304

Some liturgical translations are by Fr. Seraphim Dedes, used with permission. Others are taken from *Greek Orthodox Holy Week and Easter Services,* compiled and translated by Fr. George L. Papadeas, published by Patmos Press, South Daytona, Florida, 1996 edition.

Quotations from the Divine Liturgy come from *The Divine Liturgy of St. John Chrysostom,* translated by the faculty of Holy Cross Greek Orthodox School of Theology (Brookline, MA: Holy Cross Orthodox Press, 1985) and *The Divine Liturgy of Our Father Among the Saints Basil the Great,* translated by the faculty of the Holy Cross Greek Orthodox School of Theology (Brookline, MA: Holy Cross Orthodox Press, 1988). Used with permission.

Front cover icon licensed from iStock: PaoloGaetano
Stock photo ID: 480132648

ISBN: 978-1-955890-68-7

Library of Congress Control Number: 2024938581

To the three clergymen who have inspired
my love of the Divine Liturgy:

His Eminence Metropolitan Methodios of Boston
Fr. John Zanetos (of blessed memory)
Fr. James T. Adams (of blessed memory)

Table of Contents

Preparing for Worship

The Liturgy of the Word

The Liturgy of the Faithful

Acknowledgments

In February 2015, a parishioner approached me with an idea about creating a prayer team of parishioners who would commit to praying for the church and for me on a daily basis during the upcoming Lenten period. I have always enjoyed writing and decided that I would write a daily reflection and send it to whoever joined the prayer team. I had hoped that thirty people would participate, and my intention was to do this for forty days. Over 150 people joined the prayer team, and as Lent came to an end, they asked me if I would continue the daily reflections. So I did.

Now, many years into this practice, I write on various topics related to prayer, the Orthodox Faith, and the Christian life. This is the ninth book that has come out of the daily reflections of the prayer team.

I wish to thank those who have helped and encouraged me in this project:

His Eminence Metropolitan Alexios of Atlanta, of the Greek Orthodox Archdiocese of America, for his prayers and blessings.

The three liturgical mentors to whom this book is dedicated: His Eminence Metropolitan Methodios of Boston, Fr. John Zanetos (of blessed memory), and Fr. James T. Adams (of blessed memory)—who modeled solid liturgics for me and, more importantly, gave me a love for the divine services of our Church.

Father Aris Metrakos, my spiritual father, mentor, coworker, and friend, who graciously consented to write the foreword for this book.

Ancient Faith Publishing for offering me a chance to publish this book under their name: to Melinda Johnson for signing off on this project; to Donna Ryan for coordinating this project; to Lynnette Horner and Deacon Irenaios Anderson for their invaluable help in painstakingly editing the manuscript.

The many parishioners of St. John the Baptist Greek Orthodox Church in Tampa, Florida, for their support of the prayer team and encouragement to move forward with this project.

All the members of the prayer team for reading my reflections, for your prayers, and for your encouragement.

The Orthodox Christian Network (OCN) for posting my writings.

Father Seraphim Dedes for his permission to use his translations of the liturgical services.

The family of the late Fr. George Papadeas at Patmos Press for permission to use his translations of the liturgical services.

His Grace Bishop Athenagoras of Nazianzos for helping me secure permission from the Greek Orthodox Archdiocese of America to use their translation of the liturgical services.

My parents, Nicholas and Barbara (of blessed memory), for taking me to church faithfully, for encouraging me to serve in the altar, and for helping me to develop my writing skills.

My son, Nicholas, who already enjoys writing, for his unconditional love and for the beautiful stories he tells.

My wife, Lisa, for her support of my ministry, for the many sacrifices she makes for our family, and for her encouragement to write.

Finally, and most especially, I thank the Lord for the great blessing to serve as a Greek Orthodox priest, for His grace to stand before the holy altar and celebrate the Divine Liturgy, and for giving me a talent to write and a desire to share that gift through this project. I am thankful for the continued inspiration He provides and for this blessing He has given me to share my thoughts on the Divine Liturgy of St. John Chrysostom.

> *For every good and perfect gift is from Above, coming down from You, the Father of Lights.*
>
> —From the Divine Liturgy of St. John Chrysostom, adapted from James 1:17

Foreword

When I was at seminary, there was a rite of passage in the final year called the "senior interview." The student sat at a conference table with the assembled members of the faculty, each of whom came armed with questions intended to determine the candidate's worthiness for graduation and ordination. One of my professors challenged me with the following: "A person asks you, 'What does it mean to be an Orthodox Christian?' You have only one sentence in which to answer. What would you say?"

My response came without hesitation: "Come to Divine Liturgy."

They allowed me to graduate, so I guess they liked my answer. Regardless, decades later I would not change one word of my response. I remain convinced that the Divine Liturgy defines us as Orthodox Christians.

In the Liturgy, we gather as the Body of Christ. No one can follow the Way in isolation. It is only in our relationships with one another that we live as Christians. To be an Orthodox Christian is to stand in fellowship with one's brothers and sisters while giving glory to the Triune God.

The Divine Liturgy proclaims the centrality of Holy Scripture to the Faith and challenges all who have ears to hear to be attentive to the words of the Bible, internalize their message, and apply their teachings to their own lives. Not only is there a prescribed set of readings for each day of the ecclesiastical year, but the petitions, prayers, and hymns of the service are explications, explanations, and direct or paraphrased quotations of the Bible.

The Divine Liturgy is in a certain sense a classroom. The homily teaches, inspires, and encourages the worshipper. At the same time, the *gestalt* of the otherworldly physical surroundings, beautiful music, and sweet-smelling incense reminds us that indeed the Kingdom of God is at hand. Spending time in this ethereal classroom equips us to lead a life that is holy, peaceful, blameless, and sinless, and to proclaim to the world that we have seen the Light.

Above all, the Divine Liturgy comprises our alpha and omega as Orthodox Christians, for this service is our eucharistic celebration. Receiving the Body and Blood of Christ is the central and defining act of Orthodox Christianity. The notes that I took when studying liturgical theology in the 1980s capture these words of Fr. Alkiviades Calivas:

> In the Eucharist we share in the most intimate fashion in the life of Christ. It is the essential and characteristic worship of the Church. It is where we become over and over again the Body of Christ. It is connected to all of the sacraments, showing all the sacraments to be corporate in nature.

Once we embrace the crucial and essential role that the Divine Liturgy plays in the life of the Church and the salvation of the believer, it is reasonable to ask ourselves how we should embark on the process of learning more about the Liturgy.

The Liturgy can and should be studied historically. Without this perspective, we run the risk of treating our worship the way some Christians treat the Bible: one day it dropped out of the sky in its current form, wrapped in a plastic bag. Our central service has a history. We presuppose that the first liturgies consisted of synagogue worship combined with the Eucharist and readings from the books that would become the New Testament. Scholars seem confident that once the Liturgy was formalized, it began with the faithful and clergy assembling outside the church, proceeding in together, and commencing worship with the reading of Scripture, not with people trickling in long after the clergy have begun the service in quasi-isolation.

At the same time, focusing too heavily on history can tempt us to become card-holding members of an ecclesiastical museum who are occasionally allowed limited access. The Church has a history, but she is not a museum. The Body of Christ is not cast in stone. She is alive and at work in the hearts of all who have put on Christ and received the seal of the gift of the Holy Spirit.

We can pull apart the Liturgy as students do with a cadaver in anatomy class. We can separate and then dissect this magnificent service. We can know each part's nomenclature, function, etiology, and teleology, but there is a limit to the utility of this approach. The dismembered body on the autopsy table is a vague and distorted shadow of the beauty of the human form as captured by Michelangelo's *David*.

Knowing all the fixed and moveable parts of the Divine Liturgy and their order can be just as diminishing to our appreciation of the beauty of Orthodox worship. In our earnestness to become liturgical experts, we run the risk of reducing this life-changing experience—which is, to be sure, inordinately greater than the sum of its parts—to a disembodied collection of words and music.

Even worse, the well-intentioned person who becomes liturgically pedantic can degenerate into a critic who is liturgically pharisaic. After all, if I come to church straining to make sure that the correct antiphonal verses are being chanted, wringing my hands when the chanter reads the incorrect epistle, and rolling my eyes when the choir sings a hymn out of order, I am not so different from the pathologist who laments over the arteriosclerosis of a forty-something killed in an automobile accident.

To understand the most efficacious approach to the study of the Divine Liturgy and the internalization and application of this experience, it is useful to take a detour into some of the theory that shapes the way we develop and design religious education classes, retreats, and camp curricula.

Learning can be approached cognitively or affectively. Cognitive learning happens on the left side of the brain. It is the business of apprehending stuff: multiplication tables, dates in history, verb conjugations in a foreign language. Affective learning is tied to our emotions, or, as Orthodox Christians would say, the heart.

Our job as religious educators is not so much to impart information but to change the heart. As such, we design lessons wherein we avoid lecturing and spend more time asking people to consider how the material to which they are being exposed makes them feel.

There is a wonderful, positive symbiosis between cognitive and affective learning. When we present a piece of information and then challenge the student to identify an emotion associated with this lesson, he or she is more likely to retain and apply the concrete material that has been presented. In this process, we both transform the heart and inform the mind.

This is the beauty of this volume's approach to the Divine Liturgy. Each section of the service is identified and analyzed but from the perspective of how a specific part of Liturgy has the potential to change our hearts and direct our lives. The ideas and reflections resonate with our emotional longing for God, making us eager both to read the next chapter and participate in the next Divine Liturgy.

By approaching the Divine Liturgy this way, Fr. Stavros not only touches our hearts but avoids petrifying the Liturgy into a museum piece or distorting this defining act of worship into a series of parts. The author reminds us again and again that participation in this eucharistic celebration revitalizes us. The Liturgy is alive because Christ is alive and in our midst. The reader will soon discover that

Fr. Stavros approaches his role as liturgist with the fear of God, faith, and with love.

Consequently, far from dissecting the Liturgy as a coroner would, Fr. Stavros joins each section to the next with his own love for Christ and His people and the firm conviction that the Kingdom of God is at hand.

Every time we gather for the Divine Liturgy, we join one another in a passage from the mundane to the ethereal, the worldly to the heavenly, and the temporal to the eternal. This beautiful collection of reflections serves both to illuminate and guide us in that journey.

Fr. Aris P. Metrakos
Proistamenos, Holy Trinity Greek Orthodox Church
San Francisco, CA

Introduction

"Where do you find this stuff in Scripture?"

I have been asked this question many times by non-Orthodox people who have attended the Divine Liturgy at the Greek Orthodox church where I serve.

The simple answer is that nowhere in the Bible will you find references to pews, pulpits, or church architecture. Some people worship in an A-frame church building with pews and a pulpit in the center, where there are ten minutes of praise music and a forty-five-minute sermon, and they claim to be practicing *sola scriptura*, "Scripture alone," meaning that whatever they are doing is found in Scripture. But this is not true.

Of course, it is true that the Bible doesn't mention chalices and patens, icons and icon screens, and that there are no references to a Small Entrance or a Great Entrance. However, virtually every line of the Divine Liturgy has a scriptural basis. This is why each reflection in this book begins with a passage of Scripture that is related to the line of the Liturgy that is being discussed.

The Liturgy of St. John Chrysostom

Saint James the Apostle authored the first eucharistic service of the early Christian Church in about AD 70. Saint Basil the Great then edited the work of St. James into what is today known as the

Divine Liturgy of St. Basil the Great, which is celebrated ten times per year: on the Sundays of Lent, Holy Thursday, Holy Saturday, Eve of Nativity, Eve of Theophany, and on January 1 (the Feast of St. Basil). Saint John Chrysostom further edited the Divine Liturgy of St. Basil the Great, and his shorter version is the Divine Liturgy that we celebrate on most Sundays and feast days of the church year. Unless otherwise noted, the reflections in this book are drawn from the 2015 translation of the Divine Liturgy of St. John Chrysostom, approved by the Ecumenical Patriarchate for use by the Greek Orthodox Archdiocese of America (GOA). All references and quotes from the Divine Liturgy of St. Basil the Great are from the GOA's 1988 edition.

If you attend the Divine Liturgy in a parish of another jurisdiction—such as Antiochian, Orthodox Church in America, Serbian, etc.—you will find that some translations differ. There are also a few changes in rubrics, and in some circumstances, small additions or deletions in content. However, the structure and meaning of the Liturgy is the same throughout the world.

A Note on Scripture Translation

Unless otherwise noted, all Scripture quotations are from the Revised Standard Version (RSV) translation of the Bible. In the GOA, this is the translation from which we read the epistle and Gospel passages at divine services.

A Note on the Numbering of the Psalms

The Orthodox Church primarily uses translations from the Greek version of the Old Testament, known as the Septuagint, rather than translations from the Hebrew editions. The Septuagint (also known as the LXX) is the version of the Old Testament used in many quotations found in the New Testament, and the numbering of the psalms in the Septuagint differs from that found in Psalters and Bibles translated from the Hebrew. For example, one of the most prevalent psalms in Orthodox worship is Psalm 50 (in the Greek numbering). In Hebrew numbering—the numbering used in most translations of the Bible—it is Psalm 51. In these reflections, when a psalm is titled Psalm 50/51, the "50" refers to the Greek numbering, and the "51" refers to the Hebrew numbering.

The Purpose of This Book

> [Jesus] said, "To you it has been given to know the secrets of the kingdom of God; but for others they are in parables, so that seeing they may not see, and hearing they may not understand."
>
> —Luke 8:10, referring to earlier prophecy of Isaiah 6:9

This book is not a theological book, though it contains some theology. It is also not a history book, though it contains some history. I wrote this book to help readers understand what they should be doing and thinking while the Divine Liturgy is being offered and to assist them in praying the Liturgy.

I am neither a scholar nor a theologian but rather a parish priest who loves to celebrate the Divine Liturgy. I've loved the Liturgy for as long as I can remember. The first thing I loved was not the words or their meaning; I was in love with the rituals. I loved the vestments, the vessels, the sights, and the sounds. I still like these things. But rituals are not enough to sustain anyone's interest, even a priest's. There is a meaning and purpose behind every ritual and behind every phrase and action of the Divine Liturgy. Each is designed to draw the mind, the heart, and the soul to certain thoughts and prayers. Some are corporate thoughts—when the priest prays for peace in the world, we are all supposed to be thinking of the same thing. But when he prays for forgiveness of sins, we can call to mind our own sins.

For too many years I have stood at the altar and watched people witness the Divine Liturgy without being real participants in it. Perhaps this is why Orthodox Christians are perpetually late or miss the service altogether. After all, it is just a ritual that will be repeated virtually the same way next week, right? Yet when we examine the petitions and actions of the Divine Liturgy, we realize that each one calls us to participate. The word *liturgy* comes from two Greek words—*leitos*, meaning "people," and *ergon*, meaning "work." Liturgy literally means "the work of the people" and implies that worship is a divine work for all of us. Whether by offering a response—note that every Liturgy book says "people" next to each response, not "choir" or "chanter"—or by joining our prayers with the prayers of the service, the faithful in attendance indeed have a lot of work do.

When we come to worship and truly do the work of the people, when we pray the service, it becomes more than a ritual; it becomes alive, and we feel as though we belong to the Divine Liturgy, and the Divine Liturgy belongs to us.

The Liturgy is a parable. To the untrained eye and the unopened heart, it is a ritual involving a man in robes, a choir, altar servers, processions, incense, and candles. As Christ said in His reference to Isaiah, one can see but not see, hear but not understand. However, to the one whose heart is open, whose eye is trained, and who yearns to experience God, the Liturgy opens the gates to the Kingdom of heaven and allows the most ordinary of people to leave the world for an hour or so each week and enter heaven for a short time.

The purpose of this book is not to take the mystery out of the service but to help you understand and appreciate the mystery that unfolds before you each time the Liturgy is celebrated. It is said that knowledge is power. This book will arm you with the knowledge of how to pray the Divine Liturgy so that it will become more powerful and meaningful in your life.

Format

The format of the book is this: each line and hymn of the Divine Liturgy will be examined. Since most of the Liturgy is taken either directly or tangentially from Scripture, a Scripture passage will follow each petition or liturgical hymn. The reflection will then discuss how to pray that petition or hymn.

I love serving the Divine Liturgy. I've loved it my whole life. But it's only in more recent years that I've come to love *praying* the Liturgy. It is my fervent hope that these reflections will help you to love the Divine Liturgy even more and understand how to pray it each time you attend.

—Fr. Stavros Akrotirianakis
February 2024
Tampa, Florida

Preparing for Worship

Why It's Necessary to Go to Church & Participate in Worship

For where two or three are gathered in my name, there am I in the midst of them.

—Matthew 18:20

Is it necessary to go to church? The simple answer to this question is yes. My explanation for this answer, however, will not come from theology or Scripture. I'm going to share this answer from a personal experience of not going to church.

The parish where I serve offers a live stream of services for those who are unable to attend, such as people who are shut-ins or who are sick. Some people live in areas of the country—or the world—who don't have access to Orthodox churches and who worship via live stream. There was a blizzard in New York one week, and hundreds of people who couldn't get out of their houses tuned into our services.

On one Sunday, even I tuned in.

I was recuperating from surgery the previous week and unable to attend church. Sunday morning came, and I decided I was going to watch the live stream—partly out of curiosity about what was going on in my absence, but mostly because it was Sunday morning. What else was I going to do besides the Divine Liturgy—read the paper, watch sports? Sunday is the day we honor the Lord through worship, so I decided to experience worship in the best way I could.

I sat on my recliner and watched. I was home alone, as my family had gone to church. When the priest read the Gospel, I made myself get up and stand. When the people recited the Creed, I stood up and recited it as well. The rest of the time, I lay down.

I learned two lessons through this experience.

The first thing I learned is that without participating, the Liturgy didn't grab me. I wasn't really participating at home—I was just watching. I said to myself, "I'm so glad that I'm the celebrant on Sundays because I get to participate." Of course, one doesn't need to be a priest, serve in the altar, or sing in the choir to participate, but you do need to put something into worship in order to get something out of it. I didn't get much out of the live-stream experience because I didn't put much into it. And it's not something I would choose to watch Sunday after Sunday.

The second lesson I learned is that watching the Liturgy by myself didn't really feel like church. I felt isolated. At one point, I confess, I even texted with another parishioner who was also home that week recovering from surgery. We both commented on how weird it felt to be watching the service alone. At the end of our exchange, we both texted, "Thanks for *going to church* with me today."

The church is the people. The people who stand together, who pray together, who *are* together.

I watched the Liturgy alone, and I didn't receive Communion because there was no priest in my living room to offer it to me. I experienced worship, but I didn't receive Christ in the Holy Eucharist—which is the centerpiece, climax, and purpose of the Divine Liturgy.

Why is it necessary to go to church? Because this is where we commune with Christ, and this is where we stand with others who are experiencing the same journey, the same struggle.

Why is it necessary to participate? Because merely watching the same thing over and over again quickly causes us to lose interest. But participating in worship, on deeper and deeper levels, only piques our interest more.

A General Service to Fit Every Specific Need

> And my God will supply every need of yours according to his riches in glory in Christ Jesus.
>
> —Philippians 4:19

As I was writing the middle chapters of this book in September 2017, Hurricane Irma struck the state of Florida and much of the southeastern United States. My family and I had left our home a couple of days beforehand, not knowing whether we'd have a home to return to. Prior to leaving, my staff members and I packed up the church and wondered what we'd find of our sanctuary after the storm had passed. Fortunately for our community and my family, the damage was minimal. Because of the hurricane, our parish missed one Sunday service. When the storm had passed, I decided that we should celebrate the Divine Liturgy on a Tuesday evening to thank God for protecting us and to ask for His help in the recovery efforts for our city, state, and region.

As we were celebrating the Liturgy, I found my mind focusing on very specific things related to the storm as I prayed the service. As we prayed "For this holy house," I thought about how grateful I was that our church was spared. "For favorable weather" took on a whole new meaning as I prayed for no more hurricanes to come our way. "For those who travel" made me think of the many people who had evacuated and were still trying to make their way home. "For our deliverance from all affliction, wrath, danger, and necessity" brought to mind the people who were in need of all these things.

I'm sharing this because we often think of the Divine Liturgy as a generic service. It doesn't mention specific names or needs. However, our unique concerns—in this case, the recovery from Hurricane Irma—can be wrapped into the text of the service. In other words, we can celebrate the Liturgy and always fit our own needs into its general prayers.

The Divine Liturgy speaks to any circumstance in life—recovery from a hurricane, a serious illness, anxiety, doubt, even joy and contentment. This is what makes the service so beautiful and timeless. The same prayers and petitions can be offered time and time again, but they can be heard in different ways by different people because we can bring specific needs to mind as we offer these prayers. The Divine Liturgy was a lot more meaningful to me the day after a hurricane because my mind was focused on the words of the service and how they related to our immediate situation. If you bring to mind the issues related to your life and your personal situation as you participate in the Liturgy, you will find new ways to get more out of this beautiful service.

We Come to Celebrate— A Spiritual Glendi

> Let us, therefore, celebrate the festival, not with the old leaven, the leaven of malice and evil, but with the unleavened bread of sincerity and truth.
>
> —1 Corinthians 5:8

When we gather for the Divine Liturgy, the proper verb used for the service we are offering is "celebrate." We *celebrate* the Divine Liturgy. The priest (or bishop) presiding over the service is called the celebrant. Any other clergy members present are called the concelebrants.

The use of the word *celebrate* is intentional. Think of the times we use this word in our lives: We celebrate birthdays and holidays. We don't "offer" them or "mark" them. We celebrate them. We have parties. We experience great anticipation for them. We put on our best clothes. We clean our houses. We decorate. This is how we should approach each Divine Liturgy—as a celebration. This is why we put on our best Sunday clothes, why we should go to bed at a reasonable hour the night before, why we should arrive on time or early, and why we should come with joy. For what greater celebration can there be than worshiping Christ and receiving Him?

One hierarch of the Church once described the Divine Liturgy as a "spiritual *glendi*." *Glendi* is a Greek word that describes a party that lasts for hours—where we eat and talk and laugh and dance, and no one is in any rush to leave. The Divine Liturgy should be like this: we partake of Communion, we sing—in some liturgical traditions like in Africa, the parishioners actually dance—and no one is in any rush to leave.

When people arrive late or don't participate, when the service feels stale, it is hard to see it as a celebration. However, when people come with enthusiasm, when they participate and understand, the character of the service changes to the celebration that the Lord intends for us to have with Him each time we gather for the Divine Liturgy.

The Liturgy of the Word

It Is Time to Serve the Lord

Glory to God in the highest, and on earth peace among men with whom he is pleased!

—Luke 2:14

Just about anything significant in life requires preparation. Thus, before we begin the Divine Liturgy, before we call down the Holy Spirit upon ourselves and our Gifts, before we step forward to receive Holy Communion and have an intimate encounter with Christ, we make significant preparation. This sets the stage for us to enter into the Kingdom of God and reminds us why we are here and what we are doing.

Before the Divine Liturgy begins, the celebrant priest offers a series of prayers. First, he prays the Kairos—a short, private service where he asks God to enable him to celebrate the Liturgy. Praying the Kairos is an act of leaving humankind's time and entering God's time (*kairos*), of leaving the world and temporarily entering God's Kingdom.

Next, he offers a prayer as he puts on each article of his vestments. Once he is vested, the priest celebrates the service of the Proskomide, or the preparation of the bread and wine that will become Holy Communion. The Kairos, vesting, and Proskomide usually take place before the Matins (Orthros) service, which usually precedes the Divine Liturgy.[1] The Matins service concludes with the singing of the doxology.

As the doxology is about to conclude, the priest offers a series of prayers that are set in motion by a prompt, usually from the deacon:

It is time to serve the Lord.

Imagine if this were your mantra every morning when you woke up—if the first words out of your mouth and in your mind were, "It is time to serve the Lord." Imagine if you said that as you sat at your desk at work to begin the day. Any time is a good time to serve the Lord.

The priest begins his final preparation for the Divine Liturgy with an exclamation that is the beginning of every service in the Church, a statement blessing God:

Blessed is our God, always, now and forever and to the ages of ages. Amen.

Because before we do anything, we invoke the name of God.

And next is a more specific prayer, this one to the Holy Spirit. It is the Holy Spirit who effects all the sacraments. It is the Holy Spirit who will be called upon during the Divine Liturgy to transform bread and wine into the Body and Blood of Christ. The grace of the Holy Spirit is what looses and forgives sins in the Sacrament of Confession. His grace consecrates a wedding, blesses the waters of baptism, and blesses the oil of holy unction. The grace of the Holy Spirit is imparted through holy chrismation. The grace of the Holy

1 In Slavic traditions, the Matins service often occurs at night, grouped with Vespers in a form of Vigil.

Spirit heals what is infirm and completes what is lacking in each person, and it allows a man to be ordained into the holy priesthood to celebrate the divine services. Thus, the first prayer of the Divine Liturgy, which occurs before the first audible words of the service, is a prayer to the Holy Spirit. This prayer begins many of our services, and is generally used at the beginning of our prayers to call the Holy Spirit down to be present with us:

Glory to You, our God, glory to You.

Heavenly King, Comforter, the Spirit of Truth, present in all places and filling all things, treasury of blessings and Giver of Life, come and abide in us, cleanse us from every stain, and save our souls, O Gracious One.

On a personal and practical level, any Christian can use this prayer to the Holy Spirit as a part of daily prayers. When we gather in our parishes, particularly for meetings and decision-making events, this is the most appropriate prayer, asking the Holy Spirit to shower us with His wisdom.

The Good News of the Nativity of Christ was shared with the shepherds at Bethlehem through a hymn of the heavenly host, which is also offered before the Divine Liturgy begins:

Glory to God in the highest, and on earth peace among men with whom He is pleased. (Luke 2:14)

Note that this prayer does not say "on earth, peace, good will to *all* men." Peace is a gift to those who are of good will, who are doing what is pleasing to God. This is a reminder to us to be people who seek to please the Lord and in return are given the grace to experience the peace of God.

Lord, open my lips and my mouth shall show forth Your praise. (Ps. 50/51:15)

The priest in front of the holy altar also offers this prayer as the Divine Liturgy begins. It, too, is another short prayer that can be uttered by clergy and laity alike, within the service and outside of it. We should pray this before speeches, meetings, and difficult conversations. If the Lord is in control of our lips—the part of us that gets us in the most trouble—and our lips seek to show forth God's praises, then our lives will be more God centered, peaceful, and successful. This is a good prayer to utter multiple times a day.

As the Divine Liturgy is about to begin, the priest prays the following words as a reminder to him and to all of us that our church is not just a building in our city but the temple of God's glory:

Standing in the temple of your glory, we feel as though we are in heaven, O Theotokos. Open to us the gate of your mercy and salvation.

We are not standing merely in our town; we are standing temporarily in heaven itself. This prayer is addressed to the Theotokos, who looks down on our congregation from the icon over the altar known as the *Platytera* (Greek for "wider" or "more spacious"). She is the bridge from earth to heaven and is our spiritual mother. So, we ask her to open the gate of mercy and salvation to us.

I will close this first reflection with the prayer that the priest offers as he prays Kairos before the Divine Liturgy, laying aside all worldly cares so that we may receive the King of all. It is a prayer of disengagement from everything and everyone, an act of putting our focus on the most important thing we do in this life: partaking of the Holy Eucharist, in preparation for eternal life.

Lord, Lord, stretch forth Your hand from Your Holy Dwelling place on High and strengthen me for the forthcoming service, that I may stand without condemnation before Your awesome judgment seat and celebrate Your sacrifice which is without blood. For Yours is the power and the glory to the ages of ages. Amen.[2]

2 From *The Order of the Divine and Holy Liturgy* (Brookline, MA: Holy Cross Orthodox Press, 1987), 6–7.

The Great Litany

Blessed is the Kingdom of the Father and of the Son and of the Holy Spirit, now and forever and to the ages of ages.

> Now after John was arrested, Jesus came into Galilee, preaching the gospel of God, and saying, "The time is fulfilled, and the Kingdom of God is at hand; repent, and believe in the gospel."
>
> —Mark 1:14–15

The most important word of the Divine Liturgy is found in the first line of the service. It is the word *now.* Why is that so important? Because most people think of the Kingdom of God in either past or future tense but not as a present reality. We think back to God creating the world and to the ministry of Christ. We think to the future and what it will be like when and if we are allowed to enter the Kingdom of God. We tend not to think of the Kingdom in the present. And yet, when Christ came to earth, He said in several places, "The kingdom of heaven is at hand" (see Matt. 3:2; 4:17; 10:7). The Kingdom was obviously present in the Person of Jesus Christ, who came to earth two thousand years ago. And it is continually present in the celebration of the Holy Eucharist.

In instituting the Eucharist, Jesus took bread and said, "This is my body," and he took the cup and said, "This is my blood" (Matt.

26:26–28). By receiving His Body and Blood, we are united with the Kingdom of God. Christ is present in our midst and in us. So, the beginning line of the Divine Liturgy is an invitation to this banquet. It is an invitation to be present with Christ, right here and right now. We hope to enter His Kingdom and live there forever. But forever can seem like a long time in the future. Through the Divine Liturgy, we enter the Kingdom *now*.

The call to the Divine Liturgy is also a call to leave the world temporarily. Time stops; we do not measure it in minutes and seconds. We transcend time, and we transcend our roles in life: we cease to be teachers or spouses or parents or doctors, and we stand as children in the presence of our Father. We leave our home, our jobs, and our cities, and we enter into God's Kingdom, God's world.

Orthodox church sanctuaries are intentionally ornate because they are built to resemble heaven on earth. On the walls of the church we see the saints and angels. In the dome, we see the icon of our Lord Jesus Christ, the Savior of all, looking down upon us. The church sanctuary is a dedicated space used only for worshiping God. It is not used for social functions or other events. The furnishings of the altar are made with precious metals because they hold the most precious things—the Word of God in the Gospel and Christ Himself in Holy Communion.

From the outset of the Liturgy, we acknowledge the Trinity—the Father, the Son, and the Holy Spirit. We acknowledge the divinity of the Trinity, calling the Trinity "blessed." We acknowledge the power of God when we refer to His Kingdom. We acknowledge that God is timeless when we speak of His Kingdom now and forever and to the ages of ages. And we speak of the Kingdom as a present reality through the word *now*. That's why it's important to arrive on time for the Divine Liturgy—because the first line is actually the most important one. It is God's invitation to us to leave our lives, our world, our stresses, and our challenges, and to enter into His Kingdom.

Amen!

> "Blessed be the LORD, the God of Israel, from everlasting to everlasting!" Then all the people said, "Amen!" and praised the LORD.
>
> —1 Chronicles 16:36

The word *amen* means "let it be so." "Amen" is offered at the end of every prayer, in public and in private. In the context of worship, the priest leads the prayer of the Divine Liturgy—or prayers to bless food, to bless a house, in confession, at a wedding, etc. But the "amen" always belongs to the people. That is because the people play an integral part in worship. As the priest prays to God, the people complete the prayer with the "amen," asking God that what was offered in prayer may come to pass. Many times Scripture refers to all the people saying "Amen" and praising the Lord (see 1 Chron. 16:36; Neh. 5:13; Rom. 11:36, 15:33 and elsewhere).

The opening line of the Divine Liturgy, which we addressed in the previous reflection, invites people into the blessed Kingdom of the Father and the Son and the Holy Spirit now and forever and to the ages of ages. The response of the people is "Amen"—the first of numerous "amens" that the faithful will offer during the Divine Liturgy.

Let it be so.

In peace, let us pray to the Lord.

> Depart from evil, and do good; / seek peace, and pursue it. / The eyes of the Lord are toward the righteous, / and his ears toward their cry.
>
> —Psalm 33/34:14–15

After the announcement in the beginning of the Divine Liturgy that the Kingdom of God is now present, we begin our corporate worship by entering into prayer together. And the first prayer of the Liturgy—and most other services—is a prayer for peace. After all, how can we pray effectively if we are not at peace—with God, with others, and with ourselves?

One really important ingredient in praying, whether in a corporate worship setting or alone, is to be in peace. Yes, it is possible to pray while driving, or jogging, or moving, but we should also have times when we are physically at peace and still so that we can communicate with God. What does it say to God if we can pray only while in motion? It says that prayer can only be part of multitasking—never a primary pursuit. We must schedule some time where prayer is the only "task" we are engaging in. Learning to sit in peace—even with distractions, even with a list of tasks waiting for us—is a challenge, for sure.

Peace is so important and integral to prayer and worship that in the Divine Liturgy, the word *peace* appears more than twenty times. Peace is in this first prayer and also in the last prayer of the service, so that we begin and end whatever we are doing in peace. This should be the goal of every task—beginning the day, beginning the workday: to begin and end in peace.

Finally, with the exception of the Creed and the Communion prayers, the Divine Liturgy is an act of corporate worship. It is not "me" praying but "us." Hence, we repeatedly hear "let *us* pray to the

Lord." And so as we pray for peace for ourselves as individuals, we also pray that those around us will have peace as well.

Lord, have mercy.

> Have mercy on us, O Lord, have mercy on us, / for we have had more than enough of contempt.
>
> —Psalm 122/123:3

The Divine Liturgy begins with a set of several petitions called the Great Litany, which ends with a prayer to the Holy Trinity. The response to the end of the litany is "Amen," but the response to each of the petitions is "Lord, have mercy."

Mercy refers to offering a gift to someone who doesn't deserve it. For instance, how many times in movies have we seen a king or a ruler spare someone's life as an act of mercy? When we think about the sinful state of humanity—or when I think even of my own sinful state—I wonder, *What business do I have to be asking anything of God? What motivation does He have to grant whatever I am so unworthily asking of Him?*

The answer is mercy. His mercy is the only reason that we dare ask. His mercy is why He answers.

In Psalm 102/103:8 we read, "The Lord is merciful and gracious, / slow to anger and abounding in steadfast love." So, because of His grace and love, we ask the Lord to have mercy and to grant the petitions we are bringing before Him. In this first sequence, "In peace, let us pray to the Lord" and the response "Lord, have mercy," I sometimes think the following: *I am a sinful person, and this past week I have taken peace from many people. Yet I come to You, Lord, asking for peace. I don't deserve peace. But have mercy on me and bring me peace anyway.* The same goes for the other petitions. How can we dare ask the Almighty God for anything? Because we know that He is full of mercy and that He answers prayer. So, when the priest offers the prayer for peace and we answer "Lord, have mercy," we are essentially saying, "Lord, have mercy on us and bring us peace."

Another thought about mercy comes from one of the prayers of the Sacrament of Holy Unction: "For as great is Your majesty, so is Your mercy." If God's majesty is infinite, then so is His mercy! How comforting that is!

"Lord, Have Mercy" Is the Prayer

> Sing praises to God, sing praises! / Sing praises to our King, sing praises!
>
> —Psalm 46/47:6

A priest at summer camp gave a sermon I will never forget. It was so profound, to me at least, that I wanted to include his ideas in this book. He spoke about the importance of congregational singing, and his thesis was that the responses *are* the prayers during the litanies offered by the priest or deacon. The petitions themselves are simply prompts to remember certain things in prayer. When the priest or deacon says, "For the peace from above and for the salvation of our souls, let us pray to the Lord," he is prompting the congregation to pray for these things, and the people answer in prayer, "Lord, have mercy." In other words, the people answer the request by praying, "Lord, have mercy and offer us the peace from above and the salvation of our souls."

Imagine if the clergy offered a set of petitions and no one responded to any of them—no one took action. The words would fall flat. This is why it is necessary for people to be present to offer the responses to the prompts—in essence, to offer the prayers of the service. The priest offers prayers throughout the service that are inaudible or not heard by the faithful. However, it is the faithful who offer audible prayers in the form of "Lord have mercy" and "Grant this, O Lord," which are sung throughout the service.

As "the work of the people," worship is *meant* to be work, not just something we watch. And part of this work of the Divine Liturgy is for the faithful to pray the responses to the petitions throughout the service.

For the peace from above and for the salvation of our souls, let us pray to the Lord.

> For the kingdom of God is not food and drink but righteousness and peace and joy in the Holy Spirit.
>
> —Romans 14:17

After the first petition of the Divine Liturgy calls us to gather for prayer in peace, the second petition then brings our focus to two things—the peace from above and the salvation of our souls. There are many kinds of peace—military peace, peace of mind, political peace—but the greatest is the peace from God, the peace that surpasses all understanding (Phil. 4:7). Before we request anything else, we ask for the peace of God to come into us.

Next we pray for is the salvation of our souls, which is the overall goal of our lives. And in the context of community, it's not just our own personal salvation we are after but also the salvation of *all* our souls.

Years ago, when I was first ordained, I was offering petitions at a service of the Blessing of the Five Loaves, and the metropolitan, whom I was serving as his deacon, was present. In one of the petitions, the names of many people are commemorated. As I prayed, I recalled that after the names are offered, the priest says something. My service book stopped with the names, and nothing was written afterward. I knew that was incorrect. It came to my mind that I should finish the petition by saying, "For their health, let us pray." I will always remember the lesson I learned when the metropolitan corrected me rather forcefully: "What good is health without salvation? It's for their health and *salvation* that we are praying."

As we begin our prayer of the Divine Liturgy and enter into God's Kingdom here and now, we first pray for the prerequisite to prayer: peace. As we read in Romans 14:17, the Kingdom is not about material food and drink but rather righteousness and peace and joy. These virtues are the gateway to our salvation, so we pray for peace as the gateway to the Divine Liturgy. But the number-one thing we pray for, the number-one goal for our lives, is salvation.

For the peace of the whole world, for the stability of the holy churches of God, and for the unity of all, let us pray to the Lord.

> "The hour is coming, indeed it has come, when you will be scattered, every man to his home, and will leave me alone; yet I am not alone, for the Father is with me. I have said this to you, that in me you may have peace. In the world you have tribulation; but be of good cheer, I have overcome the world."
>
> —John 16:32–33

The services of the Church call on us to pray first for peace for ourselves. But this is not where the prayer ends. Not only must we be motivated to seek peace for ourselves and salvation for our souls, we must work for peace in the whole world. In order to do this, we must seek to be peace*makers* instead of peace-*takers*.

Certain people light up a room when they walk into it. But other people bring tension and stress with them when they walk into a room. We have the ability to choose which kind of person we will be—a light-up-the-room person or a stress-out-the-room person. Peace in the world emanates from each person's choice.

The Church can't be a vehicle for peace if it is at war or is unstable. So, as we pray for peace in the world, we also pray for the stability of the holy churches of God—for our churches to remain vigilant, orderly, and authentic.

The psalm tells us, "Behold, how good and pleasant it is / when brothers dwell in unity" (Ps. 132/133:1). We should grieve that the many Christian churches are divided rather than united. Can the churches ever be united into one body? Perhaps not. But can churches express a unity of faith and purpose and offer meaningful contributions to the world? Most definitely yes. While we should always pray for the unity of the churches rather than their continued division, we should also pray that churches come together for common good deeds that benefit our world.

For this holy house and for those who enter it with faith, reverence, and the fear of God, let us pray to the Lord.

> And Jesus answered him, "Blessed are you, Simon Bar-Jona! For flesh and blood has not revealed this to you, but my Father who is in heaven. And I tell you, you are Peter, and on this rock I will build my church, and the powers of death shall not prevail against it. I will give you the keys of the kingdom

> of heaven, and whatever you bind on earth shall be bound in heaven, and whatever you loose on earth shall be loosed in heaven."
>
> —Matthew 16:17–19

We now turn our attention to our local church community, and we pray for some very specific things. First, we pray for our church building, that it may stand safe and strong. We pray for each person who is part of our parish. We pray for everyone who has gathered to worship with us.

And for what are we praying? We are praying for the strengthening of our collective faith—that we may be faithful in our practice of Christianity, that we may be consistent, and that we may be confident. We are praying for reverence and that we have a healthy respect for what we are doing, for God's commandments, for one another—as we are all in His image—and for the words we offer in worship. If we pray to "glorify God with one voice and one heart," then as we go about our daily lives, we must live with a voice and a heart that glorifies God.

Finally, we are praying that our experience of God through worship will transform us and change us for the better. We need a balance between fear of God and joy that we are His children. To live in the fear of God means that we recognize Christ as our Lord, both as the God of mercy and the God who will judge the totality of our lives. This is an inclusive petition for us and for those who are part of our community.

As we offer this prayer, we should think about all the different people in our parish—those who are sick, those who lead the various ministries, those we know, and even the people we do not know. All have come here to grow in their faith. All are part of the same spiritual family. Let us get to know each person in our spiritual family. Let us take care of one another. Before we can take the Word of God beyond the bounds of our community, let us make sure that we are talking about Him and living out His Word by helping others *within* the bounds of our community.

For pious and Orthodox Christians, let us pray to the Lord.

> "Therefore you also must be ready; for the Son of man is coming at an hour you do not expect. Who then is the faithful and wise servant, whom his master has set over his household, to give them their food at the proper time? Blessed is that servant whom his master when he comes will find so doing."
>
> —Matthew 24:44–46

There is a difference between being pious and being pietistic. *Pious* has to do with being a faithful Christian, which starts with being humble. *Pietism,* or religiosity, has to do with flaunting our Christianity. Christ was careful to warn His followers to be pious but not pietistic. In Matthew 6:1–8, Jesus said:

> Beware of practicing your piety before men in order to be seen by them; for then you will have no reward from your Father who is in heaven.
>
> Thus when you give alms, sound no trumpet before you, as the hypocrites do in the synagogues and in the streets, that they may be praised by men. Truly, I say to you, they have received their reward. But when you give alms, do not let your left hand know what your right hand is doing, so that your alms may be in secret; and your Father who sees in secret will reward you.
>
> And when you pray, you must not be like the hypocrites; for they love to stand and pray in the synagogues and at the

> street corners, that they may be seen by man. Truly, I say to you, they have received their reward. But when you pray, go into your room and shut the door and pray to your Father who is in secret; and your Father who sees in secret will reward you.
>
> And in praying do not heap up empty phrases as the Gentiles do; for they think that they will be heard for their many words. Do not be like them, for your Father knows what you need before you ask him.

The Scriptures encourage us repeatedly not only to hear God's Word but to *do* God's Word, and to do it in a way that brings glory to Him, not to ourselves. That's why it has always been hard for me to understand the practice of philanthropy when it involves having one's name put on something. If someone donates money for an icon and places his or her name on that icon, the donor is exchanging money for recognition. The Lord wants us instead to offer ourselves with humility.

If we have a beautiful prayer rope around our wrist, or beautiful icons in our homes, or wear an expensive cross around our necks but rarely pray, rarely worship, and rarely serve others, we are pietistic but not pious. To be pious, or faithful, means to pray or to give for the glory of God, expecting no earthly reward. This petition reminds us that true Christianity is about an authentic relationship with Christ and humble service to others.

There is certainly nothing wrong with wearing a prayer rope or wearing a cross or having nice icons in our homes. But it is not the religious things we own that make us pious Christians. These things are merely tools that we use to help us grow in our faith.

For our Archbishop *[Name]*, for the honorable presbyterate, for the diaconate in Christ, and for all the clergy and the people, let us pray to the Lord.

> Do not neglect to do good and to share what you have, for such sacrifices are pleasing to God. Obey your leaders and submit to them; for they are keeping watch over your souls, as men who will have to give account. Let them do this joyfully, and not sadly, for that would be of no advantage to you. Pray for us, for we are sure that we have a clear conscience, desiring to act honorably in all things.
>
> —Hebrews 13:16–18

The next petition of the Divine Liturgy is a prayer for the leaders of the Church. The Orthodox Church is hierarchical, with several layers of leadership—from our patriarch to our archbishop, metropolitan, parish priest, and lay leaders. In the Orthodox Church, the local parish comes under the leadership of a bishop ("metropolitan," "archbishop," and "patriarch" are titles given to bishops) and his local representative, the priest.

This petition commemorates all three orders, or ranks, of the clergy. The first rank is that of the deacon, whose primary role is to assist in the services. The second rank is that of the presbyter, whose primary role is to celebrate the services and sacraments of the Church. We commonly call the presbyter the "priest." So, why use the word *presbyter*? That is because in the Greek language, the word for "clergy" is *ierosini,* which translates as "the priesthood." Each member of the clergy is a member of the ierosini, or the priesthood.

The third rank of the clergy is the bishop, whose primary role is to teach the faithful. He is the shepherd who leads the flock. In this petition, we mention all three ranks of the priesthood, including the specific metropolitan of our metropolis, who is referred to in ecclesiastical language as "archbishop."

Christ revealed Himself as the "Good Shepherd" (John 10:11), and He commissioned the apostles to be the shepherds and leaders of the Church. They were the first bishops. As the Church began to grow, they needed assistance in caring for the poor. In Acts 6:1–4, we read:

> Now in these days when the disciples were increasing in number, the Hellenists murmured against the Hebrews because their widows were neglected in the daily distribution. And the twelve summoned the body of the disciples and said, "It is not right that we should give up preaching the word of God to serve tables. Therefore, brethren, pick out from among you seven men of good repute, full of the Spirit and of wisdom, whom we may appoint to this duty. But we will devote ourselves to prayer and to the ministry of the word."

From this passage, we glean that the work of the Church consisted of two things: preaching the Word of God and feeding the hungry. Seven deacons were chosen and ordained to assist in food distribution while the apostles, the "bishops," concentrated on preaching the Word—their primary job to this day. The Church grew even larger as the apostles planted many new communities where they could not be constantly present. This led to the creation of the order of the presbyter, to serve in the community in place of the bishop.

This is how the Church operates today. Every Orthodox church is under the authority of a bishop, who is the ultimate authority in the church, for he assigns each parish its presbyter (priest), who administers the community on his behalf. To further administer the community effectively, deacons serve in many churches, assisting the presbyter.

The role of the clergy is not to be dictators over the people but to be leaders for us to follow. Heirarchy and obedience are important in the Orthodox Church. The hierarchy maintains apostolic succession, an unbroken line to the apostles, while obedience to the hierarchy maintains this order and continuity. Nowadays the concept of obedience gets a bad rap in a world that craves independence, yet in our daily lives, we submit obediently to our doctor, our dentist, and the engineers who build our roads and set the speed limit in order for us to live healthy and orderly lives. Refusing to obey anything would lead to a life of chaos. I don't know much about medicine, so I submit to the expertise of my doctor. And I trust that his advice will lead me to a healthy life.

Following the leadership of the clergy leads to more stability in the Church and more success in spreading the gospel. Of course, even the best-intentioned clergy are human beings and make mistakes. So, it is important to pray for the clergy as they lead us. Over the years, I have taken much comfort in the prayers people have offered for me.

The priesthood is also somewhat a lonely life. There is usually no local peer group for priests, and in my parish I'm the only one. Many decisions I make, especially in pastoral situations, are made with no one else around except the people to whom I am ministering. It's hard to get every pastoral encounter, every sermon, and every interaction right. And this is where your prayers come in.

Thank you for your prayers. Keep them coming.

The following prayer from the Psalms is also offered as a prayer by each member of the clergy before the Divine Liturgy, when they wash their hands before serving.

I wash my hands in innocence,
    and go about thy altar, O Lord,
singing aloud a song of thanksgiving,
    and telling all thy wondrous deeds.

O Lord, I love the habitation of thy house,
  and the place where thy glory dwells.
Sweep me not away with sinners,
  nor my life with bloodthirsty men,
men in whose hands are evil devices,
  and whose right hands are full of bribes.

But as for me, I walk in my integrity;
  redeem me, and be gracious to me.
My foot stands on level ground;
  in the great congregation I will bless the Lord.
(Psalm 25/26:6–12)

For our country, the president, all those in public service, let us pray to the Lord.

Then the Pharisees went and took counsel how to entangle him in his talk. And they sent their disciples to him, along with the Herodians, saying, "Teacher, we know that you are true, and teach the way of God truthfully, and care for no man; for you do not regard the position of men. Tell us, then, what you think. Is it lawful to pay taxes to Caesar, or not?" But Jesus, aware of their malice, said, "Why put me to the test, you hypocrites? Show me the money for the tax." And they brought him a coin. And Jesus said to them, "Whose likeness and inscription is this?" They said, "Caesar's." Then he said to them, "Render therefore to Caesar the things that are Caesar's, and to God the things that are God's."

—Matthew 22:15–21

When Jesus told His followers to render to Caesar what is Caesar's, He was endorsing the authority of the state. Imagine what would happen if we didn't have a country or a government. We would have chaos. Without civil authorities, we wouldn't have roads on which to travel, schools in which to learn, firefighters and police officers to keep us safe, or water, electricity, and so many other valuable services. The Church concerns herself with preaching the gospel, preaching morality, and bringing the Kingdom of God to earthly life. The state is supposed to provide the means for us to live safely and in a healthy manner, to learn, to transact business, and so on. We have a duty to support the work of the Church with our stewardship. We have a duty to support the work of the state both with taxes and with following its laws.

Without making a political statement, I've noticed an increasing gray area between the work of the state and the work of the Church. In many ways, the state has infringed on the work of the Church, dictating morality on many levels. People have worked to enact laws that limit the work of the Church. Thus, we must continue to pray for those in civil authority, that the Lord may always speak to their hearts and guide their actions.

The Divine Liturgy provides us an opportunity to offer a magnificent prayer for the entirety of humanity, to the small and large pockets of society. When I offer this petition "for all in public service," I often think singularly of our president and what he does, the power he holds, the influence he wields. Other times, I think about people in our armed forces, such as the tank driver out in the hot desert in the Middle East who is far away from his family. I think of the kids who are missing their mommy or daddy and of the spouses at home who pray for a safe return. I think of our firefighters and police officers, heroes who run into harm's way to keep others safe.

Many thoughts can come to mind with this petition. I'm sure if you meditate on it, you will come up with many as well. Try carrying a different thought into each Divine Liturgy in preparation for this petition. That will keep the service from becoming stale. I often wish we could add a great pause after each phrase so we can truly reflect on those we are praying for. But as you hear each petition, and particularly this broad one for our leaders and for those who serve, reflect on at least one of its many aspects each time it is offered.

For this city and parish, for every city and land, and for the faithful who live in them, let us pray to the Lord.

> I will look with favor on the faithful in the land, / that they may dwell with me; / he who walks in the way that is blameless / shall minister to me.
>
> —Psalm 100/101:6

People often complain that the Divine Liturgy is always the same. That is true to some extent, though hymns and Scripture readings change at each service. But the Divine Liturgy is complete. We cover many areas of life in the Liturgy, and in this petition, we focus directly on the places we live and on our parish community.

As we pray this petition, bring to mind some aspects of your life within your community: your job and your coworkers, your school and your classmates, your kid's baseball team, the teller at the bank, the clerk at the store, or any number of people with whom you interact daily.

We bring to mind our city and also every city and country in the world. We pray especially for the faithful people who dwell everywhere on earth. We pray that the Faith will spread everywhere. We pray that it takes root and is established on a solid foundation wherever it is planted. This is a good time to bring to mind those who live in areas where Christians are persecuted—for their safety and for the protection of all churches and communities that are under oppression in dangerous areas.

I know a priest from Uganda who attended Holy Cross Greek Orthodox School of Theology in the United States and currently is serving in his homeland as an Orthodox priest. He told me that in his village, people would walk miles to go to church, even though they lived in an area where military guerillas regularly disrupted life and were especially hostile to the Church. Every Sunday, before the Divine Liturgy, the people of his parish gathered and offered two prayers. The first was a prayer of thanks that they had lived another week. The second was a prayer for protection that they could get through the service without any attacks. This story gives new meaning to "every city and land." The words bring to mind the sufferings of Christians whose joy in Christ is tempered by constant fear of persecution.

Can you see how this *one* petition provides so many possibilities for prayer? If you prayed for one of these things at each service, you could approach this petition in at least ten different ways during ten Divine Liturgies—truly a far cry from "the same and the same." The petitions in the Liturgy are a testament to the ways a few precious words can bring so much to our minds, our hearts, and our prayers.

For favorable weather, for an abundance of the fruits of the earth, and for peaceful times, let us pray to the Lord.

> The Lord will open to you his good treasury the heavens, to give the rain of your land in its season and to bless all the work of your hands.
>
> —Deuteronomy 28:12

People have often asked what we should be thinking about during the petitions. I hope these short reflections on "praying the Divine Liturgy" are giving you some concrete ideas. A natural question that follows the question of *what* to think about during the petitions is *how* to stay focused. One practice that I have found helpful is to have a "slideshow" of the petitions playing in my mind. So, on this petition for "favorable weather, abundance of the fruits of the earth, and for peaceful times," some of the slides that have passed through my mind include these images:

- people in a developing country, traveling to find water
- news reports of floods
- news accounts of natural disasters
- the farmer in the Midwest taking care of his crops
- the truck driver transporting the farmer's crop to the city
- the family hiking in the mountains

There are many others. The point of the slideshow exercise is that when I'm praying various petitions, I try to visualize the people for whom I am praying. Even if I don't know their names, I am made aware of their situations via news reports and my own life experience regarding the struggles of those who live in various climates.

As we pray this petition, we should pray for adequate rain for places that get too much or too little of this precious commodity. This is a good time to pray for our environment and for the conservation of our natural resources. It is also appropriate for us to reflect on our own personal stewardship of our natural resources. Like the other petitions, this one is so rich with material that we could each come up with different mental slides each time it is offered and still not run out of possibilities for prayer.

For those who travel by land, sea, and air, for the sick, the suffering, the captives and for their salvation, let us pray to the Lord.

> And the LORD went before them by day in a pillar of cloud to lead them along the way, and by night in a pillar of fire to give them light, that they might travel by day and by night.
>
> —Exodus 13:21

Again, our Church offers a wide variety of issues and people to remember in this one petition, giving us variety in praying the service. "And air" was added to the Divine Liturgy in the past century—evidence that the wording does change ever so slightly as there is need. This is another good petition for using a mental slideshow. Often when I pray this, I am thinking of specific people I know who are traveling as well as individuals in our community who are sick.

The Divine Liturgy, however, is an act of all the people of a community on behalf of all the people in the world. So, we offer a global prayer for the millions of people on earth—the overwhelming majority of whom we do not know by name—who are sick or suffering. Many people in poorer parts of the world do not have access to medical care, and this petition provides an opportunity to pray for them and for those who have the means to bring medical relief to them. People in the world are suffering in many different ways—the poor, homeless, orphans, and so on—and this is a good time to bring them to mind and to prayer. At any given time, people are being held unjustly in captivity. And then there are those who are justifiably imprisoned who need our prayers for their repentance and salvation. In many areas in the world Christians are not safe to practice their faith; they are held "captive" by oppressive governments who are bent on stamping out Christianity. We pray for them here as well.

It is interesting to note that we are not praying for safety, freedom, liberation, or vindication for any of the groups mentioned in this petition. We are not praying for material gain or recovery. We are praying for the greatest need—salvation. Perhaps someone who is suffering will never get better; the person in poverty may never get rich. But salvation is very much in God's plan for every human soul.

For our deliverance from all affliction, wrath, danger, and distress, let us pray to the Lord.

> Answer me when I call, O God of my right! / Thou hast given me room when I was in distress. / Be gracious to me, and hear my prayer.
>
> —Psalm 4:1

As we near the end of the Great Litany, the final petition is sort of an "all of the above" request, asking the Lord to deliver us from *all* affliction, wrath, danger, and distress, as these difficulties threaten the following:

- our personal peace
- the peace in the world
- the unity of our Church
- our church community
- the clergy
- the leadership of our nation
- the community in which we live
- the weather
- travelers
- those who are sick or suffering

Affliction includes physical and mental illness, poverty, loneliness, and other crosses that people carry.

Wrath, or anger, includes present or potential anger within ourselves, as well as the anger or potential anger from others. Hence, we pray for deliverance from these experiences so that peace will be present throughout our lives and our relationships.

Danger comes in many forms—from natural disasters and from the less obvious, such as temptation to gossip—and everything in between.

Distress is the opposite of abundance or even adequacy. We pray to have the adequate, if not abundant, amounts of the things we need—food, shelter, friends, and material sufficiency. (Notice I did not say "wealth.") This petition, just as the petitions before it, has wide-ranging application. It also serves as a "catch-all" for anything that may not have been covered in the previous petitions.

Help us, save us, have mercy on us, and protect us, O God, by Your grace.

> Help me, O Lord my God! / Save me according to Thy steadfast love!
>
> —Psalm 108/109:26

Concluding this opening set of petitions is a prayer that will be repeated several times in the Divine Liturgy. This is not a general prayer, such as the ones for good weather or safe travel. This prayer is very personal. It is a cry to God from the heart. It is said in the plural, because the Divine Liturgy is a corporate prayer. And we are praying for help, salvation, mercy, and protection for everyone around us.

We can think also of this prayer in the singular: Help *me*, save *me*, have mercy upon *me*, and protect *me*, O God, by Your grace. Now, try reading this another way, with the emphasis on the actions of God, almost screaming it out: *Help* me, *save* me, *have mercy* on me, and *protect* me, O God, by Your *grace*.

Prayed properly, this petition cries to God for the things that we desperately need and that He bestows so freely. We offer this petition so often that perhaps we hear it with complacency rather than with urgency. We need help from God because there are certain kinds of help that only God can provide. We need God to guide us to salvation because in no way can we guide ourselves there alone. We need His mercy because only God's mercy can overcome our sinfulness. And we need His protection because only He can safeguard our souls. This final prayer of the Great Litany is for ourselves—for help, salvation, mercy, and protection—key ingredients we need for the journey of today, this week, and this life, on our pilgrimage to eternal life.

Commemorating our most holy, pure, blessed, and glorious Lady, the Theotokos and ever-virgin Mary, with all the saints, let us commend ourselves and one another and our whole life to Christ our God.

> Then Jesus, crying with a loud voice, said, "Father, into thy hands I commit my spirit!" And having said this he breathed his last.
>
> —Luke 23:46

At the conclusion of these long sets of petitions in our Church, we always commemorate the Virgin Mary. Since we will explore this petition several times in our journey through the Divine Liturgy, I will focus on a different part of it each time.

At an Orthodox summer camp in which I participate, we have an exercise called the trust fall. A person stands on a platform about six feet high. Behind him or her, people have assembled below the platform. The person on the platform falls backward without looking, and the people catch that person. It takes a great deal of faith to fall where you can't see, trusting that you'll be caught without being hurt. A few campers have a really hard time doing this; some actually decline to take part, since this activity is very scary, especially for first-timers.

The ultimate trust fall is when we close our eyes in death and fall out of life, trusting that we will land in the hands of God. We will all participate in this exercise, the falling out of life, whether we want to or not. We have no choice. So, we prepare for the end of our lives by doing a little "trust fall" each day. That trust fall is called "commending," or committing ourselves to Christ. Can I fall into His arms by trusting in Him enough to keep His commandments today, believing that if I stay faithful, I will have the strength to endure the day in a better way than I could without them?

The Church, through this petition, calls on us to examine our commitment to the Lord, first for today and eventually for our whole life. But our whole life is too long a span to grasp. If today is the first day of the rest of our lives, then to commit our lives to Christ begins with a decision to commend ourselves to Him today. So, as we pray this petition, put the focus on today: *What is my commitment today? How am I demonstrating that commitment to myself and to others today?*

For to You belong all glory, honor, and worship, to the Father and to the Son and to the Holy Spirit, now and forever and unto the ages of ages. Amen.

> To the King of ages, immortal, invisible, the only God, be honor and glory for ever and ever. Amen.
>
> —1 Timothy 1:17

Every set of petitions concludes with an *ekphonesis,* a statement that gives glory to God. So, now that we have completed the Great Litany, making our many petitions to God for His help and mercy, we conclude our prayers by giving glory, honor, and worship to God.

What about my life? Am I glorifying God in what I do? Am I bringing Him honor? This is a great measure by which to make decisions. If I am doing something that dishonors the name of God, then I should not continue with that.

Glory is something that exalts the name of God so that people hear His name and think positive thoughts: God is almighty, good, benevolent, merciful.

Honor means to show "high respect" or "great esteem."[3] In honoring someone, we give praise and recognize that person as unique. In giving honor to the Lord, we recognize His unique position as our Lord, Savior, and Creator and offer to Him praise and recognition of His greatness.

Worship should be given only to God. We give compliments to one another, we thank others, and we praise in the sense of offering profound thanks to others, but worship belongs to God alone. Worship places something higher than us, and it is God alone who should rank above us.

---

3 *Oxford Languages* website, https://languages.oup.com.

The priest offers silent prayers throughout the Divine Liturgy. Today's prayer is one he offers either during the petitions (if they are being offered by a deacon or another priest) or during the hymn that follows the petitions. Though these hymns are uniquely part of the Divine Liturgy, some of them, including this one, can be prayed at any time by anyone. Just change the third person to first person, and this prayer can become personal for you.

> Lord, our God, whose dominion is incomparable and glory incomprehensible; whose mercy is immeasurable, and love for mankind ineffable: Look upon us and upon this holy house in Your loving-kindness, and grant to us and to those who pray with us Your abundant mercy and compassion. For to You belong all glory, honor, and worship, to the Father and to the Son and to the Holy Spirit, now and forever and to the ages of ages. Amen.

The Antiphons

Through the intercessions of the Theotokos, Savior, save us.

> And Mary said, "My soul magnifies the Lord, and my spirit rejoices in God my Savior, for he has regarded the low estate of his handmaiden. For behold, henceforth all generations will call me blessed."
>
> —Luke 1:46–48

This beautiful hymn to the Virgin Mary has often caused confusion for people regarding her status. We know that worship belongs to God alone, and we do not worship the Virgin Mary or the saints. Instead, we venerate her and praise her as the Mother of God and as the spiritual mother of us all. It is only Jesus Christ who saves us, so we lean on the Theotokos ("God-bearer") as an intercessor for us with her Son and our God.

What is an intercessor? One who intervenes on behalf of someone else. Let's say, hypothetically, that I want to send a message to the ecumenical patriarch. I do not know the ecumenical patriarch. But our metropolitan knows him, and I know our metropolitan. So, I would ask the metropolitan to intercede on my behalf and deliver my message. Ultimately, the exchange is between me and the patriarch—my need is conveyed to him. But the message is given by using an intercessor—in this case, the metropolitan—who knows him better than I do.

This is the role of the Virgin Mary. She knows the Lord Jesus Christ in a closer way than we do. Yet she is a human being like us, and we relate to her. So, we are asking someone who lived like us to intercede for us.

Let's make this even simpler to understand: when we are sick or are having surgery, many times we ask someone to pray for us—to intercede with God on our behalf. If we can ask one another to pray, then we should ask first and foremost the Theotokos to intercede on our behalf.

The hymn below puts the first antiphon in reverse order, acknowledging that it is only our Savior who saves us. But the intercessions of the Virgin Mary and all the saints assist us in the pursuit of our salvation.

> O Virgin Theotokos, rejoice, Mary full of grace. The Lord is with you. Blessed are you among women, and blessed is the fruit of your womb; for you have borne the Savior of our souls.[4]

Again and again, in peace, let us pray to the Lord.

> Pray constantly.
>
> —1 Thessalonians 5:17

In the advertising world, depending on which report you quote, people need to see an ad for a product between seven and twelve times before they will buy it. Long before statistical reports were available,

4 From *Lenten Vespers*, translated by Fr. Seraphim Dedes.

the Church seems to have understood this, because she added this petition to pray in peace several times in the Divine Liturgy.

Saint Paul exhorts us to pray without ceasing. What does that mean? That we are to pray all day long? Is that even possible? This verse has been interpreted several ways. There is the literal "pray constantly," which in the monastic context is the primary focus of the monk or nun.

But what about the rest of us? The Fathers of the Church write that work is prayer. So, this verse—to pray unceasingly—reminds us that our work should glorify God. Whether we are a lawyer, a doctor, a teacher, a parent, a coach, or a homemaker, all our work can and should be done for the glory of God.

On a practical level, I read this verse as saying that we should not cease our prayers, even for one day. We should practice our habit of prayer without ceasing. We should not miss a morning to pray as we begin the day; or an evening to pray as we end the day; or a meal, where we thank God for the food we are to receive; or an activity, where we ask God to be with us and bless us.

And remembering the first petition of the Divine Liturgy, our prayers should be offered again and again, but in peace. Peace in the world begins with the peace of God coming into our hearts and then into the hearts of those around us. We each play an integral part in this, by being peacemakers and advocates for peace!

Help us, save us, have mercy on us, and protect us, O God, by Your grace.

Do not forsake me, O Lord! / O my God, be not far from me! / Make haste to help me, / O Lord, my salvation!

—Psalm 37/38:21–22

This petition for the help, salvation, mercy, and protection of God is another that is stated multiple times in the Divine Liturgy. We've all had days where the above-quoted psalm describes our needs. We feel forsaken by friends, coworkers, the world in general, and perhaps even by God Himself. This plea appears in the Divine Liturgy so often because the Church recognizes that life in this world is tough, and we need God's reinforcement not once but many times. This repetition helps us remember that the Lord is here to assist us in negotiating the stormy seas of life. He offers us the help, safety, mercy, and protection that we all desperately need.

So, when life is hard, remember the Lord's nearness and pray this petition. These words are repeated so frequently in our liturgical services precisely because the Church understands the difficulties that befall each human life. We are reminded and comforted by the thoughts that our God is helpful, merciful, and protecting, and He stands ready to help each of us make our way to salvation.

Commemorating our most holy, pure, blessed, and glorious Lady, the Theotokos and ever-virgin Mary, with all the saints, let us commend ourselves and one another and our whole life to Christ our God.

> The prayer of a righteous man has great power in its effects.
>
> —James 5:16

One of the titles for the Virgin Mary that the Church uses often in the Divine Liturgy is *Theotokos,* which means "God-bearer." This is a beautiful name because it describes not only the Virgin Mary but all of us. We are all called to be God-bearers. How do we bear God? By being like the Virgin Mary.

When the Theotokos was visited by the archangel Gabriel and told that she would bear Christ within her womb, her response was very simple: "Behold, I am the handmaiden of the Lord, let it be to me according to your word" (Luke 1:38). Through those words, Mary showed obedience. Her response was all about the Lord and not about her. She didn't question God's will for her life. She stepped forward and embraced it.

And our response needs to be the same in our lives. We need to be obedient to God, to make life more about Him than about us, to have faith and to trust rather than questioning everything. This is how we become a Theotokos, a God-bearer, ourselves. As believers who are sealed with the gift of the Holy Spirit, we each carry God, so we try to honor the One who already dwells within each of us.

The prayer which follows is the "Magnificat," a hymn taken from the Matins service of the Church. It is based on Mary's song of praise in Luke 1:46–55:

> My soul magnifies the Lord, and my spirit has rejoiced in God my Savior,
>
> for he has regarded the lowly estate of his maidservant; For behold, henceforth all generations will call me blessed;
>
> for he who is mighty has done great things for me, and holy is his name. And his mercy is on those who fear him from generation to generation.
>
> he has shown strength with his arm, he has scattered the proud in the imagination of their hearts, he has put down the mighty from their thrones, and exalted the lowly; he has filled the hungry with good things, and the rich he has sent empty away.
>
> He has helped his servant Israel, in remembrance of his mercy, as he spoke to our fathers, to Abraham and his seed forever.

> Greater in honor than the Cherubim, and in glory greater beyond compare than the Seraphim; you without corruption gave birth to God the Word, and are truly Theotokos. You do we magnify.[5]

For Yours is the dominion, and Yours is the Kingdom and the power and the glory, of the Father and of the Son and of the Holy Spirit, now and forever and to the ages of ages.

> This was the dream; now we will tell the king its interpretation. You, O king, the king of kings, to whom the God of heaven has given the kingdom, the power, and the might, and the glory, and into whose hand he has given, wherever they dwell, the sons of men, the beasts of the field, and the birds of the air, making you rule over them all—you are the head of gold.
>
> —Daniel 2:36–38

We each spend a lot of time concerned about our own dominion, kingdom, power, and glory. Think about how much effort we spend to own a home: forty percent or more of our income goes to maintaining a place to live. That amounts to hundreds of hours a year spent paying to exercise our dominion over our bit of real estate. We also spend a lot of time maintaining our little kingdoms—cleaning, lawn mowing, and regular repairs. Then there is the major maintenance—replacing a roof or a pool pump or buying new lawn equipment.

5 Translated by Fr. Seraphim Dedes.

Next there is power. Most of us spend time, effort, and worry trying to solidify our place in the workforce. We struggle for advancement, and sometimes we put others down so we can rise up. Sometimes we worry about power, obsess over it, and lose sleep over it. Many times we are angry or disappointed that after reaching a certain age or years of employment, we don't have the power we think is our due.

And what about glory? We all like hearing our name called for something good. We all like recognition.

This ekphonesis (ending phrase) of a small litany that prays for peace is a powerful reminder. If we want the peace of God to permeate us, we must give Him the dominion, power, and glory in our lives. We need to make our lives about Him, rather than about us. That's why *Yours* is used twice: "For *Yours* is the dominion, and *Yours* is the kingdom and the power and the glory." These traits belong to the Holy Trinity—Father, Son, and Holy Spirit. And they belong to the Holy Trinity not only forever but *now* as well.

Below is the inaudible prayer offered by the priest before the end of this litany. It puts the focus on God instead of us and asks the Lord to bless those who bless Him with the way they live their lives.

> Lord, our God, save Your people and bless Your inheritance. Protect the fullness of Your Church. Sanctify those who love the beauty of Your house. Glorify them in return by Your divine power, and forsake us not who have set our hope in You. For Yours is the dominion, and Yours is the kingdom and the power and the glory, of the Father and of the Son and of the Holy Spirit, now and forever and to the ages of ages. Amen. (Prayer of the Second Antiphon)

Save us, O Son of God, *[risen from the dead / Who are wondrous in Your saints]*, we sing to You, Alleluia.

> And when he got into the boat, his disciples followed him. And behold, there arose a great storm on the sea, so that the boat was being swamped by the waves; but he was asleep. And they went and woke him, saying, "Save, Lord; we are perishing."
>
> —Matthew 8:23–25

The word *antiphon* means "to sing with a different voice." The antiphons of the Liturgy are hymns in which, in the early Church, half of the congregation would sing a verse, then the other half would sing the next verse, alternating back and forth. The second antiphon of the Divine Liturgy consists of two hymns: "Save Us, O Son of God" and "Only Begotten Son." The first hymn puts the emphasis solely on Christ, while the second hymn references Christ in relation to the rest of the Holy Trinity.

The first hymn is sung in one of three ways:

1. **Save us, O Son of God, risen from the dead, we sing to You, Alleluia.**
   We sing these words, with the phrase "risen from the dead," on resurrectional days: most Sundays and during the forty days after Pascha. This hymn is a plea to save us—an acknowledgment that our salvation comes about only through our Lord Jesus Christ.

2. **Save us, O Son of God, Who are wondrous in Your saints, we sing to You, Alleluia.**
   On most non-Sundays outside of the paschal season, we sing this hymn with the phrase "who are wondrous in Your saints." The reference to the saints shows that we offer veneration to them, but

we give worship to and find the hope of our salvation only in the Person of Jesus Christ. The saints gave the greatest glory to God, and so we acknowledge their importance while at the same time giving supremacy to the Lord.

3. **Save us, O Son of God**
. . . who were born of a Virgin (Christmas),
. . . who were baptized by John in the Jordan (Theophany),
. . . who were transfigured in Glory (Transfiguration),
we sing to You, Alleluia.
On major feast days of the Church, a different and unique formula is added to this hymn: a reference to the feast we are celebrating. The hymn in all its variations is a reminder that we cannot take our eyes off the prize of salvation. It's when we take our gaze away from Christ that we, like Peter walking on the water, start to sink (Matt. 14:29–31). As long as we keep our eyes on Him, we will not fail. And if we ever are sinking, the opportunity to be saved is as close as praying to the Lord, "Save me," and trusting that He will do exactly that.

Hymn: Only Begotten Son and Logos of God

Glory to the Father and to the Son and to the Holy Spirit, now and forever and to the ages of ages. Amen.

Only begotten Son and Logos of God, being immortal, You condescended for our salvation to take flesh from the holy Theotokos and ever-virgin Mary and, without change,

became man. Christ, our God, You were crucified and conquered death by death. Being one of the Holy Trinity, glorified with the Father and the Holy Spirit: Save us.

> For God so loved the World, that he gave his only Son, that whoever believes in him should not perish but have eternal life.
>
> —John 3:16

> In the beginning was the Word, and the Word was with God, and the Word was God.
>
> —John 1:1

> And now, Father, glorify thou me in thy presence with the glory which I had with thee before the world was made.
>
> —John 17:5

This hymn is probably the most important hymn of the Divine Liturgy, along with "We Have Seen the True Light," which we sing right after Holy Communion. This is certainly the most theological of the hymns of the service. It identifies God as Trinity—Father, Son, and Holy Spirit. It identifies Jesus Christ by the many names ascribed to Him: only begotten Son, Word of God, and Christ our God.

The essence of our salvation is Christ, the Word of God, who became incarnate as a man through the Virgin Mary, yet He remained God. The Gospel of John 1:1, quoted above, says, "In the Beginning was the Word [referring to Jesus Christ as being pre-eternal with the Father and the Spirit and being part of the creation], and the Word was with God, and the Word was God." In John 17:5 (among other places), this concept is restated as Christ asks His Father to "glorify thou me in thy own presence with the glory which I had with thee before the world was made." Again, the pre-eternal Christ exists forever with the Father and the Spirit.

Through the Incarnation, Jesus Christ became a human being, was crucified, resurrected, and trampled down death by death. John 3:16 sums up the entire New Testament: "For God so loved the world that he gave his only Son, that whoever believes in him should not perish but have eternal life." And this hymn really summarizes the Divine Liturgy. We gather to partake of the Body and Blood of the crucified and risen Christ because our salvation comes through Him. Hence the last phrase of the hymn: "save us."

The Holy Trinity is perhaps the most complex Christian concept to understand. This hymn explains it in a succinct way. If you learn to sing it, you will have the story of salvation easily available to ponder and review often.

Again and again, in peace, let us pray to the Lord.

> Jeremiah the prophet said to them, "I have heard you; behold, I will pray to the Lord your God according to your request, and whatever the Lord answers you I will tell you; I will keep nothing back from you."
>
> —Jeremiah 42:4

Again! Again we have to pray this prayer? Again, Fr. Stavros, you are writing about this petition?

The answer is yes. Why does the Divine Liturgy repeat this so many times? Because it includes the two things that seem to elude us the most in our Christian lives—prayer and peace.

When we were children, prayer was a rote practice. We prayed at meals, maybe. Nightly prayers, once in a while. My generation never really learned how to pray. We listened to the priest pray in church. There were opening and closing prayers at the end of church events. But I can't recall ever hearing anything inspirational about prayer. And as I have gone through life, prayer has been an obligation, sometimes a chore. Then it became a habit, and only in recent years has it become a joy.

To the one who hasn't discovered its power, prayer seems more like mumbling something to an unseen, unanswering God. Prayer is a recourse that is available when you have nothing else to rely on, and many people turn to prayer only in times of crisis.

At summer camp, we spend a lot of time in prayer. We schedule a fifteen-minute time alone with God every day, where everything stops and we sit in silence and prayer. We don't have to make the time at camp; it is provided for us. We say prayers before and after every meal, and we offer prayers throughout the day at various events. As the week wears on, small prayer groups start with counselors or campers. Sometimes people stand in a circle; sometimes they might even hold hands. Sometimes one person in the group will pray, and at other times everyone in the circle will offer something. And no one ever says, "What? We have to pray again?"

As an Orthodox Christian for my whole life, with more than twenty years as a priest, I have to say that we as Orthodox Christians have really missed the boat on prayer, both privately and with others. So, writing on this petition "again and again" is a good reminder to *me* about the importance of prayer, and I hope to you as well. Prayer is beautiful, powerful, and comforting.

I remember a priest one time giving a sermon on prayer, and he compared it to chocolate ice cream. He said, "I can describe ice cream only so much—it is cold, it is sweet—but then you have to try it for yourself. And it's the same thing with prayer. Many have written books on prayer, but at some point, you just have to try it for yourself. Then you will know its power."

Now, to peace. If someone asked me, "What's the one thing you want to change about your life?" I would answer, "To have more peace." Certainly, it would be nice if there were greater peace in the world, but on a more personal and selfish basis, I'd love to have more peace in my own life. I'd like to have less stress and more peace. I'd take peace over money any day. What good is all the money in the world if you are stressed out? Doctors will tell you the key to living a long life is diet and exercise, but even more important is managing stress. And the answer to that is finding peace.

If I want peace from others, I've got to bring peace to others. Prayer and peace are what we need most in our lives. As I mentioned earlier, marketing executives tell us that it takes seven to twelve touches (commercials and other ads) for a message to sink in with a consumer. Even the authors of the Divine Liturgy understood that! We need to be reminded, "again and again."

Help us, save us, have mercy on us, and protect us, O God, by Your grace.

> And Peter answered him, "Lord, if it is You, bid me to come to You on the water." He said, "Come." So Peter got out of the boat and walked on the water and came to Jesus; but when he saw the wind, he was afraid, and beginning to sink he cried out, "Lord, save me." Jesus immediately reached out his hand and caught him, saying to him, "O man of little faith, why did you doubt?"
>
> —Matthew 14:28–31

Most of us are familiar with the story of Peter walking on water—or trying to (Matt. 14:22–33). A storm, with its wind and waves, was tossing about the tiny boat that carried Peter and the other disciples. He may have had concerns about the integrity of the boat and whether he and his friends would survive to see the morning. And then in the midst of all this, Jesus appears, walking on the water.

Peter doesn't question Jesus' ability to walk on the water, but he does question who this person is. Assured that He is Jesus, who makes possible what seems impossible, Peter eagerly goes to his Lord and Savior—in this case, a real savior from the storm. He sees the Lord as his safe haven and eagerly gets out of the boat and starts to walk on the water. He manages pretty well—that is, until he takes his eyes off of the Lord. Distracted now by an earthly concern, in that moment of doubt Peter begins to sink. Now, certain of his demise, he cries out to the Lord, "Save me." And Jesus immediately does just that.

Peter's cry can be seen in two ways. It can be seen as a cry of desperation: "Nothing else is going right. I'm desperate and have nowhere else to turn." Or it can be seen as a cry of confidence: "I believe, and even though I've messed up and I've doubted, I still believe, and I know that You, Lord, will not forsake me." If Peter really had no faith, he wouldn't have gotten out of the boat to walk to Jesus in the first place. And when he started to sink, he would have begun frantically swimming rather than calling on the name of the Lord. So, let's give Peter some credit here. Like all of us, he had his moments of doubt. But even in doubt and in a posture of failure, he had enough faith to cry to the Lord, to repent, and to believe.

I love St. Peter because he is like all of us—a man who is trying to believe. A man who makes mistakes. A man who repents and is restored. A man who gets it right in the end. Peter sinks and is called a doubter. Later, he questions, and Jesus says, "Get behind me, Satan!" (Matt. 16:23). Peter fell asleep in the garden when Jesus needed a friend to watch with Him (Matt. 26:40). Peter denied Christ when it counted (Matt. 26:69–75). But Peter is paramount among the apostles and one of our Church's greatest saints.

We hear this petition—"Help us, save us, have mercy on us, and protect us, O God, by Your grace"—many times in the Divine Liturgy. It is a reminder that we will have many failures and setbacks, just like Peter, and that the Lord will be here for us when we cry out to Him, as Peter did when he sank in the sea.

Let Us Commend Ourselves and One Another

Commemorating our most holy, pure, blessed, and glorious Lady, the Theotokos and ever-virgin Mary, with all the saints, let us *commend* ourselves and *one another* and our whole life to Christ our God.[6]

> And one of the scribes came up and heard them disputing with one another, and seeing that he answered them well, asked him, "Which commandment is the first of all?" Jesus answered, "The first is, 'Hear, O Israel: The Lord our God, the Lord is one; and you shall love the Lord your God with all your heart, and with all your soul, and with all your mind, and with all your strength.' The second is this, 'You shall love your neighbor as yourself.' There is no other commandment greater than these."
>
> —Mark 12:28–31

6 [Emphasis mine.]

As we continue our journey through the Divine Liturgy, we come across another petition that is repeated several times throughout the service; in fact, this petition is found in most of the services of the Orthodox Church. Today's takeaway concerns committing not only ourselves but also our neighbors to Christ.

The two great commandments, upon which all the Law and the Prophets are based, are the commandments to love God and to love our neighbors. We can love our neighbors in many ways. First, we should see God in our neighbors and serve them as if we are serving God Himself. Second, we should love our neighbors as we love ourselves; we should care for our neighbors as we care for ourselves. To put it plainly, if you are making a sandwich for your neighbor, make a sandwich that you'd want to eat. If you are mowing your neighbor's lawn (which I enjoy doing), treat that lawn as if it were your own—meaning, give it your best effort.

Another way for us to love our neighbor is something we don't think about very often. We should be concerned for our neighbor's salvation. How many of us have been going to church for years, sitting in the same section near the same people, talking to the same friends at coffee hour, and moving in the same social circles? And how many of us, in our small group of friends, have ever brought up the topic of salvation?

When someone dies, many people say something like, "When we all get there, we'll keep playing cards every Friday." This is actually a very secular and, in my opinion, disrespectful view of heaven. Standing in the presence of God will evoke a sense of awe, not a desire to play cards. But seriously, in the social groups where we spend the most time, how often do we talk about salvation?

Do you feel a group setting is too big for that discussion? Well, how about talking one on one with someone about salvation? Have you ever asked someone who is dying if there is anything you can do for them in a spiritual way to help them prepare for death? If the answer is no, don't worry; that's probably the answer most people would give.

As we pray through the Divine Liturgy and internalize what each line means for our lives, this petition should remind us to commend ourselves to Christ and to help our neighbors to commend themselves to Him also. We should strive to feel more comfortable talking about the Lord. If I were dying, I'd want someone to talk about Him with me, to ask me about my salvation, and to give me an opportunity to give testimony while I still can.

Salvation is not just about our own souls; our spiritual journey includes our neighbors. We should be concerned with their salvation as much as our own. And this starts with making opportunities to pray for our neighbors and to talk about salvation with them, committing ourselves to Christ and helping our neighbors commit to Him as well. And when we are having a hard time committing our lives to Christ, our neighbors in turn should be there for us to offer encouragement.

For You, O God, are good and love mankind, and to You we offer glory, to the Father and to the Son and to the Holy Spirit, now and forever and to the ages of ages.

> For we ourselves were once foolish, disobedient, led astray, slaves to various passions and pleasures, passing our days in malice and envy, hated by men and hating one another; but when the goodness and loving kindness of God our Savior appeared, he saved us, not because of deeds done by us in righteousness, but in virtue of his own mercy, by the washing of regeneration and renewal in the Holy Spirit.
>
> —Titus 3:3–5

As the Divine Liturgy progresses, we end the second small litany with the "exclamation" of the ekphonesis—the traditional ending to every set of petitions. Each exclamation is different because there are so many ways to describe and glorify God. This exclamation praises God as *agathos* ("good") and *philanthropos* (in most translations of the Divine Liturgy, this word is translated as "loving," but from this word in Greek, we get the words "philanthropic" and "philanthropy").

Philanthropic (and all associated words) literally means "friend of man." God is philanthropic to all people, meaning He welcomes all people to Him. In like manner, we are supposed to be philanthropic. Ideally, everyone should be our friend. Of course, that is not possible or even practical, but we should approach people in a way that is friendly and welcoming. Every Sunday at church, we encounter people who are new. Do we welcome them or stay away from them?

We encounter new people all the time in life. Look carefully at yourself and ask this question: *Am I a welcoming and encouraging person who lets people in, or am I stand-offish, with a hard shell that few people can break through?* Most people give off a vibe as either one or the other. Make it a goal to work on your vibe. If your vibe says, "I'm welcoming, accessible, and safe," then you will have a greater opportunity to be the philanthropic person that the Lord calls us to be. The Lord is welcoming, accessible, and safe, and He asks the same from us. In fact, one of the first steps in being able to love our neighbor is developing ourselves to be a philanthropos, a friend of people, instead of someone who is not welcoming.

When we think of philanthropy, we also think about charitable giving. Charitable giving has no expectation of return or reward. It is joyful, selfless giving. No matter what we own in life, we are supposed to give some of it back, joyfully, to those who are less fortunate than we are. We develop this sense of philanthropy as we come to understand that everything we have is a gift from God, that nothing we have is truly ours; everything we own is His gift entrusted to us.

The inaudible prayer printed below precedes this ekphonesis. It is a beautiful prayer offered quietly by the priest in the altar that reminds us we do not need to be gathered in large numbers to experience the power of God. He stands even in the midst of two or three. The prayer asks God to be philanthropic to us by answering our prayers for our benefit (not necessarily according to our desires), to grant us knowledge of His truth (including how to become more philanthropic, as He is), and to grant us the greatest gift—eternal life in the world to come.

> Lord, You have granted us to offer these common prayers in unison and have promised that when two or three agree in Your name, You will grant their requests. Fulfill now, O Lord, the petitions of Your servants as may be of benefit to them, granting us in the present age the knowledge of Your truth, and in the age to come eternal life.
>
> For You, O God, are good and love mankind, and to You we offer glory, to the Father and to the Son and to the Holy Spirit, now and forever and to the ages of ages. Amen.

Come, Let Us Worship!

Wisdom. Arise. Come, let us worship and bow down before Christ. Save us, O Son of God, risen from the dead (or *who are wondrous in Your saints*), we sing to You, Alleluia.

> O come, let us worship and bow down, / let us kneel before the LORD, our Maker!
>
> —Psalm 94/95:6

Much can be written about the part of the service we are examining today. Historically, the Small Entrance, or the Entrance of the Holy Gospel, is the first action of the Divine Liturgy. In the early Church, the Liturgy began in the narthex. At the time of the Small Entrance, the faithful entered the nave for the first time, and the clergy entered the altar for the first time. The only remaining vestige of this practice can be seen when the bishop serves: he enters the altar for the first time during the Small Entrance. In modern times, the Small Entrance is simply a brief exit from the sanctuary with the priest, preceded by altar servers, carrying the Gospel to the center of the solea.

As the priest makes this entrance, a hymn called an *apolytikion* is sung as he exits the altar. There are eight resurrectional apolytikia that rotate each Sunday, as well as a special apolytikion for each day of the Church year. So, on a weekday feast day, the apolytikion of the saint or an event in the life of Christ or the Virgin Mary is sung at this point in the Divine Liturgy. (This is the practice in the Greek Orthodox Church, where I serve. Other jurisdictions offer the apolytikion [sometimes called a troparion] only after the Small Entrance, while offering the Beatitudes before the entrance.)

When the priest comes to the center of the solea, as the apolytikion concludes, he offers a blessing toward the altar with the words, "Blessed is the entrance of Your saints, now and forever and to the ages of ages. Amen." The word *agios* is translated as both "saints" and "holy ones." The subtle message is this: may we, the ones who are striving to be holy (and yes, this is a call to all of us) make our entrance into worship today—now—in church and forever, in the Kingdom of God.

After the hymn concludes, the priest raises the Gospel and says, "Wisdom. Arise." This is to call our attention to what is going on. The Gospel, the Word of the Lord, stands high above us, reminding us that the truth of the Lord should stand at the forefront of every life. We are then directed to "worship and bow down before Christ." As the priest bows his head, the parishioners also bow their heads.

Why bow? A bow is a sign of respect and reverence. We've all seen in movies that everyone bows to the king or queen. The monarch is seen as the supreme ruler. No one would dare *not* bow. No one would dare disobey. The lifting up of the Gospel book is a reminder to us that we are to bow before Christ as our God and as our Lord. We are to bow in respect, admiration, and worship. We are to bow in obedience. We are not asked to bow before anyone else but our Lord. And while we reverence the saints of the Church, worship is given only to the Lord. Later on in the service, the priest will say, "Let us bow our heads unto the Lord." He won't ask us to bow to any saint—only to the Lord.

When we speak of Jesus Christ as our Savior, the connotation is that *we* are the beneficiaries of something. He gives. We receive. But when we speak of Jesus Christ as Lord, the connotation is that *we* give our glory, admiration, worship, and obedience to Him, and He receives them from us. We often think of Christ our Savior as the one who is going to "save me," the one who is going to "give me" salvation. But how often do we think of Christ as our Lord, the one to whom *we* give?

As we see the Gospel, the Good News (*Evangelion* in Greek), we are to worship Christ and have thanks in our hearts that through Him we can be saved. But also, as we bow before the Gospel book, we are reminded that Christ is our Lord. Not only are we to bow to Him in our liturgical ritual, but we are to bow to Him in obedience every day of our lives, not just on Sundays.

As noted in an earlier reflection, this entrance hymn, "Come, let us worship," includes "risen from the dead" on Sundays. It includes "who are wondrous in Your saints" instead on many weekdays. However, on feast days of the Lord, the entire hymn will be replaced by something related to the feast. For instance, at Christmas the entrance hymn is this:

> From before the morning star I have begotten You; the Lord has sworn a promise which He will not retract. You are a priest forever after the order of Melchizedek (Ps. 109/110:4). Save us, O Son of God, who were born of a Virgin, we sing to You, Alleluia.

On Theophany, we sing the following hymn:

> Blessed is He who comes in the name of the Lord (Matt. 21:9). God is the Lord and has revealed Himself to us. Save us, O Son of God, who were baptized by John in the Jordan, we sing to You, Alleluia.

These feast-day entrance hymns remind us of the purpose of the day's gathering. At the Nativity, we are celebrating the Incarnation of the pre-eternal God, the Word (Christ) becoming flesh and dwelling among us. At Theophany, we are celebrating the manifestation (appearance) of God as Trinity.

Below is the inaudible prayer that the priest offers as he carries the Gospel in the Small Entrance:

> Master, Lord our God, who has established the orders and hosts of angels and archangels in heaven to minister to Your glory, grant that holy angels may enter with us, that together we may celebrate and glorify Your goodness. For to You belong all glory, honor, and worship, to the Father and to the Son and to the Holy Spirit, now and forever and to the ages of ages. Amen.

Let Us Sing: A Reflection on Congregational Singing

> Let the word of Christ dwell in you richly, teach and admonish one another in all wisdom, and sing psalms and hymns and spiritual songs with thankfulness in your hearts to God.
>
> —Colossians 3:16

This reflection is not about a specific line of the Divine Liturgy but addresses the subject of hymns and singing. Following the Small Entrance, several hymns are sung. Although some people claim the Divine Liturgy is the same each time, this section of the service varies. Following the Small Entrance, the apolytikion of the day is repeated. On Sundays, after the resurrectional apolytikion, usually a hymn for the saint of the day follows. Then the hymn of the saint or feast of the church is sung, and finally the *kontakion* (hymn of the season), which relates to the season of the Church year.

The Church offers three kinds of hymns:

1. *Hymns that praise God*
   For instance, the hymn, "Holy, holy, holy, Lord Sabaoth, heaven and earth are filled with Your glory," doesn't seek anything from God; it offers praise and glory to Him.

2. *Hymns that ask God for things*
   The one we hear most often is "Lord, have mercy." Another example is "Save us, O Son of God, risen from the dead (or who are wondrous in Your saints), we sing to You, Alleluia." These hymns ask the Lord for specific requests.

3. *Hymns that teach*
   The majority of hymns fall into this category. The most well-known of the teaching hymns is "Christ is risen from the dead, by death, trampling down upon death, and to those in the tombs, He has granted life." This hymn does not praise God, nor does it ask God for anything. It explains to us what the Resurrection is all about.

We've all had the experience of a catchy tune sticking in our heads. A hymn like "Christ Is Risen" is sung many times during the paschal season so that it will stay in our minds and in our hearts. If anyone asks what you believe about the Resurrection, the answer is twenty-two words: "Christ is risen from the dead, by death trampling down upon death, and to those in the tombs, He has granted life."

Before people could read—which wasn't until a few centuries ago—how did they learn? Through pictures and songs, just like little children. My son learned the alphabet not by studying letters but with the alphabet song. He learned about animals and colors through pictures. We learn our Faith through icons and through hymns.

We are meant to sing the hymns! It's not just the priest or the choir or the chanter who is supposed to sing the hymns and responses of the Church. They are for everyone! As discussed earlier, the word *liturgy* comes from two words, *leitos* and *ergon*, which literally means "the work of the people." Worship is not entertainment where we sit back and watch the proceedings. Worship is work—serious work. We are meant to praise God with one voice, which means we are to stand and sing together.

I remember going to a performance of Handel's *Messiah* one year at Christmastime. Before the concert, which was held in a large Protestant church, the audience was asked to rise and sing "O Come, All Ye Faithful." From my seat in the balcony, I watched the crowd of seven hundred strong rise as one and sing loudly this beautiful Christmas carol. I almost could feel the building shake; it was alive with a multitude of voices singing praises to God.

A choir is necessary because we need musical leadership. But a handful of people in a choir doing all the singing is not the way God intends for us to worship.

A few years ago I gave a sermon about congregational singing during church. I prepared a contest in which I played various fight songs from different colleges and asked alumni of those colleges in our parish to stand up and do what came naturally to them. The

University of Florida alumni did the gator chomp, and the Florida State alumni did the tomahawk chop.

Then I asked everyone to stand up and do what came naturally to them. I intoned, "Let us pray to the Lord." And I heard a tentative and cacophonous "Lord, have mercy." The point of this sermon was that at a college football game, when the band starts playing the fight song, two things happen: a) No one sits down and ignores the song—everyone gets into it; and b) Everyone knows exactly what to do. The band provides the leadership, but the student body provides the energy.

We need the same response in our churches. The choir is like the band; they lead. But the rest of us need to follow. We need to learn what to do. Singing needs to become almost instinctive for us. Then when we hear a petition we will offer the proper response, doing what comes naturally to us.

Can you imagine if the band played and no one cheered? There would be no energy, no enthusiasm, and maybe no fans.

What happens when the choir sings and we don't join in? There is no energy, no enthusiasm, and perhaps one day—no people.

We don't have to join the choir to sing. We don't have to have a great voice to sing. Saint Paul tells us in Ephesians 5:18–19, "Be filled with the Spirit, addressing one another in psalms and hymns and spiritual songs, singing and making melody to the Lord with all your heart."

Psalm 71:8 (NKJV) reads "Let my mouth be filled *with* Your praise / *And with* Your glory all the day." Meditate on this verse throughout the day today. Think about it before every conversation you have today and before every decision you make.

The Glory of the Lord

Let us pray to the Lord. Lord, have mercy. . . .

For You, our God, are holy, and to You we offer up glory, to the Father and to the Son and to the Holy Spirit, now and forever, and to the ages of ages.

> Moses said, "I pray thee, show me thy glory." And he said, "I will make all my goodness pass before you, and will proclaim before you my name 'The Lord'; and I will be gracious to whom I will be gracious, and will show mercy on whom I will show mercy."
>
> When Moses came down from Mount Sinai, with the two tables of the testimony in his hand as he came down from the mountain, Moses did not know that the skin of his face shone because he had been talking with God. And when Aaron and all the people of Israel saw Moses, behold, the skin of his face shone, and they were afraid to come near him.
>
> —Exodus 33:18–19; 34:29–30

The word *glory* appears several times in the Divine Liturgy. Almost every time we invoke the name of the Holy Trinity, we are offering up glory. What does this word mean? Well, it is hard to define and quantify. In the Book of Exodus, Moses asked God to "show me Your glory." And God told Moses that He would place Moses in a cleft in a rock then walk by, placing His hand over the cleft. After He passed by, He would remove His hand and let Moses see His back but not His face.

Even this small glimpse was enough. When Moses came down from the mountain, having seen the glory of God, he looked different:

"the skin of his face shone because he had been talking with God" (Ex. 34:29). The people of Israel could not look right at him.

In the Gospel accounts of the Transfiguration, we read that Jesus "was transfigured before them [three of His disciples], and his face shone like the sun, and his garments became white as light" (Matt. 17:2). And His disciples were not able to look upon Him.

The glory of God is something that we cannot fully comprehend. We know that His glory is more incredible than anything we can imagine. And we know that His glory changes people. It changed Moses. It changed the disciples.

So, what does it mean to give God glory? It means that we acknowledge His majesty and give Him honor through worship and praise, since He alone is deserving of these things. We bring God glory through our obedience to His commandments and our efforts to acquire His attributes and virtues—like love, patience, forgiveness, and joy—and showing these to others. We experience God's glory in our own humility before Him. We experience it in prayer, in Holy Communion, in nature. And we experience God's glory when we open our hearts and let them be touched by God.

People who are filled with God's glory are changed. Life's rough patches become smoother and easier to endure with God's glory. The inner beauty that God instilled in each of us shines forth when we become one with God's glory. As we hear this line of the Divine Liturgy, may it remind us about the glory of God. May we pray that His glory be bestowed upon each of us and that it change us in a positive way.

The prayer that precedes this ekphonesis is offered silently by the priest. It is worth examining because it describes attributes of God, which He has made accessible to us.

> O Holy God, Who is resting among the holy ones, praised by the Seraphim with the thrice-holy voice, glorified by the

Cherubim, and worshiped by every celestial power, You have brought all things into being out of nothing. You have created man according to Your image and likeness and adorned him with all the gifts of Your grace. You give wisdom and understanding to the one who asks, and You overlook not the sinner, but have set repentance as the way of salvation.

You have granted us, Your humble and unworthy servants, to stand even at this hour before the glory of Your holy Altar of sacrifice and to offer to You due worship and praise. Master, accept the Trisagion Hymn also from the lips of us sinners, and visit us in Your goodness. Forgive all our voluntary and involuntary transgressions, sanctify our souls and bodies, and grant that we may worship You in holiness all the days of our lives, through the intercessions of the holy Theotokos and of all the saints who have pleased You throughout the ages.

For You, our God, are holy, and to You we offer up glory, to the Father and to the Son and to the Holy Spirit, now and forever, and to the ages of ages. Amen.

Holy God, Holy Mighty, Holy Immortal, have mercy on us.

And the four living creatures, each of them with six wings, are full of eyes all round and within, and day and night they never cease to sing, "Holy, holy, holy, is the Lord God Almighty, who was and is and is to come!"

—Revelation 4:8

This hymn is called the Trisagion Hymn. *Agios* means "holy" in Greek. So, *Trisagion* means "three times we say holy."

The first part of the Divine Liturgy that we have studied thus far is called the Liturgy of the Word. It includes petitions. It includes hymns. And it concludes with Scripture readings and a homily. As we begin the transition from petitions and hymns to the reading of sacred Scripture, this hymn builds the bridge for us. It first glorifies God, although the words are not descriptive about His nature. It doesn't say, "Holy is God, Holy and Mighty," as some translations incorrectly state. It addresses God—Holy God, Holy Mighty, Holy Immortal—and then asks God to "have mercy on us." The words both give glory to God and ask Him for mercy.

During the singing of this hymn, the priest offers the prayer examined in the previous reflection ("To You we offer up glory"). While we sing, we should be thinking about the majesty of God. We should think not only of the power of God but of His timelessness. He created everything. He has redeemed everything through the ministry of Jesus Christ. And He has provided us with the tools we need to sustain us until He comes again—namely, the Church, which has given us the Divine Liturgy and the opportunity to partake of Holy Communion, and the Scriptures, which give us the message of salvation. Indeed, this is a powerful moment of the Liturgy.

The Trisagion Hymn is another example of a hymn that is simple and repetitive. This hymn is recited at almost every service: during Matins and Vespers, in morning and evening prayers. In most prayer books, it is the first prayer listed. This is so that these words will play in our minds and our hearts throughout the day. As we remember our Holy, Mighty, and Immortal Lord, we remember that we are in need of His mercies, and we remember that He bestows them so freely upon His people.

Here is another liturgical note: the Trisagion Hymn is altered on occasion. On Theophany, the Feast of St. John the Baptist, the Saturday of Lazarus, Holy Saturday, Pascha, all of Bright Week, the

Leave-Taking of Pascha, Pentecost, the Feast of the Holy Spirit, and Christmas, this hymn is replaced by the following: "All those who have been baptized into Christ have put on Christ. Alleluia." In the ancient Church, baptisms occurred in large groups on baptismal days in the context of the Divine Liturgy. The feasts mentioned above were days when baptisms traditionally were conducted, so this baptismal hymn replaced the Trisagion Hymn. In modern times, baptisms often are performed privately throughout the year. The "All those who have been baptized" hymn is still sung at each baptism but has also been preserved on the aforementioned days. Then on September 14 (Feast of the Holy Cross) and the third Sunday of Lent (Veneration of the Holy Cross), the following replaces the Trisagion Hymn: "Your Cross we venerate, O Master, and Your holy Resurrection we glorify."

Below are a set of prayers commonly known as the Trisagion Prayers, with the Trisagion Hymn as the first four lines. The Trisagion Prayers customarily are part of our morning and evening prayers and are very appropriate for every Christian to pray on a daily basis.

Holy God, Holy Mighty, Holy Immortal, have mercy on us.

Holy God, Holy Mighty, Holy Immortal, have mercy on us.

Holy God, Holy Mighty, Holy Immortal, have mercy on us.

Glory to the Father and to the Son and to the Holy Spirit, now and forever and to the ages of ages. Amen.

All Holy Trinity have mercy on us; Lord, forgive our sins; Master, pardon our iniquities; Holy One, visit and heal our infirmities for the glory of Your name.

Lord have mercy, Lord have mercy, Lord have mercy.

Glory to the Father and to the Son and to the Holy Spirit; now and forever and to the ages of ages. Amen.

Our Father, who art in heaven, hallowed be Thy name. Thy Kingdom come, Thy will be done, on earth as it is in heaven. Give us this day our daily bread, and forgive us our trespasses, as we forgive those who trespass against us. And lead us not into temptation but deliver us from evil.

For Thine is the Kingdom and the power and the glory of the Father and of the Son and of the Holy Spirit, now and forever, and to the ages of ages. Amen.

Dynamis!

> His divine power has granted to us all things that pertain to life and godliness, through the knowledge of him who called us to his own glory and excellence, by which he has granted to us his precious and very great promises, that through these you may escape from the corruption that is in the world because of passion, and become partakers of the divine nature.
>
> —2 Peter 1:3–4

This prompt is given by the priest or deacon after the Trisagion Hymn has been sung three times. The people then respond by singing the hymn one final time. *Dynamis* is one of those words in Greek that we simply can't translate. Various attempts at translation include: "Again, fervently," "Again," "With strength," "With power," and "Louder." People have even joked and made translations like "Sing it again," "Do it with gusto," or "Give it all you got!"

As you hear the prompt "Dynamis" in the liturgy, several things can come to mind that relate to power. The first is that the words we are singing have power. There is great power in singing "Holy God, Holy Mighty, Holy Immortal, have mercy on us," and to call upon the name of the Lord. Describing God as holy, mighty, and immortal proclaims Him as powerful. Walking hand in hand with God throughout our lives brings power to our days.

What do I think when I say the word *dynamis?* Well, I wish one day that the congregation would all sing at the top of their collective lungs about how great our God is. "Dynamis" may prompt the choir to sing a little louder, but many in the congregation still stand in silence. Just think about how powerful the experience would be if everyone sang as loudly as they could in the church. And think about how much power there would be if everyone took that same gusto and brought it to their everyday lives, never missing an opportunity to help or encourage or give witness in the name of the Lord.

So many people are sending out loud messages through protests and demonstrations. What's stopping us from raising Orthodox Christian voices to demonstrate for truth, to witness for the Lord we serve? And on the micro, private level, what stops us from calling on the name of the Lord with our families in prayer and with our friends in conversation? "Dynamis!" is a collective cry to the congregation: God is power, and God's power can change our lives. With God's power, we can help change the lives of others. "Dynamis!" is the cry to ramp up our efforts this week so that with each passing week, we become more confident in the power of the Lord.

From dynamis comes the word *dynamic*. To be dynamic means to be inspiring, to lead by example, and to encourage others to think in your way of thinking. Dynamis is a reminder that our Faith isn't just some heirloom we dust off on Sundays, but a living force that is constantly at work. Our Faith is not static; it is dynamic. Likewise, we are not supposed to be static Christians but rather dynamic Christians who eagerly come to church to learn and who eagerly leave church ready to live out the gospel, setting an example and spreading its message.

The Scripture Readings

Let Us Be Attentive!

> Hear, O sons, a father's instruction, / and be attentive, that you may gain insight; / for I give you good precepts: / do not forsake my teaching.
>
> —Proverbs 4:1–2

Two New Testament Scripture readings are part of each Divine Liturgy. One is from either the Acts of the Apostles or an epistle. The other is from one of the Gospels.[7] Every time a reading is introduced in a service, the reader tells us the book from which it is taken but not the specific chapter and verse. For instance, we may hear, "The epistle is from St. Paul's Letter to the Romans," but the chapter and verses are not stated. Chapters and verses weren't added to the Scriptures until the fifteenth century.

---

7 The Pre-Sanctified Liturgy during Great Lent includes two Scripture readings from the Old Testament, from Genesis and Proverbs. During Holy Week at the Pre-Sanctified Liturgy, readings are taken from the Old Testament books of Exodus and Job, and a Gospel lesson is added. Old Testament prophecies are read at many Vespers services, while New Testament scriptures are part of nearly every other service in the Orthodox Church—Paraklesis, baptism, wedding, funeral, Matins, etc. I share this to point out that Scripture readings are part of nearly every service in the Orthodox Church, though we may read only from the Old Testament or only from the New Testament in a particular service.

After a reading is introduced in the service, the priest or deacon gives the prompt, "Let us be attentive." We are told to pay attention. Why? Aren't these writings from the first century? Why are they important today?

We are told to pay attention because the things that affected the early churches still impact our Church today. For instance, when St. Paul writes in 1 Corinthians 13:3, "If I give away all I have, and if I deliver my body to be burned, but have not love, I gain nothing," this message that love is the greatest of virtues rings as true for the Church in the twenty-first century as it did in the first. These lessons from the epistles are timeless.

In Galatians 5:22–23 we read, "But the fruit of the Spirit is love, joy, peace, patience, kindness, goodness, faithfulness, gentleness, self-control; against such there is no law."

In Titus 3:9 we read, "But avoid stupid controversies, genealogies, dissensions, and quarrels over the law, for they are unprofitable and futile."

In Romans 5:3–5 we read, "More than that, we rejoice in our sufferings, knowing that suffering produces endurance, and endurance produces character, and character produces hope, and hope does not disappoint us."

The messages in each of these passages are applicable to our lives today. Saint Paul and others wrote to the churches of the first century and continue to speak with solid spiritual advice to today's churches and today's parishioners. It is amazing how the Spirit inspired the authors of the epistles to write things that are timeless in their value.

Remember this: It is not enough to merely hear what is read. It is important to apply what we hear to our lives—to be not only hearers but also doers of the Word (James 1:22–25). This is why we must be attentive—attentive to what is proclaimed and attentive to apply these words to our everyday lives, to our everyday decisions, in our everyday challenges.

Wisdom. Arise. Let us hear the Holy Gospel. Peace be with all.

> Stand therefore, having girded your loins with truth, and having put on the breastplate of righteousness, and having shod your feet with the equipment of the gospel of peace; besides all these, taking the shield of faith, with which you can quench all the flaming darts of the evil one.
>
> —Ephesians 6:14–16

When the epistle reading has concluded, the priest blesses the person who offered the reading. We then turn our attention toward the reading of the Gospel. The word *wisdom*, or *sophia* in Greek, is stated without qualification or explanation. There is no "This is wisdom" or "These are words of wisdom you are about to hear." That message is implied.

Orthoi can mean "to rise," "to listen," or even "to pay attention." From a practical perspective, this part of the service is where people rise after sitting during the epistle reading. But from a spiritual perspective, the words are a reminder for our hearts and minds to rise to attention, "to hear the Holy Gospel."

But before reading the Gospel, the priest imparts a blessing of peace to the congregation. This blessing, "peace be with all," is said three times during the Divine Liturgy—before the Gospel reading, before the confession of faith (the Creed), and before Holy Communion.

The word *peace* has already been used five times up to this point of the Divine Liturgy, and we are again reminded of peace for two reasons: First, the gospel of Christ is a message of peace. Nowhere does the gospel say to take up arms against a neighbor or to be unkind or cruel to people. Rather, the central message of the gospel is one of salvation: "For God so loved the world that He gave His only Son, that whoever believes in Him should not perish but have eternal life" (John 3:16). The greatest commandments in the gospel revolve around love:

> But when the Pharisees heard that he had silenced the Sadducees, they came together. And one of them, a lawyer, asked him a question, to test him. "Teacher, which is the great commandment in the Law?" And he said to him, "You shall love the Lord your God with all your heart, and with all your soul, and with all your mind. This is the great and first commandment. And a second is like it, You shall love your neighbor as yourself. On these two commandments depend all the law and the prophets." (Matthew 22:34–40)

Access to salvation and doing acts of love revolve around our pursuit of peace. The gospel of salvation is essentially the gospel of peace—hence the reminder to us that whatever will be read in the gospel passage on a particular day calls us to peace.

The second reminder as we hear the blessing "peace be with all" is for us to have peace in our minds at this moment. If we have been distracted during the service, we need to clear our thoughts so we can absorb the words. Again, on a practical level, much of the Divine Liturgy is the same each time the service is celebrated. But the Scripture readings vary. They are unique to each service. Therefore, our hearts and minds should be clear of thought so we can pay attention. I remember as a child being taught that during the Gospel passage we were not to move. This is why all activity in the church stops: people do not light candles, enter the nave, or move around during the reading of the Holy Gospel.

In the last reflection we considered the importance of attentiveness. We listen closely because the ultimate purpose of the Gospel reading is for us to become not only hearers of the Word but also doers of the Word. In Luke 11:28, Jesus says, "Blessed rather are those who hear the word of God and keep it!" In order to do God's Word, we must first hear it. And in order to hear the Word, we must be at peace and ready to listen.

Today's prayer comes from the Divine Liturgy. The priest offers it inaudibly before the reading of the Gospel, but it is a great prayer to say before reading any Scripture, even outside the context of the service. It should be a part of your prayer life each day, each time you open the Bible:

> Shine in our hearts, O Master who loves mankind, the pure light of Your divine knowledge, and open the eyes of our mind that we may comprehend the proclamations of Your Gospels. Instill in us also reverence for Your blessed commandments so that, having trampled down all carnal desires, we may lead a spiritual life, both thinking and doing all those things that are pleasing to You. For You, Christ our God, are the illumination of our souls and bodies, and to You we offer up glory, together with Your Father, who is without beginning, and Your all-holy, good, and life-creating Spirit, now and forever and to the ages of ages. Amen.

The reading is from the Holy Gospel according to [*Matthew, Mark, Luke or John*]. Let us be attentive. Glory to You O Lord, Glory to You.

> A sower went out to sow his seed; and as he sowed, some fell along the path and was trodden under food, and the birds of the air devoured it. And some fell on the rock; and as it grew

> up, it withered away, because it had no moisture. And some fell among thorns; and the thorns grew with it and choked it. And some fell into good soil and grew and yielded a hundredfold. . . . Now the parable is this: The seed is the word of God. The ones along the path are those who have heard; then the devil comes and takes away the word from their hearts, that they may not believe and be saved. And the ones on the rock are those who, when they hear the word, receive it with joy; but these have no root, they believe for a while and in time of temptation fall away. And as for what fell among the thorns, they are those who hear, but as they go on their way they are choked by the cares and riches and pleasures of life and their fruit does not mature. And as for that in the good soil, they are those who, hearing the word, hold it fast in an honest and good heart, and bring forth fruit with patience.
>
> —Luke 8:5–8, 11–15

A Gospel lesson is part of every Divine Liturgy of St. John Chrysostom and St. Basil the Great.[8] When the priest introduces the Gospel reading, he says, "*The* reading is from the Holy Gospel," not "A reading." The reason for this is that the Scriptures that are read in the services come from a prescribed lectionary with readings assigned to every Sunday, every feast day, and every day of the year. You can go to any Orthodox Church in the world on a given Sunday or feast day and hear the same Gospel reading.

The following list shows how the Gospel readings work in the calendar:

8 There is no Gospel reading at the Pre-Sanctified Liturgies during Lent. However, there is a Gospel reading during the Pre-Sanctified Liturgies that are offered during Holy Week.

- Paschal season: Primarily from the Gospel of John
- After Pentecost: Generally from the Gospel of Matthew. Depending on how early Pascha and thus Pentecost fall, there may be anywhere from ten to fifteen Sundays of Matthew before September 6.
- Feast of the Universal Exaltation of the Precious and Life-Giving Cross (September 14): The Sundays before and after have their own specific readings, then from September 22 through mid-December, we read from the Gospel of Luke.
- Sundays surrounding Christmas and Theophany: Their own readings
- Theophany through the beginning of the Triodion period (pre-Lent): Generally from Matthew
- Triodion Sundays and Lent: Their own specific readings
- Great Lent: The Gospel of Mark is read predominantly on weekends. During the weekdays, other than the Feast of the Annunciation, there are no daily Gospel readings but rather Old Testament scriptures, primarily from the Book of Genesis and the Book of Proverbs.
- Feast day on a Sunday: The Gospel of that feast replaces the regular Sunday Gospel reading, which is skipped for the year. For example, if the Dormition of the Theotokos is on a Sunday, which also happens to be the eighth Sunday of Matthew, then the Gospel reading for the eighth Sunday of Matthew is skipped, and the Gospel of the Dormition is read in its place.
- Other major feast days: Each its own unique Gospel as well as epistle reading

Of course, you don't need to memorize this schedule. The point in sharing this information is so you know that the Gospel readings are not at the discretion of the priest but are set according to the church calendar. The Kanonion, a formalized list of what is read each Sunday of the upcoming year, is sent to every GOA priest from the Ecumenical Patriarchate in the fall of each year.

Scripture reading is important in the life of every Orthodox Christian. In prayer, we speak to God. In reading Scripture, we hear the words of God to us. Scripture reading should be part of our *daily* routine. It should not be limited to what we hear in church on Sundays.

I've heard an acronym for the word *Bible*: "Basic Instructions Before Leaving Earth." The Bible includes the history of God's people from the beginning of time through the creation of the early Church. It includes the saving message of Jesus Christ. It includes moral precepts and guideposts for life. Some have described the Bible as a love letter from God to His children. Whether you read a selection from the daily readings (which can be found on the websites of the various Orthodox jurisdictions), read a whole chapter, or read a just few verses, make time to read something of the Bible each day. The Psalms, for instance, include every emotion. It is good to read this book and catalogue the emotions it evokes in you.

If you've never read the Bible, the four Gospels are a good place to start. The epistles give advice to modern churches just as they did for early ones. And the Old Testament Book of Proverbs has helpful advice for daily living.

The story of the sower, which I quoted above, is a parable—a story with a hidden meaning and a life application. The application of this parable is easy to identify, though harder to put into practice. If the seed is the Word of God, then we are supposed to hold it fast in a good and honest heart and bring forth fruit from that seed. We are not supposed to be like seed that falls on thorns, getting choked by the cares of life or falling away in times of temptation.

It has been customary in the Divine Liturgy for the priest to deliver the homily, or sermon, after the reading of the Gospel to help us interpret the Scripture and tell us how to apply the passage to our lives. In many parishes, the sermon is given at the end of the service for pastoral reasons or practical ones. Regardless of the timing of the homily, the priest is always supposed to preach—to teach the people and deepen their understanding of Scripture.

The Liturgy of the Faithful

Ever Guarded by Your Might

[Grant] that, ever guarded by Your might, we may ascribe glory to You, to the Father and to the Son and to the Holy Spirit, now and forever and to the ages of ages. Amen.

> Blessed be the God and Father of our Lord Jesus Christ!
> By his great mercy we have been born anew to a living hope
> through the resurrection of Jesus Christ from the dead,
> and to an inheritance which is imperishable, undefiled, and
> unfading, kept in heaven for you, who by God's power are
> guarded through faith for a salvation ready to be revealed in
> the last time.
>
> —1 Peter 1:3–5

As we conclude the Gospel reading, we end the first part of the Divine Liturgy, known as the Liturgy of the Word, in which the reading of the words of God through the sacred Scriptures is central. The second part of the service is called the Liturgy of the Faithful, when faithful believers present their gifts of bread and wine, confess their faith, call the Holy Spirit down to consecrate the Gifts, then receive the Gifts through Holy Communion.

After the Gospel reading, the priest makes ready for this second part of the Liturgy by placing the Gospel toward the back of the altar table. He then opens a cloth called the *antimension* and spreads it over the front part of the table. *Antimension* means "instead of the table," and this cloth is essential to celebrate the Divine Liturgy. When the Liturgy is celebrated outside of the church temple—for example, at summer camp or in a nursing home—the antimension can be placed on any table, transforming it into a suitable altar.

On the antimension is an icon of the *Epitaphios* (literally "in the tomb"), which shows Christ being lowered from the Cross and being placed in the Tomb. This icon is a smaller version of the icon that rests in the Tomb of Christ (also called the Epitaphios) on Holy Friday. For the forty days of Pascha, this embroidered cloth is placed on the altar beneath the antimension.

After the Scriptures have been read and the people have absorbed the power and strength that comes from them, the priest offers a transitional line, that "ever guarded by Your might" we may continually give glory to God in the Trinity, now and forever.

As we can see in these reflections, virtually every line of the Divine Liturgy has its basis in Scripture. Many times, in fact, we find scripture readings that closely match a line in the Divine Liturgy, such as the line for today. The words echo the passage quoted above from 1 Peter, which offers up glory to God and mentions Jesus Christ. The line from the Liturgy also mentions the Holy Spirit, proclaiming that God's power guards us through faith for a salvation that is ready to be revealed fully at the end of time.

The Divine Liturgy reveals God's power in the here and now. It allows us to stand in His presence in the here and now. It allows us to partake of His divine nature in the here and now. And it helps to grow, guard, and preserve our faith for our entrance into eternity. This is why the words of the Liturgy ask God to grant that we *always* be guarded by His power, now *and* forever.

The prayer today is called the Second Prayer of the Faithful. It is generally offered inaudibly by the priest during the reading of the epistle, and in some churches, the priest offers the prayer out loud after the reading of the Gospel. The prayer concludes, as do all the prayers of the service, with an ekphonesis, a statement offering glory to the Holy Trinity, which is highlighted in this reflection.

> Again and countless times we fall down before You, and we implore You, O Good One, Who loves mankind: That You, having regarded our prayer, may cleanse our souls and bodies from every defilement of flesh and spirit, and grant to us to stand before Your holy Altar of sacrifice, free of guilt and condemnation. Grant also, O God, to those who pray with us, progress in life, faith, and spiritual understanding. Grant that they always worship You with awe and love, partake of Your Holy Mysteries without guilt or condemnation, and be deemed worthy of Your celestial kingdom.
>
> That, ever guarded by Your might, we may ascribe glory to You, to the Father and to the Son and to the Holy Spirit, now and forever and to the ages of ages. Amen.
>
> Let us, who mystically represent the Cherubim and who sing the thrice-holy hymn to the life-creating Trinity, now lay aside every worldly care. So that we may receive the King of all.

Laying Aside Every Worldly Care

Let us, who mystically represent the Cherubim and who sing the thrice-holy hymn to the life-creating Trinity, now lay aside every worldly care. So that we may receive the King of all.

> But Martha was distracted with much serving; and she went to him and said, "Lord, do you not care that my sister has left

me to serve alone? Tell her then to help me." But the Lord answered her, "Martha, Martha, you are anxious and troubled about many things; one thing is needful. Mary has chosen the good portion, which shall not be taken away from her."

—Luke 10:40–42

Today begins several reflections on the Cherubic Hymn, as well as the prayers and actions of the priest during the singing of the hymn. So, let us begin with the practical and work our way to the inspirational.

The Liturgy of the Faithful begins with a presentation of the Holy Gifts and their transfer to the holy altar. What do we mean by *transfer?* Well, first let us step back in time and look at the early Church.

Back then, the communities were often much larger than the parishes of today, with multiple clergy serving. When people went to church, they would enter the narthex and find two large rooms next to it. One room on the right side was the baptistry with a baptismal pool, which would be used only a few times a year for mass baptisms. On the left side of the narthex was a room called the *skevofilakion,* or the room of the "holy vessels" (*skevi*). A priest, called the *economos,* was in charge of this room and the property of the church, and he received the gifts offered by parishioners.[9]

Upon entering the narthex, the faithful would give an offering to the economos—wine, bread, oil, incense, candles—the things needed to conduct the service. This is where the tradition of making an offering comes from, though in the ancient Church the offerings

9 Priests are given titles as they accrue seniority and service. These titles are largely honorary, since most priests serve by themselves in parishes. One of these honorary titles is *economos,* and another is *protopresbyter,* or archpriest. The only title that materially changes the role of the priest is the title *pnevmatikos,* because only someone who has been given this title can hear confessions. A confessor also wears the diamond-shaped vestment over his right knee. Those who are not confessors do not wear this piece of vestment.

included not only money but these other items as well. The economos would then prepare the gifts of bread and wine. At the time of the Great Entrance, the deacons of the church would process down the side aisle, pick up the gifts in the narthex, proceed up the center aisle, then give them to the protopresbyter to be placed on the altar. Over the years, a table to the left side of the altar, called the table of the *prothesis,* replaced the skevofilakion.

At the prothesis, the priest prepares the bread on the *diskos* (or paten), places wine in the chalice, and prepares the Gifts for the Divine Liturgy. At the time of the Great Entrance, he exits the altar, goes down the left aisle to the narthex, and then up the center aisle.[10] Though the transfer of the Gifts is only a few feet—from the prothesis to the altar—the ancient processional route is still used. This procession is what we call the Great Entrance, with altar servers walking in front of the priest carrying candles, fans, a cross, and a censer.

Before the Great Entrance can take place, the priest offers a prayer, censes the church, and prepares to bring the Gifts. He also offers several other prayers here, which we will examine in future reflections.

While all this is going on, the people sing the Cherubic Hymn, which makes two important points. First, it reminds us that we are about to stand in the place of the angels. How is that possible? In Isaiah 6, we read the following:

> In the year that King Uzziah died I saw the Lord sitting upon a throne, high and lifted up; and his train filled the temple. Above him stood the seraphim; each had six wings: with two he covered his face, and with two he covered his feet, and with two he flew. And one called to another and said:

10 When a bishop is present and serving, the Gifts are presented to him, and he places them on the altar.

"Holy, holy, holy is the LORD of hosts; the whole earth is full of his glory." (Isaiah 6:1–3)

In Isaiah's vision of heaven, the angels surround the throne of God, singing the thrice-holy hymn. Likewise we, the faithful, are about to set aside our worldly cares so that we too can stand in the presence of God, temporarily entering into heaven and assuming the role of the angels. We do this in a mysterious way; we can't explain scientifically how this happens. So, we mystically represent the cherubim, and we sing the thrice-holy hymn to the life-creating Trinity because we are preparing to receive the King of all, our Lord Jesus Christ, in the Sacrament of Holy Communion.

The hymn reminds us what is needed for us to do this: we must set aside our worldly cares. We are all like Martha in the Scripture passage above. Stress and hurry are just a part of life. We almost feel guilty if we are not scurrying around doing something. This hymn not only gives us permission to set aside our earthly concerns but almost demands that we do so. If we can't set aside earthly cares, at least for a little while each day in prayer, and for a little while each week in worship, then we *are* going to miss out on the only needful thing—intimacy with our Lord. It is time spent at His feet that gives us the strength and the wisdom to do our "running around" successfully.

It is in this quiet time with Christ, setting aside our worldly cares and to-do lists, that we can each become Mary in a Martha world.

A Prayer to Be Worthy

No one bound by carnal desires and pleasures is worthy to approach, draw near, or minister to You, the King of Glory.

For to serve You is great and awesome even for the heavenly powers. Yet, because of Your ineffable and immeasurable love for mankind, You impassibly and immutably became man. You, as the Master of all, became our high priest and delivered unto us the sacred service of this liturgical sacrifice without the shedding of blood.

Indeed, Lord our God, You alone reign over the celestial and the terrestrial; borne aloft on the cherubic throne, Lord of the Seraphim and King of Israel, the only holy and resting among the holy ones. I now beseech You, who alone are good and inclined to hear: Look down upon me, Your sinful and unprofitable servant, and cleanse my soul and heart of a wicked conscience; and enable me, by the power of Your Holy Spirit, clothed with the grace of the priesthood, to stand before Your holy Table and celebrate the Mystery of Your holy and pure Body and Your precious Blood.

I come before You with my head bowed, and I implore You: Turn not Your face away from me, nor reject me from among Your children, but make me, Your sinful and unworthy servant, worthy to offer these Gifts to You.

For You are the One who both offers and is offered, the One who is received and is distributed, O Christ our God, and to You we offer up glory, with Your Father, who is without beginning, and Your all-holy and good and life-creating Spirit, now and forever and to the ages of ages. Amen.

> And I heard the voice of the Lord saying, "Whom shall I send, and who will go for Us?" Then I said, "Here am I! Send me."
>
> —Isaiah 6:8

During the singing of the Cherubic Hymn, several things happen. First, the priest offers the prayer above, which we will discuss here. Then he offers incense, recites Psalm 50/51, and prepares for the Great Entrance.

Today's reflection is the longest one thus far. This prayer is of extreme importance to me as a priest, so please allow me a few extra minutes to explain it line by line. The prayer applies not only to clergy, with its insight into the holy priesthood, but to the laity because of its insight into what it means to be an obedient and faithful Christian.

The celebrant priest prays these words with extreme humility as he prepares to offer the Gifts of bread and wine to become the Body and Blood of Christ and then administer them to the people.

No one bound by carnal desires and pleasures is worthy to approach, draw near, or minister to You, the King of Glory.

No priest can ever be worthy of approaching the holy altar to celebrate the Divine Liturgy. No human being is ever worthy to partake of Holy Communion. It is only by the mercy of the Lord that anyone can dare approach to touch the divine Christ in the Eucharist. Yet if no one approaches for Holy Communion, then no one experiences the joy and the unique oneness with Christ that He called us to when He instituted the Holy Eucharist. And if no one serves as a priest, then no sacrament can be celebrated. Thus we approach our Lord's presence in the Gifts with great humility.

For to serve You is great and awesome even for the heavenly powers.

Even the angels in heaven cannot do what we are doing. For the angels surround the throne of God, standing near Him; but in the Divine Liturgy we, the human beings, touch the living God.

Yet, because of Your ineffable and immeasurable love for mankind, You impassibly and immutably became man.

In the words of St. Athanasios, "For He (Christ) was incarnate that we might be made god; and He manifested Himself through a body that we might receive an idea of the invisible Father; and He endured the insults of human beings, that we might inherit incorruptibility. He Himself was harmed in no way, being impassible and incorruptible and the very Word and God."[11] Christ took on human flesh yet remained God—perfect Man and perfect God.

You, as the Master of all, became our high priest and delivered unto us the sacred service of this liturgical sacrifice without the shedding of blood.

Christ came to serve and to minister, giving us His own Body and Blood. Prior to the time of Christ walking the earth, a large part of worship involved offering up animals as sacrifices. But with Christ's death on the Cross and His shedding of His blood for us, we no longer offer blood sacrifices. Instead, the priest serves Holy Communion to the people of God.

Indeed, Lord our God, You alone reign over the celestial and the terrestrial; borne aloft on the cherubic throne, Lord of the Seraphim and King of Israel, the only holy and resting among the holy ones. I now beseech You, who alone are good and inclined to hear.

We give glory to the Lord our God and ascribe honor only to Him. Only He rules over the heavens and the earth. Only He is seated

---

11 *On the Incarnation: An English Translation of St. Athanasius the Great of Alexandria*, trans. John Behr (Yonkers, NY: St. Vladimir's Seminary Press, 2011), 107.

on the throne of the cherubim (an order of angels); only He rules over the seraphim (another order of angels). He is the one who dwells amid the saints in heaven, and He alone models what is good. He is always ready to hear our prayers.

Look down upon me, Your sinful and unprofitable servant, and cleanse my soul and heart of a wicked conscience; and enable me, by the power of Your Holy Spirit, clothed with the grace of the priesthood, to stand before Your holy Table and celebrate the Mystery of Your holy and pure Body and Your precious Blood. I come before You with my head bowed, and I implore You: Turn not Your face away from me, nor reject me from among Your children, but make me, Your sinful and unworthy servant, worthy to offer these Gifts to You.

How can a human being, entangled in his own sins and struggles, somehow step forward from the people and celebrate the divine services? How can any of the clergy dare hold these elements in their own hands? If any priest thought long and hard about what he holds, he'd run away and spend his life begging for God's mercies for doing this even once. And yet, without priests there can be no Divine Liturgy. *Someone* has to go forth for the people to perform this task. So, before doing the greatest work that a human being can do—to hold the Lord God in his hands—the priest prayerfully acknowledges that he is "sinful and unworthy" and that he is a "servant." He "implores God" to look upon him, to "cleanse [his] soul and heart of a wicked conscience."

In the service of ordination to the holy priesthood, the bishop prays that the "divine grace (of the Holy Spirit), which heals what is infirm and completes what is lacking," may come upon the man being ordained. So, the priest calls on that power of the Holy Spirit who once vested him with the grace of priesthood to again come upon him, allowing him to stand without condemnation before the holy altar to celebrate the Sacrament of Holy Communion. The priest bows his head and implores God not to turn His face away from him or reject him and his prayer but to make him worthy for this moment in time to offer the Gifts.

For You are the One who both offers and is offered, the One who is received and is distributed, O Christ our God, and to You we offer up glory, with Your Father, who is without beginning, and Your all-holy and good and life-creating Spirit, now and forever and to the ages of ages. Amen.

The concluding statement of the prayer is that Christ is both the One who is offering the Gifts and the One being offered. He is the One who receives our prayers, and yet He is the One who will be distributing Himself to us in Holy Communion.

For me, this is the most beautiful and powerful prayer of the Divine Liturgy. It reaffirms my calling to serve as a priest and forces me to utter words of extreme humility and unworthiness, with the hope that these words will be the cornerstones of my ministry—not only at the Divine Liturgy but away from it as well. In my humble opinion, this prayer can be altered with a few changes to become a beautiful prayer offered by the priest or the people outside of the Liturgy.

And so, with great humility, I offer these words again so that *you* can pray it as today's prayer. May it serve to remind you and me that when we are intertwined in worldly desires and pleasures, none of us is worthy to approach Christ for Holy Communion, to approach Him in prayer, or to be His minister through our respective roles. Therefore, we must try to "lay aside every worldly care" on a daily basis—not just on Sunday mornings—through prayer, obedience to the commandments, and charity. Then we can experience a continual "communion" (union) with Christ, both in church and outside of it.

Pray the following prayer for yourself. The words in italics are my changes.

No one bound by carnal desires and pleasures is worthy to approach, draw near, or minister to You, the King of Glory. For to serve You is great and awesome even for the heavenly powers. Yet, because of Your ineffable and immeasurable love for mankind, You impassibly and immutably became man. You, as the Master of all, became our high priest and delivered unto us the celebration of *the Divine Liturgy*.

Indeed, Lord our God, You alone reign over the celestial and the terrestrial; borne aloft on the cherubic throne, Lord of the Seraphim and King of Israel, the only holy and resting among the holy ones. I now beseech You, who alone are good and inclined to hear: Look down upon me, Your sinful and unprofitable servant, and cleanse my soul and heart of a wicked conscience; and enable me, by the power of Your Holy Spirit, clothed with the grace of *my baptismal garment*, to stand *in Your Holy Church* and *receive* Your holy and pure Body and Your precious Blood.

I come before You with my head bowed, and I implore You: Turn not Your face away from me, nor reject me from among Your children, but make me, Your sinful and unworthy servant, worthy to *receive* these Gifts.

For You are the One who both offers and is offered, the One who is received and is distributed, O Christ our God, and to You we offer up glory, with Your Father, who is without beginning, and Your all-holy and good and life-creating Spirit, now and forever and to the ages of ages. Amen.

Let my prayer arise as incense before You, and the lifting up of my hands as an evening sacrifice.

—Adapted from Psalm 140/141:2

After saying the previous prayer, the priest offers incense over the entire church and all the holy things—first the altar (the throne of God) on all four sides, the crucifix behind the altar, and the table of oblation (prothesis) to the left, where the Holy Gifts have been prepared. He then exits the sanctuary and censes the bishop's throne, which also represents the throne of God. Next he censes the icons on the icon screen three times each—Christ, the Theotokos, St. John the Baptist, the festal icon of the church, and the icons of the archangels Michael and Gabriel.

Next, the priest censes the people. Why? Are the people holy images like the icons? Absolutely! In Genesis 1:26–27, we read,

> Then God said, "Let us make man in our image, after our likeness; and let them have dominion over the fish of the sea, and over the birds of the air, and over the cattle, and over all the earth, and over every creeping thing that creeps upon the earth." So God created man in his own image, in the image of God he created him; male and female he created them.

We are created for holiness. So, when the priest is censing, two things should cross our minds. First, because we are created in God's image and likeness, the priest is censing us just as he is censing the icons. Are we pursuing holiness? Are we striving to be godly in our lives?

The second thing we should do is "let our prayers arise as incense." This is one of the moments in the Divine Liturgy when it is okay to offer a personal prayer. For most of the service we pray corporately, offering prayers for whatever is being lifted up at that moment (e.g., for peace in the world, for our country, etc.). But this moment, as the incense is rising to heaven, is a good opportunity to pray for things that are personal to us. As the choir is singing for us to "lay aside every worldly care, so that we may receive the King of all," we can take this moment to call to mind the worldly concerns that keep us away from Christ and offer those to Him as well.

To bow or to make the sign of the cross—which is correct? Some hotly debate this subject, which in my humble opinion is foolish. As St. Paul wrote in his Epistle to Titus (3:9), "Avoid stupid controversies." This one could certainly qualify. We bow out of reverence to God, who made us in His image and likeness. But as we offer a prayer to rise along with the incense, we most certainly can make the sign of the cross as we would after any prayer. Thus, to do either or both is acceptable.

Incense is offered at other parts of the Divine Liturgy—at the conclusion of the Proskomide, during the preparation of the Holy Gifts before the Liturgy begins, after the Small Entrance when a hierarch is serving, over the Gospel prior to its reading, over the whole church during the Cherubic Hymn, over the Gifts after they are consecrated, and over the remains of Holy Communion after it is distributed. Incense is offered at just about every other service in the church as well.

We can burn incense in our homes as well during daily prayers, with the symbolism of the prayers rising as incense. Orthodox worship combines all the senses, including that of smell. When I imagine what the scent of heaven might be, I often think of the church after services. If we leave the church and then enter again minutes later, the unmistakable smell of incense greets us, the fragrance that symbolically carries our prayers up to heaven.

For today's prayer, I share with you the priest's prayer as he blesses the incense before offering it over the icons and the people.

We offer You incense, O Christ our God, as an offering of spiritual fragrance. Accept it before Your heavenly altar and send down upon us in return the grace of Your Holy Spirit, now and forever and to the ages of ages. Amen.[12]

Having Beheld the Resurrection of Christ

Having beheld the Resurrection of Christ, let us worship the holy Lord Jesus, the only sinless one. Your Cross, O Christ, we venerate, and Your holy Resurrection we praise and glorify. For You are our God; apart from You we know no other; we call upon Your name. Come, all faithful, let us venerate the holy Resurrection of Christ; for behold, through the Cross, joy has come to the whole world. Ever blessing the Lord, let us praise His Resurrection; for having endured the Cross for us, He destroyed death by death.

> Therefore, since we are surrounded by so great a cloud of witnesses, let us also lay aside every weight, and sin which clings so closely, and let us run with perseverance the race that is set before us, looking to Jesus the pioneer and perfecter of our faith, who for the joy that was set before him endured the cross, despising the shame, and is seated at the right hand of the throne of God.
>
> —Hebrews 12:1–2

12 From *The Order of the Divine and Holy Liturgy* (Brookline, MA: Holy Cross Orthodox Press, 1987), 22–23.

This beautiful statement is offered three times every Sunday. During the Matins service, between the reading of the Matins Gospel and the chanting of Psalm 50/51, the priest or the chanter reads it. The priest recites it as he begins to offer incense during the Cherubic Hymn, and again after he receives Holy Communion, while he prepares to distribute the Gifts to the faithful. These words are also read at every Matins service throughout the paschal season.

It is interesting that we find the words *joy* and *cross* in the same sentence both in this liturgical line and in the above-quoted scripture. We usually think of the Cross associated with pain or with shame, but this prayer reminds us that the Cross, for the Christian, is a symbol of joy. It is the symbol of our hope. Our salvation comes from the Cross. It is the place where we are now; we are to take up our cross and follow today. And it is the place where we are going: when we've carried our cross with the same dignity and obedience with which Christ carried His, when we die to our personal wants by carrying our cross, then when we die physically in this life, we will be resurrected to everlasting life.

Today's prayer is the most well known hymn of the church year. The Resurrection is part of every Divine Liturgy. Thus, the hymn of the Resurrection should always be close at hand. Even though it is only chanted during the forty days of Pascha, this hymn should come to our minds often, reminding us of the joy and the hope of the Resurrection and serving as a teaching tool. For this hymn neither glorifies the Lord nor petitions Him for anything. Rather, it teaches us in a succinct way why the Resurrection is of utmost importance and what is the true meaning of the Christian Faith. Sing or hum this hymn a few times, and remember the joy of Pascha while anticipating the joy of *our* personal Pascha, which we await at the end of our lives.

Christ is risen from the dead, by death, trampling down upon death and to those in the tombs, He has granted life.

Truly the Lord is Risen!

Create in me a clean heart, O God, and renew a steadfast spirit within me.

—Adapted from Psalm 50/51:10 (Matins service)

When my computer freezes up, is running slowly, or is just not doing what I want it to do, the first thing I try is to reboot it, and many times the problem is fixed. It is simple: hit a couple of keys, wait a few minutes, and generally I am back in business.

Do you ever feel like you need to press the reset button on your life? Well, there is a prayer specifically for this, and it is Psalm 50/51, the "Psalm of Repentance." *Repentance* means reorienting toward God. So, when you've done wrong, or when you just want to do better, Psalm 50/51 is a great prayer to pray.

This is the first mention of the psalms in these reflections on praying the Divine Liturgy, so we should note that the psalms are 150 poems that capture every human emotion: joy, anger, disappointment, hope. Many times when we are praying, we struggle to find the right words to capture our feelings at a particular moment. If you read the psalms, you can make a list of the emotions that each one evokes in you and then keep an index of them to read in times of need.

The psalms are a part of just about every service in the Orthodox Church. That's because worship by nature involves and evokes emotion, and by including the psalms, the Church helps us to manage our feelings. For instance, at evening Vespers we read Psalm

103/104, the Psalm of Creation. As the day is about to end and another begins, we acknowledge that God made everything—the sun, the moon, the stars. Psalm verses are used during the antiphons, and in some jurisdictions, Psalm 102/103 and Psalm 145/146 are sung in their entirety in place of the first and second antiphons.

Psalm 50/51 is part of the daily Matins service, the daily Small Compline service, and usually part of the Third Hour service. If we were praying the daily monastic cycle of services, Psalm 50/51 would be recited three times per day. The reason for this repetition is our constant need for repentance. The Lord, through this beautiful psalm, gives us a chance to reboot our spirits a few times per day.

Psalm 50/51 is part of the Divine Liturgy, and the priest says it inaudibly as he is offering incense during the Cherubic Hymn—that's why his lips are moving as he is censing. Why this particular psalm? Because the priest is calling to mind his own repentance as he is about to carry the Holy Gifts to the altar in the Great Entrance. It is a great psalm to pray on a daily basis, before receiving Holy Communion, or even during the Divine Liturgy. Some versions of the Cherubic Hymn are very long and are very difficult to sing. Praying Psalm 50/51 or offering personal prayers are two things to do while the incense is being offered. This psalm is also appropriate to pray any time we feel the need for repentance or a new spiritual start.

There is great meaning in the verses of this psalm. Verse 10 is probably the most well-known: "Create in me a clean heart, O God, / and put a new and right spirit within me." This verse can be repeated over and over when you feel like you've done wrong and want God to forgive you.

Verse 7, "Purge me with hyssop, and I shall be clean; / wash me, and I shall be whiter than snow," is prayed at the end of every Orthodox Christian funeral service as the body of the deceased is anointed with oil.

Verse 15, "O Lord, open thou my lips, / and my mouth shall show forth thy praise" is prayed by the priest, inaudibly, just before every Divine Liturgy begins.

Verses 16–17 read, "For thou hast no delight in sacrifice; / were I to give a burnt offering, thou wouldst not be pleased. / The sacrifice acceptable to God is a broken spirit; / a broken and contrite heart, O God, thou will not despise." These words give hope in times of sorrow. When our heart has been broken and is humble and contrite over sin, this is the sacrifice that is pleasing to God. God is not necessarily looking for material sacrifices but for a change in our hearts, to turn them to please Him rather than pleasing ourselves and others.

For today's prayer, pray Psalm 50/51 in its entirety. I used to read this psalm daily before being ordained, to the point that I memorized it. Today, it is just a thought away in times of sorrowful repentance. It is something I try to pray with conviction at each Divine Liturgy, realizing my need for a cleaner heart, a more steadfast spirit, and a humbler countenance. When I pray Psalm 50/51 at the Divine Liturgy, I feel less hypocritical in celebrating the service because I realize that the Fathers of the Church included it to help the priests recognize that even the most faithful of us fall short every day. We are all in need of God's mercies and our personal repentance. Combining this with the priestly prayer we examined two reflections ago puts me in proper spiritual alignment to move to the climax of the service.

But you don't have to be a priest or be at church to get something out of praying this psalm. It's good for a spiritual boost or spiritual reboot any time.

Have mercy on me, O God, according to thy steadfast love;
according to thy abundant mercy blot out my transgressions.
Wash me thoroughly from my iniquity, / and cleanse me from my sin!

For I know my transgressions, / and my sin is ever before me.
Against thee, thee only, have I sinned, / and done that which is evil in thy sight,
so that thou art justified in thy sentence / and blameless in thy judgment.
Behold, I was brought forth in iniquity, / and in sin did my mother conceive me.
Behold, thou desirest truth in the inward being; / therefore teach me wisdom in my secret heart.
Purge me with hyssop, and I shall be clean; / wash me, and I shall be whiter than snow.
Fill me with joy and gladness; / let the bones which thou hast broken rejoice.
Hide thy face from my sins, / and blot out all my iniquities.
Create in me a clean heart, O God, / and put a new and right spirit within me.
Cast me not away from thy presence, / and take not thy holy Spirit from me.
Restore to me the joy of thy salvation, / and uphold me with a willing spirit.
Then I will teach transgressors thy ways, / and sinners will return to thee.
Deliver me from bloodguiltiness, O God, / thou God of my salvation,
and my tongue will sing aloud of thy deliverance.
O Lord, open thou my lips, / and my mouth shall show forth thy praise.
For thou hast no delight in sacrifice; / were I to give a burnt offering,
thou wouldst not be pleased.
The sacrifice acceptable to God is a broken spirit; / a broken and contrite heart, O God,

thou wilt not despise.
Do good to Zion in thy good pleasure; / rebuild the walls of Jerusalem,
then wilt thou delight in right sacrifices, / in burnt offerings and whole burnt offerings;
then bulls will be offered on thy altar.
(Psalm 50/51)

God, be gracious to me, a sinner, and have mercy on me.

> But the tax collector, standing far off, would not even lift up his eyes to heaven, but beat his breast, saying, "God, be merciful to me a sinner!"
>
> —Luke 18:13

In the Divine Liturgy and the other divine services of the Orthodox Church, the priest performs several small prostrations—bending at the waist and touching the ground with the fingers of his right hand. This happens before the Liturgy begins, before the Small Entrance, before the Consecration of the Gifts, and before the priest receives Holy Communion. It also happens before the Great Entrance. As the priest finishes censing, he makes three prostrations before the holy altar table.

What does the priest say when he makes a prostration? It is a version of the Jesus Prayer. There is a tradition in the Orthodox Church of the Jesus Prayer, which is, "Lord Jesus Christ, Son of God, have mercy on me, a sinner." Both the Jesus Prayer and the prayer the priest is offering during prostrations have their origin in the publican's prayer in the Parable of the Publican and Pharisee as told in the Gospel of Luke.

In this parable, we are introduced to two men who went to the temple to pray. The Pharisee prayed "with himself," extolling his virtues and thanking God that he was not like the "unrighteous" tax collector. The tax collector prayed in humility, asking God for His mercies. The moral of the parable is that the Lord hears the humble prayer and not the haughty one.

So, as he prepares to pick up the Holy Gifts to carry them in the procession, the priest is asking God for His graciousness and mercy, as even he must acknowledge his own sinfulness and need of these essential blessings from the Lord.

Likewise, all of us should pray the Jesus Prayer each day as a way to continually ask for God's mercies and forgiveness. If you say the Jesus Prayer enough, it becomes like the song that just can't get out of your head. It will stay in your mind all day long and will be with you as you make decisions, have conversations, and engage in activities. Keeping the thought of the Lord in your mind constantly will make it easier to keep Him at the forefront of a Christ-centered life.

You can offer this prayer repetitively. Some people offer their prayer with every two breaths: "Lord Jesus Christ (inhale), Son of God (exhale), have mercy (inhale) on me, a sinner (exhale)." You can pray it using a prayer rope, making a revolution or two around the circle.[13]

The prayer rope is also a witness for your faith. It is a good conversation starter because people will ask what it is. But it is also a good tool for accountability, for yourself and to others. Wearing a prayer rope around your wrist may slow you down from raising that fist in anger or using that hand to do something that is not pleasing to God. You can also pray the Jesus Prayer and insert the names of other people: "Lord Jesus Christ, Son of God, have mercy on Your

13 Most prayer ropes, or *komboskini* in Greek, have thirty-three knots and are worn on the wrist. The number thirty-three represents Christ's years on earth.

servant (name)." Try praying for thirty-three names—one for each knot on the prayer rope—of people you know. And if you run out of names, try praying for thirty-three kinds of people, like "Lord Jesus Christ, Son of God, have mercy on (teachers / the military / doctors / firefighters)" and so on.

Here is another practical application that I use personally. When I bend down to tie my shoes or pick up something from the floor (which is often), I offer the prayer that I offer in church: "God be gracious to me, a sinner, and have mercy on me." Continually invoking the name of God has a great benefit for us, even when we offer it without thinking. He continues to bless us, and we continue to bless Him.

Today's prayer is the Jesus Prayer. Try repeating this for five minutes. Spend four minutes praying this for yourself, and spend one minute inserting the names of your loved ones and friends.

Lord Jesus Christ, Son of God, have mercy on me, a sinner.

The Great Entrance

Getting Ready

Lift up your hands to the holy place, / and bless the LORD.

—Psalm 133/134:2

God has gone up with a shout, / the LORD with the sound of a trumpet.

—Psalm 46/47:5

We have entered into the Liturgy of the Faithful, the second half of the service where the Gifts will be consecrated and we will partake of them. The priest now prays several short prayers as he prepares for the Great Entrance. After his prostrations before the holy altar, he venerates the antimension (the cloth), which he opened after the Gospel reading and upon which the Holy Gifts will be placed.

We venerate images of holiness. I have been asked by people who are not familiar with the Orthodox Church, "Why do you kiss pictures on pieces of wood or cloth?" And my answer is that we don't kiss pictures on wood; we venerate images of holiness. For these are not mere pictures; they are images of holy people—our Savior, the Theotokos, the saints. And we venerate them: we show them extreme respect and adulation, not for the images themselves but to show proper reverence and respect for the people depicted in them.

As the priest venerates the antimension, he offers two short but beautiful prayers. One references the Parable of the Publican and the Pharisee, which we discussed in the previous reflection. The other references the Parable of the Prodigal Son. These two parables, both from the Gospel of Luke, are read on the first two Sundays of the Triodion—the three-week period that precedes Great Lent. The Parable of the Publican and the Pharisee is about the virtue of humility. The Parable of the Prodigal Son is about our need for repentance and the forgiveness that God so graciously offers to us. These prayers are as follows:

> Like the Prodigal Son, I have sinned before You, O Savior; receive me as I repent, O Father, and have mercy on me, O God.
>
> With the voice of the publican I cry out to You, O Savior: take pity on me as You had upon him and have mercy on me, O God.

These short prayers remind the priest of his need for humility and repentance, as these prayers are inaudible and generally not known by the faithful. They are beautiful reminders for all of us and make for great, short additions to our daily prayers.

Turning toward the people, the priest says, "Those who love us and those who hate us, may God forgive us." Most people mistakenly think that before the Great Entrance, the priest is asking for forgiveness. He will do that before he receives Holy Communion, but this first time that the priest bows toward the people is a reminder that we should seek forgiveness from all, we should pray for all, we should help all, and that all have access to God's forgiveness—those who love us *and* those who hate us.

Going toward the prothesis, the priest prays one of the hymns from Holy Week, from the Service of the Bridegroom: "I see Thy Bridal Chamber adorned, O my Savior, and I have no wedding garment, that I may enter therein. Make radiant the vesture of my soul, Giver of Light, and save me." As the priest is walking toward the prothesis to pick up the Gifts and carry them in procession, he has the opportunity to gaze upon the Gifts that are our salvation. In a moment, the faithful will have this opportunity as well.

As he lifts the *aer* (the cloth that covers the gifts) and places it over his shoulders, the priest offers a verse from the Psalms: "Lift up your hands to the holy place, / and bless the LORD" (Ps. 133/134:2). As he picks up the diskos, he offers a second verse from the Psalms: "God has gone up with a shout, / the LORD with the sound of a trumpet" (Ps. 46/47:5).[14] Then he picks up the chalice and offers these words: "I will receive the cup of salvation and call on the name of the LORD" (Ps. 115/116:13), which is the Communion Hymn for all feasts of the Theotokos.

I realize that the faithful hear very few of these prayers, but they are a beautiful part of the Liturgy for the priest, which is why I wanted to share them with you. They not only comprise some meaningful preparation for the Great Entrance, but they are short prayers that we can offer outside the context of the Liturgy as well. I will list them all below for you to pray today.

> Like the Prodigal Son, I have sinned before You, O Savior; receive me as I repent, O Father, and have mercy on me, O God.
>
> With the voice of the publican I cry out to You, O Savior, take pity on me as You had upon him and have mercy on me, O God.
>
> Those who love us and those who hate us, may God forgive us.

14 This verse, incidentally, is the Entrance Hymn on the Feast of the Ascension, foretelling the Lord ascending into heaven and the trumpets being sounded at His triumphant return.

I see Thy Bridal Chamber adorned, O my Savior, and I have no wedding garment, that I may enter therein. Make radiant the vesture of my soul, Giver of Light, and save me.

Lift up your hands to the holy place, / and bless the Lord (Ps. 133/134:2).

God has gone up with a shout, / the Lord with the sound of a trumpet (Ps. 46/47:5).

I will lift up the cup of salvation / and call on the name of the Lord (Ps. 115/116:13).

May the Lord God remember all of us in His Kingdom, always, now and forever and to the ages of ages.

> One of the criminals who were hanged railed at him, saying, "Are you not the Christ? Save yourself and us!" But the other rebuked him, saying, "Do you not fear God, since you are under the same sentence of condemnation? And we indeed justly; for we are receiving the due reward of our deeds; but this man has done nothing wrong." And he said, "Jesus, remember me when you come into your Kingdom." And he said to him, "Truly, I say to you, today you will be with me in Paradise."
>
> —Luke 23:39–43

Prior to the beginning of the Divine Liturgy, the priest prepared the Holy Gifts during a service called the Proskomide. While the focus of the early part of the Divine Liturgy was petitions, hymns, Scriptures, and the sermon, it is now time to present the Holy Gifts and place them on the altar so that they can be consecrated and distributed as Holy Communion. Following the Cherubic Hymn and the priest's offering of the accompanying prayers of repentance and forgiveness, the priest is now ready to make the Great Entrance. The altar servers precede him and carry objects of great symbolism: The candles represent the light of Christ. The fans (in Greek, *Exapteryga*, or "six wings") represent the six-winged angels—the seraphim—that stand around the throne of God. This is why the fans are placed behind or near the altar table. The processional cross represents the Cross on which Christ was crucified. And the incense, of course, represents our prayers rising to heaven.

The exclamation by the priest at this most powerful moment of the Divine Liturgy is the confession of the repentant thief on the cross next to Christ. This man, who had been condemned to death, repented in his dying moments next to the Lord. His request wasn't desperation or, as I once heard a priest say, it wasn't a savvy "stealing of heaven by a thief" at the last moment. It was a moment of sincere repentance. He looked at Jesus with a sorrowful heart, knowing that he was receiving the due earthly retribution for his deeds.

The thief also experienced a moment of faith as he recognized Jesus as the Christ, whose Kingdom is not of this earth. And he made a spiritual request. He didn't ask for a material request like the other thief—to be saved physically, to cheat death, to cheat his just sentence of condemnation. Rather, he made a spiritual plea: "Remember me in Your kingdom." And the answer of the Lord showed love, mercy, and compassion as He told the thief that he would be with Him in Paradise. Jesus also said the man would be in paradise *today*.

As the priest carries the Holy Gifts through the church, the procession reminds us of Christ's journey to Golgotha.[15] The Holy Gifts

15 In Slavic practice, the priest carries the Gifts across the solea rather than through the church.

are carried as a bloodless sacrifice to the altar for us, reminiscent of animals presented for slaughter as atonement for sin in the Old Testament. And the priest's words are the simple prayer of the thief—for the Lord to remember us in His Kingdom.

While the procession is passing through the church, your eyes should follow the Gifts as you turn and face their direction. As the Gifts pass you on their way to the back of the church, make the sign of the cross, and do it again as they pass you on the way to the front.[16] While the Gifts are carried and the priest is praying for the Lord to remember everyone in His Kingdom, think of those who are near and dear to you, those in the pews around you, those whom you love and those whom you do not, as well as your priest. Bring as many people to your mind as possible at this moment. And as the priest returns to the front of the church, sing loudly the "Amen," indicating "May it be so": may the Lord our God remember everyone in His Kingdom, now and forever and to the ages of ages.

One of the beautiful traditions in our Church occurs when the bishop serves and commemorates people who are living and who have passed away. (In some jurisdictions, this commemoration occurs at every Divine Liturgy and is offered by the celebrant priest. In the GOA, it is only done by a hierarch when he is presiding.) He prays for them by name and also by need, such as those who are sick or imprisoned. This is the prayer I share with you today.

16 Here it is helpful to note that we make the sign of the cross over ourselves in the following parts of the service: whenever the name of the Holy Trinity is invoked, whenever the Theotokos is commemorated, before and after the reading of the Holy Gospel, before and after we receive Holy Communion, before and after we venerate an icon, during the words of the Institution of the Holy Eucharist, and at the Great Entrance. The cross also can be made at any time, on any petition as you wish to make it. But it should be made in a reverent way.

For our Archbishop (name), for our priest (name), and all those who serve in our church—the Parish Council, the Sunday school teachers and students, the Philoptochos, the choir, the chanters, the altar boys, and all members of our community. For our country, the president, all civil authorities, and our armed forces. For mercy, life, peace, health, salvation, visitation, pardon and remission of sins of the servant of God (any names you wish to remember). For those departed this life, in the hope of the resurrection to eternal life (list their names). May the Lord our God remember all of us in His Kingdom, now and forever and to the ages of ages. Amen.

Who is invisibly escorted by the angelic hosts. Alleluia. Alleluia. Alleluia.

> And suddenly there was with the angel a multitude of the heavenly host praising God and saying, "Glory to God in the highest and on earth, peace among men with whom He is pleased."
>
> —Luke 2:13–14

Several years ago, I had the opportunity to hear Metropolitan Kallistos Ware speak at a conference I attended. He told the story of how he once offered a Paraklesis in a small church near Oxford, England. He celebrated with only two other people who were sick and had asked for the service to be offered for them. After the service, some tourists who were Greek Orthodox came to the parish and met the metropolitan. They told him that they had stopped by earlier, had looked into the windows of the church, and saw that the place was filled with people holding candles. They hadn't wanted to come in and intrude, but they asked what kind of service he had been holding on a random weeknight. He told them it had been a Paraklesis service and that only he and two other people had been in attendance. The metropolitan said that he did not see those people with candles, but they must have been angels.

He went on to say that when priests cense the church during Matins and walk up and down the center aisle, there are many times when the pews have no people in them. In fact, at a weekday Divine Liturgy, there may only be a handful of people in the church. He reminded us that we priests should cense all the pews in the church sanctuary, even the empty ones, because the angels are sitting there with us. It was comforting to think that the church is always filled. Even at the Sacrament of Confession, when only the priest and one person are present, the church is filled with angels who are praying and rejoicing over the one sinner who has returned.

When we gather to worship in our parish, the *whole* church gathers together. We, the people of our community, worship together with the saints and the angels, as well as the souls of the righteous who have passed away. We *all* worship together. That's one of the reasons we adorn the walls of our churches with icons—to remind us of this truth.

So, as the priest turns to enter the altar with the Holy Gifts, imagine him lifted up by hundreds of angels carrying him and the Gifts to their resting place. Imagine hundreds of angels descending from heaven to stand around the altar as part of the Divine Liturgy. Imagine the angels coming and preceding the Holy Spirit, who is about to come down to consecrate the Gifts. You are not engaging in wishful thinking, because these things are happening! Your church is filled with the bodiless powers, the invisible army of angels that descends to be part of the service, and we stand in their presence.

Today's prayer is the one the priest offers as he enters the altar and places the Gifts on the altar table. It is a combination of a hymn from

Holy Friday—remember, the Great Entrance is a commemoration of the journey to Golgotha—and the concluding verses of Psalm 50/51.

The noble Joseph, when he had taken down Your immaculate Body from the tree, wrapped it in pure linen and spices, and with sorrow, placed it in a new tomb.

Do good in Your good pleasure to Zion, and let the walls of Jerusalem be rebuilt. Then You will delight in right sacrifices, in burnt offerings and whole burnt offerings; then they shall offer up bulls on Your altar [and have mercy on me, O God].

The Litany of Completion

Let us complete our prayer unto the Lord.

> That which was from the beginning, which we have heard, which we have seen with our eyes, which we have looked upon and touched with our hands, concerning the Word of Life—the life was made manifest, and we saw it, and testify to it, and proclaim to you the eternal life which was with the Father and was made manifest to us—that which we have seen and heard we proclaim also to you, so that you may have fellowship with us; and our fellowship is with the Father and with his Son Jesus Christ. And we are writing this that our joy may be complete.
>
> —1 John 1:1–4

If the Divine Liturgy were a play with many acts, this point would mark the beginning of the fifth act. So far in the service, we've had the Litanies and Antiphons (act one, if I can use the analogy), the Small Entrance with the hymns that follow (act two), the Scripture readings (act three), the Cherubic Hymn, and the Great Entrance (I would consider this an act in itself, so act four). With the offering of bread and wine now on the altar, there is a new beginning, so to speak, and with it a new litany. The Great Litany, with which we opened the Divine Liturgy, offers prayers for universal topics—peace in the world, for our country, and so on. This litany, which in Greek is called the *Plerotika*, or the Completion Litany, offers prayers for universal topics like forgiveness of sins or a life completed in repentance; however, I have always understood these petitions in a more personal way.

The Completion Litany begins with the petition, "Let us complete our prayer unto the Lord." Someone once asked me, "How can there be a petition to 'complete' the service when in the book, we're not even halfway through it? If you begin Divine Liturgy at 10 a.m., and we get to this line at 10:40 a.m., and we're going to be in church until at least 11:30 a.m., how can you have a petition to 'complete' a service that is nowhere near its end?"

The answer goes back to the beginning of the service: when we opened the Divine Liturgy with the words "Blessed is the Kingdom . . . now and forever," we opened the door for us to experience God's Kingdom in the here and now. In order to experience the Kingdom, we must first make ourselves ready to enter it through prayers and hymns and scriptures. Having passed those points of the Divine Liturgy, with the sacrifice now on the altar table, it is time to complete that opening petition to experience the Kingdom of God in the here and now through the receiving of Holy Communion.

This petition in the Litany of Completion is the first step in this next stage of the journey, which will now move much faster as it heads toward its climax. From a pragmatic perspective, there hasn't really been that much action in the first half of the service. This will change shortly with the many events that are yet to come.

For the time being, the priest stands before the altar and begins a long series of petitions. Once these petitions end, the table will be set for the Consecration of the Gifts and their reception in Holy Communion.

Plerosomen, which is translated as "complete," can also be translated as "fill." So, there are other meanings here. We are not only completing our prayers, but we are fulfilling the purpose in our gathering—bringing God's Kingdom into the present—and we do that by filling ourselves spiritually through prayer and receiving the Holy Eucharist.

So, what should we be thinking at this moment of the service? We should think about the word *complete.* And we can think of it in several ways:

- *How complete (or empty) is my spiritual life at this moment?*
- *Am I ready to be filled with God's grace through receiving Holy Communion?*
- *What is the will of the Lord for my life that I have yet to complete?*

In order to be motivated to complete something, one must first realize that something is lacking that needs to be completed. So, what is lacking in your life? And what can you do about this in the coming week?

With the service half over now, it is time to start formulating a plan in your mind for spiritual tasks to complete in the week to come, even as we move toward the end of this service with the Completion Litany.

> O Lord, rebuke me not in thy anger, nor chasten me in thy wrath. Be gracious to me, O Lord, for I am languishing; O Lord, heal me, for my bones are troubled. My soul also is sorely troubled. But thou, O Lord, how long? Turn, O Lord, save my life; deliver me for the sake of thy steadfast love. (Psalm 6:1–4)

For the precious Gifts here presented, let us pray to the Lord.

> When [the Magi] saw the star, they rejoiced exceedingly with great joy; and going into the house they saw the child with Mary his mother, and they fell down and worshipped him. Then, opening their treasures, they offered him Gifts, gold and frankincense and myrrh.
>
> —Matthew 2:10–11

The second petition in the Completion Litany directs our attention immediately to the purpose for which we have gathered: the receiving of the Gifts. Why are the Gifts precious?

- They will become the Body and Blood of Christ, so their value is immeasurable and infinite. They are indeed the most precious things we have.
- The Gifts represent the people. People bake the bread and make the wine used in the service, offering their precious resources of time, talent, and material.
- The source of these Gifts—the wheat and water that are part of the bread and the grapes that make the wine—is the hand of God Himself. He created the ingredients and gave people the talent to use them, and humans then put them together to make the Gifts. It is a precious combination—God providing for humankind and humankind working in concert with God.

The verse quoted above is from the story of the Nativity where the magi offered gifts to the Christ child. The gifts were treasures because they had material value—gold, incense, and myrrh. But they were also symbolic of Christ's purpose in coming to earth—gold for a king, incense for God, myrrh for the burial of our Savior.

The use of the word *gifts* also makes us think of the meaning of gifts: they are gestures offered with love and received with gratitude. These Gifts in the Liturgy, like many gifts in our lives, cannot be used fully without the blessings of God. So, as we present the Gifts to God, we present them with love, with gratitude, and with faith that He can, through His Holy Spirit, consecrate them so that we may receive them as the Body and Blood of Christ. Therefore, as this petition is offered, think about love, gratitude, and faith—for the precious Gifts here presented, our intention in presenting them, and the reward of offering them.

For this holy house and for those who enter it with faith, reverence, and the fear of God, let us pray to the Lord.

> Then David said to Solomon his son, "Be strong and of good courage, and do it. Fear not, be not dismayed; for the Lord God, even my God, is with you. He will not fail you or forsake you, until all the work for the service of the house of the Lord is finished."
>
> —1 Chronicles 28:20

For the second time in the Divine Liturgy, we encounter this petition. Remember that it was in the Great Litany that began the service. There is a reason for redundancy in the service: repetition helps our memorization. We are again called to remember those with whom we are praying—our church community—as well as our own disposition in prayer.

For Orthodox Christians, the sanctuary is sacred. It is space that is consecrated[17] and set aside for the strict purpose of worship. In other Christian churches, the worship space is sometimes multiuse. But for Orthodox Christians, this space is used only for worship and teaching. Thus, we pray for our sacred space.

Even more important than the space where we worship are the people with whom we worship. There is a saying that "one Christian is no Christian." Christians are relational people. The church building with no people is just a museum. It is the people who make the church a community. So, we pray that we, ourselves, and our fellow parishioners will enter into the sacred space with a disposition of faith, reverence, and fear of God. These three characteristics must be ratcheted up, so to speak, because the Holy Gifts are now on the altar, ready for consecration. Therefore, we must have even *greater faith*.

Up to this point, we've prayed, we've sung, we've listened to the words of Scripture, but now we are about to put our faith in the Holy Spirit to come down upon us and consecrate the Gifts into the Body and Blood of Christ. We need to have *greater reverence* than before, for at this moment we are surrounded not only by the saints and angels but also the Gifts. We are going to stand in the presence of Christ Himself. This requires *greater fear of God*, greater respect and awe. For we are not just gathering to pray but are coming together to touch the Divine God in the Eucharist.

We pray for these attitudes not only for ourselves but also for everyone in church with us. We should take comfort that those around us are praying for the same things. This is part of the work of the Divine Liturgy; we carry not only our needs but also the needs of others to the Lord. And the comfort of the Divine Liturgy is that others help us with our needs, and we help them. This is what the

---

17 An Orthodox church is consecrated in a formal service where relics of saints are interred in the altar.

church community is all about: to "bear one another's burdens, and so fulfill the law of Christ" (Gal. 6:2).

For our deliverance from all affliction, wrath, danger, and necessity, let us pray to the Lord.

> Many are the afflictions of the righteous; / but the Lord delivers him out of them all.
>
> —Psalm 33/34:19

This is the second of three petitions in a row that are repeated from earlier in the service. Once again, repetition helps our memorization. And these requests are important. Being a Christian does not guarantee a life free of affliction, anger (wrath), danger, and need. In fact, as we read in the psalm above, the afflictions of the righteous are many. Disease at some point affects every life. There is peril even in the most common of activities—driving a car, going to the mall. And most of us experience anger on an almost daily basis. Regarding necessity, while most of us enjoy enough food and adequate shelter, everyone suffers from emotional deficits—not receiving adequate affirmation or affection—at least some of the time.

Now, if the Lord delivers us from these things, why do we still have to deal with them? Why doesn't He just deliver us one time for all time? The answer is that *He will do just that*! That is what the Kingdom of heaven will be like: no affliction, wrath, danger, or necessity. This life is a preparation for eternal life.

The Divine Liturgy is a foretaste of the Kingdom of heaven because it contains none of these difficulties. Outside the Divine Liturgy, difficulties are a part of every life. Here on earth, the Lord helps to deliver us from the emotional and spiritual toll that these things take on us. We can be afflicted with disease, even disease that eludes physical healing, but spiritual healing is available. We can be angry, but any anger can be softened with prayer. When we feel we are in danger, the power of prayer will bring comfort. And we can suffer need. This is where the Church can step in—to help meet the needs of those who cannot meet their own. We are meant to feed the person who has no food. We are supposed to embrace the one who has no friend.

So, as this petition is offered, bring your needs to the Lord. Think of the people around you and their trials. And think about what you can do to help. Prayer, faith, and work will indeed stand us all in good stead as we prepare to enter the Kingdom of heaven, where all affliction, wrath, danger, and necessity are no more. The work of the Church is to help people survive the difficulties of life. The Divine Liturgy offers us both a break from these afflictions and a foretaste of eternal life without them.

A beautiful verse of scripture says, "And the ransomed of the LORD shall return, / and come to Zion with singing; / everlasting joy shall be upon their heads; they shall obtain joy and gladness, / and sorrow and sighing shall free away" (Is. 51:11). This joy is in store for us when we return to God, if we have stayed faithful to Him during our sojourn on earth.

Today's prayer is a hymn that the Church offers in the service of Great Compline during Great Lent. If you know this hymn, sing it a few times today. And if you don't know it, offer it as a prayer.

> Lord of the Powers, be with us; for no other helper do we have in tribulations, but You. Lord of the Powers, have mercy on us.[18]

18 Hymn from the Lenten Service of the Great Compline, trans. Fr. Seraphim Dedes, as found on the Digital Chant Stand of the Greek Orthodox Archdiocese of America. https://dcs.goarch.org.

Help us, save us, have mercy on us, and protect us, O God by Your grace.

> O Lord my God, I cried to thee for help, / and thou hast healed me.
>
> —Psalm 29/30:2

This petition is also one we have encountered before in the Divine Liturgy. In fact, it is offered five times during the service. This petition is offered so frequently because it contains four foundational things that we need from God.

First and foremost, we need salvation. The ultimate goal of life is salvation in the Kingdom of God. So, whatever help and protection God offers us in our daily lives does not compare to the salvation that we desire to receive from Him.

On our path to salvation, however, we need His help every step of the way there. That help comes from patience, discernment and wisdom to make good decisions, and divine guidance in developing the talents He has given us.

Mercy is God's patience with us. If we start to add up the sins we have committed, especially as we get older and live longer, the number is thousands or tens of thousands—a number too great to imagine. Without God's mercies and without His forgiveness of our many sins, none of us stands a chance to receive His salvation. And so we continually ask for His mercies, just as we continually ask for His help to stay strong in the face of temptations.

We also need protection. Even the greatest saints come under attack from the devil and temptation. Failures in life and the hurts that we suffer in this world can sometimes lead even the strongest person to a sense of despondency. And this is where we need

God's protection. Not that His protection can save us from failure and hurt—God will not take away our free will or the free will of others to inflict harm on us. But the area we need His protection most—where He always comes through for us—is to protect our faith in Him. So, in times when we are despondent or are losing sight of God and salvation, we ask God to protect our faith, rekindle our spirit, inspire our souls, and help us to keep our eyes on the prize.

We call upon the Lord often with this prayer not only as a petition to Him but also as a reminder to us that we *need* these things from God. No matter how strong or successful we are, we all need the help, salvation, mercy, and protection that can come only from Him. As Christians, these gifts are the greatest benefits we receive from God in this life, in preparation for eternal life.

That the whole day may be perfect, holy, peaceful, and sinless, let us ask the Lord.

> Open the gates, that the righteous nation which keeps faith may enter in. Thou dost keep him in perfect peace, whose mind is stayed on thee, because he trusts in thee. Trust in the LORD for ever, for the LORD GOD is an everlasting rock.
>
> —Isaiah 26:2–4

All the petitions and prayers of the Divine Liturgy are offered in the plural, on behalf of all the people present who are worshiping together. Yet I hear this petition and the five that follow in a personal way. This set of six petitions is not answered with the usual "Lord, have mercy," which means "Lord, have mercy, even though we do not deserve this; allow it to happen by Your grace." Instead, the responses here are a bolder "Grant this, O Lord." We are still humbly petitioning the Lord, and we are asking Him to grant us things that are incredible, if you think about it. But I hear "Grant this, O Lord" with a quiet confidence in God's ability and desire to give to us. And perhaps the reason I hear these in a personal way is that at the end of each petition, instead of saying "Let us pray to the Lord," the deacon or priest is saying, "Let us ask of the Lord."

What is the difference between praying for something and asking for something? Are they not the same? In my opinion and experience within the Divine Liturgy, we pray for many things, and not all those things are personal. For instance, I am not the president, or a civil authority, or a member of the armed forces. So, when I'm praying for these people, I am not praying for myself. Same with some of the other petitions. But when I hear these petitions we are considering today, I hear them not only in a communal way but also in a personal way. This petition and those that follow are things I personally need—and need constantly!

So, first we ask the Lord for a perfect, holy, peaceful, and sinless day. Wow, if God granted only this petition, imagine what life would be like. Of course, we must work in concert with the Lord to experience these things. So, as you hear this petition, think of the things *you* can do to make your day more perfect, holy, peaceful, and sinless, and ask the Lord to help you do those things.

So many needs fit under this petition that you could attend the Divine Liturgy with a different game plan for this prayer each time you hear it. For instance, if profanity is what keeps your day from being sinless, this petition provides an opportunity to offer a prayer to God to tame what comes out of your mouth.

If something takes away your sense of peace, ask the Lord to be present in that circumstance to help you find peace. Offer a prayer to become a person of peace, so that not only will people bring peace to you, but you will also bring peace to them.

If life is going fairly well, remember the story of the rich man who went away sorrowful because Jesus told him that he lacked one thing, and he couldn't give it up (Luke 18:18–27). Ask yourself seriously, *What do I still lack that is keeping me from a perfect relationship with the Lord?* Then resolve to do godly things in your day. God crowns effort, not success. We will never succeed in being perfect. But we certainly should be making a good effort.

Holy means "set apart." So, when we strive for holiness, we seek to be what God wants us to be and not necessarily what the world or our friends want us to be. Asking God for a holy day means asking Him for the strength to seek holiness and the perseverance to set ourselves apart from unholy things in order to grow in our faith.

Once again, this petition and those that follow it can be heard not only in a communal way but also in a personal way. We pray for a perfect, holy, peaceful, and sinless day—something that every member in the community needs—and also something I personally need. As I hear this petition, I reflect on the day's opportunities and challenges.

And with God's grace and my efforts, I pray to grow in holiness.

For an angel of peace, a faithful guide, a guardian of our souls and bodies, let us ask the Lord.

> Behold, I send an angel before you, to guard you on the way
> and to bring you to the place which I have prepared.
>
> —Exodus 23:20

The psalms speak of a guardian angel who watches over us: "Because you have made the LORD your refuge, / the Most High your habitation, / no evil shall befall you, / no scourge come near your tent. For he will give his angels charge of you / to guard you in all your ways. On their hands they will bear you up" (Ps. 90/91:9–12). Cartoons often depict a white angel sitting on the shoulder of a character, encouraging him or her to make a good decision, with a red devil sitting on the other shoulder, tempting the person to make a bad one. And while we do not depict such a thing in our iconography, we believe both that the devil comes to tempt us—not necessarily in obvious ways through a red-horned creature, but through more subtle ways—and that angels come to guard, guide, and protect us. Though we do not have a white angel sitting on our shoulder, we believe we have guardian angels, unseen protectors who guide and guard us.

The angels bring messages from God to us. The archangel Gabriel figures prominently in the Nativity narrative. In Luke 1, Gabriel tells Zacharias that he and Elizabeth would bear the forerunner of Christ in their old age: "And the angel answered him, 'I am Gabriel, who stands in the presence of God; and I was sent to speak to you, and to bring you this good news'" (Luke 1:19). The archangel Gabriel also makes the Annunciation to the Virgin Mary: "In the sixth month the angel Gabriel was sent from God to a city of Galilee named Nazareth, to a Virgin betrothed to a man whose name was Joseph, of the house of David; and the Virgin's name was Mary. And he came to her and said: 'Hail, O favored one, the Lord is with you!'" (Luke 1:26–28).

The angels were created by God. Orthodox theology identifies nine angelic orders: angels, archangels, thrones, dominions, principalities, authorities, powers, the cherubim, and the seraphim. In Colossians 1:15–16, St. Paul writes: "He (Christ) is the image of the invisible God, the first-born of all creation; for in him all things were created, in heaven and on earth, visible and invisible, whether thrones or dominions or principalities or authorities—all things were created through him and for him." And St. Basil, in the Anaphora of his Divine Liturgy, writes:

> For You are praised by the angels, archangels, thrones, dominions, principalities, authorities, powers, and the many-eyed Cherubim. Round about you stand the Seraphim, one with six wings and the other with six wings; with two they cover their faces; with two they cover their feet; with two they fly, crying out to one another with unceasing voices and ever-resounding praises.

The angels are God's messengers. In the Nativity account, a multitude of the heavenly hosts delivered the message of the Incarnation to the shepherds. We, too, are surrounded by angels.

So, this petition "for an angel of peace, a faithful guide, a guardian of our souls and bodies" asks God to send His angels to protect us, to bring us peace, to guide us in the Faith, and to keep us safe both in body and in soul. And just like those who heard the angelic message in the Gospel of Luke—Zacharias, the Theotokos, Joseph, the shepherds—we too must listen, trust, and take direction from the angels who are guiding our steps and our thoughts. As we hear this petition, we should pray also that we may be humble and trusting enough to allow ourselves to be guided and guarded by the angels.

God has sent His angels to minister to us—and He has also empowered *us* to play this role for one another. If God can work through powers that are unseen, He most certainly can work through people who are seen. We also must take on the role of angels, in the sense of encouraging people to do what is good and pleases God. If we hope to one day be with the angels, then we must learn to act like angels as well. As we hear this petition, we should think about how we can be more angelic in our lives. Today's prayer is called the Prayer of the Hours, as it is offered at the various "hours" (services done throughout the day):

> O Christ our God, who at all times and at every hour, both in heaven and on earth, are worshipped and glorified, long

suffering and plenteous in mercy and compassion; who love the just and show mercy to the sinners; who call all men to salvation through the promise of the blessings to come: Do You, the same Lord, receive also our supplications at this present time, and direct our lives according to Your commandments. Sanctify our souls; purify our bodies; set our minds right; clear up our thoughts, and deliver us from every sorrow, evil and distress. Surround us with Your holy Angels so that being guarded and guided by their presence, we may arrive at the unity of the faith and the knowledge of Your ineffable glory; for blessed are You unto the ages of ages. Amen.[19]

For pardon and remission of our sins and transgressions, let us ask the Lord.

> Then he [Jesus] opened their minds to understand the scriptures, and said to them, "Thus it is written, that the Christ should suffer and on the third day rise from the dead, and that repentance and forgiveness of sins should be preached in his name to all nations, beginning from Jerusalem.
>
> —Luke 24:45–47

The word *sin* means "to miss the mark." God has set standards by which we are to live and to conduct ourselves. Sin is when we fail to meet these standards. Sin is not only intentionally doing something wrong, it also includes failing to do something that is right. Indifference (nonaction) can be a sin. I've heard sin defined as "failure to love."

19 Translated by Fr. Seraphim Dedes.

There isn't a day that goes by when we do not sin. Sin includes our actions but can also permeate our thoughts. Our struggle against sin is called repentance, or striving to change our orientation so that we hit the mark instead of missing it. A battle between sin and repentance rages in every human soul and in every human relationship. In the soul, it is a battle between thoughts of good and evil that compete for our attention. And in human relationships, we experience a constant battle between rejoicing in our relationships and restoring them when a sinful act has occurred.

There is an important difference between the words *forgiveness* and *remission*. Forgiveness can be offered between two people and is offered from God to us. Forgiveness is an overlooking of sin. We acknowledge that the sin happened, and we offer to move on from the sin and move toward reconciliation between two people.

Remission is the greatest gift God has offered to us. Remission is a total wiping away of our sins from our souls, eliminating those sins from our life's records. If God were to keep track of our sins, there would be too many to count—and certainly plenty to keep us out of Paradise when life on earth is over. Remission of sins is possible through the Crucifixion. Saint Paul writes in Romans 6:23, "For the wages of sin is death, but the free gift of God is eternal life in Christ Jesus our Lord."

Sin is when we miss the mark and are estranged from God. But through the Cross, Jesus has shown us a new path to salvation: repenting when you make a mistake and forgiving others when they make a mistake against you.

We are all familiar with bills. When you receive your credit card bill or your utility bill, there is a paper that usually says, "Please remit with payment," asking you to send in the payment with the paper to receive credit for paying. It doesn't say that you personally have to write the check, only that a check accompanies your bill. If someone wants to pay the debt for you, the credit card company is not going to complain; they will be happy as long as your debt is paid. In our spiritual lives, we all separate ourselves from God and are estranged from Him. But He wants us to be with Him, so He forgives our sins and remits—pays the debt—for us.

When I offer this petition at the Divine Liturgy, I call to mind my own sins, and I ask God not only to forgive them but to remit them—to wipe them out from my record of life entirely. I also ask God to help me repent, to give me the wisdom and strength to orient my life toward Him, and to avoid the temptations and habitual poor behaviors that move me further away from Him.

The Sacrament of Confession offers us an opportunity in this life to take responsibility for our sins and to have them wiped out through the prayer of absolution. The sacrament is not the confession per se—even non-Christians forgive sins. The sacrament is the wiping away of our record of a sin. This happens when we own up for sins (confession), work with the priest to create a plan to lessen or eliminate the sins that have been mentioned (repentance), and receive the beautiful prayer of absolution (the remission part), where God allows us to return to the perfect state we were in when we were baptized. The Sacrament of Confession allows us to formalize our sins and take responsibility for them with a priest, who then offers us absolution.

We should also confess our sins to God on a daily basis. Thus the Divine Liturgy offers us an opportunity through this petition to call to mind our sins against one another and against God and to ask forgiveness for them, while at the same time making a plan to repent of them. On a practical level, as you hear this petition, remember your sins of the past week and meditate on how you can avoid them in the coming week. Furthermore, ask God to forgive you of these sins so that with a clear conscience you can approach for Holy Communion.

While remission of sins is an integral part of our journey to salvation, our faith, our works, and ultimately God's grace are needed. A continual confessing of our sins, genuine repentance, and God's grace to remit our sins as we ask Him for forgiveness are certainly things we need to be doing on a regular basis.

For that which is good and beneficial for our souls, and for peace in the world, let us ask the Lord.

> Bless the LORD, O my soul; / and all that is within me, bless his holy name!
>
> —Psalm 102/103:1

This petition is one of the most useful and practical in the entire Divine Liturgy. Imagine if you made every decision according to this petition:

> *Is what I am about to do good for my soul?*
> *Will my actions promote peace in the world?*

If the answer to either question is no, then you are not making a good decision. For instance, as soon as the Divine Liturgy ends in most parishes, there is a fellowship hour in the parish hall. Undoubtedly, before you leave the church premises, you will have an opportunity to gossip. Gossip is not good for your soul, and it certainly does not promote peace in the world, in the church community, in the workplace, within the family, or anywhere else. Yet we probably fall prey to this temptation more than most—many times right after the Divine Liturgy, only a short time after hearing this petition.

If we made every decision during the week according to these two petitions, we would experience not only a foretaste of heaven, but we might feel what it is like to be a saint. Many of us can't go a day without doing something that goes against this petition. That's why it is so important. That's why it is offered at every Divine Liturgy and in most other services as well.

When people complain that the Divine Liturgy is "the same and the same" every week, I often tell them that if they can follow these guidelines—for the soul's benefit and for peace—for an entire week, then they can skip the Divine Liturgy the next Sunday. Truth is, none of us can do this. When I hear this petition at each Divine Liturgy, I am reminded that I need to use it as my barometer in decision-making.

When you wonder if you are at a crossroads, remember this petition. Is this decision good for my soul? Does it promote peace in the world, or at least in my small corner of it? If the answer to either question is no, make a different decision.

That we may complete the remaining time of our life in peace and repentance, let us ask the Lord.

> For godly grief produces a repentance that leads to salvation
> and brings no regret, but worldly grief produces death.
> —2 Corinthians 7:10

Have you ever done one of those exercises where you are given a list of twenty-five items and then asked to pick which five items you would keep if you were stranded on a deserted island? And let's say that one item is a book of matches and another item is a mirror. Someone doing this exercise may think the matches are more important than the mirror because matches can be used to start a fire, and a mirror is of no use if you have no one to look good for. I would choose the mirror over the matches because you can start a fire with a mirror and use the mirror as a signal for a potential rescue. The matches will eventually be used up, and if they get wet, they can be destroyed.

Let's say that you were given a list of twenty-five things you could have in your life—a house, a large bank account, your own personal Wikipedia page (some fame), an advanced degree, a corner office, a solid marriage, children, health, peace, repentance, a nice car, many vacations, a dog, season tickets to your favorite sports team, and so on. And then you were told you could pick exactly five things from this list. What would make your top five?

I can honestly say that my top five would be repentance, peace, health, a solid marriage, and my child. Why does repentance make the top of the list? Because without it, there is no salvation; there is no eternal life in heaven. If we have no peace, then we won't be in good health or have a good family or be a good parent. Health is important; just ask someone who is limited by disease. A solid marriage is important—even more important than children—because without a stable marriage, there isn't a good foundation for raising children.

The point of this exercise is to show that the most important things in life are peace and repentance. If those aren't number one and two on your list, ask yourself why they are not. They are the keys to spiritual health, which is the necessary precursor to salvation.

Spiritual health is an important goal, and we should be pursuing peace and repentance daily. Peace is absence of conflict. As we reflected in the last petition, we should make decisions that promote peace every day, trying to de-escalate conflict rather than escalating or creating it.

Repentance is a word we have not yet encountered in the Divine Liturgy. In fact, this is the only time we will encounter this word. Repentance means "change of direction." Sin, as we've discussed, is when we miss the mark and are off target. When we repent, we point in the right direction toward our target—salvation.

In the 1960s, when the United States was racing to get to the moon, even the slightest error could send the *Apollo* spacecraft past the target and into outer space and certain destruction. So, along the way, the spacecraft would make course corrections. Without these course corrections, some large and some quite small, these missions most likely would have ended in tragedy. Our lives are the same way. We all need course corrections. Sometimes they are small, and sometimes they are significant. However, without these corrections—without repentance—we will miss the target as well.

Repentance should be formalized periodically in the Sacrament of Confession. This sacrament has two parts: the confession of sins, followed by repentance—the course correction to eliminate or lessen the sins. However, between formal confessions, our repentance should be a daily practice. *How can I be better and more accurate in my spiritual journey?* This is why the word *repentance* is included in the Divine Liturgy—to remind us of its importance, along with that of peace, throughout our lives.

And let us ask for a Christian end to our life, peaceful, without shame and suffering, and for a good defense before the awesome judgment seat of Christ.

> When the Son of Man comes in his glory, and all the angels with him, then he will sit on his glorious throne. Before him will be gathered all the nations, and he will separate them one from another as a shepherd separates the sheep from the goats, and he will place the sheep at his right hand, but the goats at the left.
>
> —Matthew 25:31–33

During the Divine Liturgy, we pray for many things: for peace; for travelers; for those who are sick; for our country, city, and parish; and for all those we know and do not know. But in our final moments, we won't be thinking of our country, travelers, or many of the things we have prayed for or have done throughout our lives. At the point when all of life's events are in the rearview mirror, the most important petition of our life will boil down to this one plea in the Divine Liturgy for "a Christian end, without shame and suffering, and a good defense before the awesome judgment seat of Christ."

Between every earthly life and the life beyond lies a judgment for each person. We will stand before the Lord as a defendant does before a judge and give an *apologia*, a defense of our life. And then the Lord will judge each person worthy of either everlasting joy or everlasting punishment.

If every prayer in our lives is answered except for this prayer for a Christian end and a good defense, then our lives have been in vain. On the flip side, we could live a life with every hope and dream unfulfilled, but if this prayer is answered, then we are set for eternity. A successful life journey ends with the granting of this petition.

Our Church is neither fatalistic nor morbid. It is realistic and compassionate, keeping the reality of earthly death in front of us at all times, because eternal life after death is our goal—to live in Christ so that we can die in faith and receive salvation in the Kingdom of God. When I am ministering to those who are dying, I am confounded by how frequently they look confused, as if they didn't think death was going to happen to them. Many times, people ask me, "What do I do now?" And when I answer them, "Prepare for a good death," they look at me like I'm from another planet. Then I refer to this petition and talk about how all of life boils down to this. The Church includes this plea in the Divine Liturgy and in other services to remind us where we are going so that when we get there—whether we are forty or fifty or ninety—we will be prepared.

The phrase *kalin apologian,* translated as "good defense," means that we need to be prepared to give a good account, defense, or apology of our life before the Lord.[20] Did we use our talents? Did we use them for His glory? Did we help our fellow human beings? Were we peacemakers or peace-takers? Are we ready to be one with God? The Divine Liturgy not only prepares us to meet the Lord—it gives us a foretaste of heaven, especially in Holy Communion—but it teaches us *how* to prepare.

We need to be Christian to the end. Many people die after lengthy sicknesses, which test our faith and our resolve. It is important to remember this petition if we have a serious or terminal illness—that above all, we must go with faith all the way to our last breath. In material terms, of course, we want our death to be painless. No one wants to suffer. Unfortunately, many people suffer in a physical way during illness. While we may not be able to escape physical suffering, we do have an opportunity to escape spiritual suffering by focusing on the Lord.

We want to come to the end of our life blameless and peaceful. This is possible when we make peace with the Lord and peace with one another. We should always try to be reconciling and forgiving with others, but this is especially important toward the end of our lives. I remember a dear friend years ago who was on his deathbed and asked to see someone so that he could ask forgiveness from him. He didn't want to die with bad feelings between him and anyone else. He left me with a powerful example.

We reconcile with the Lord through the Sacrament of Confession, which is the opportunity to own up for our shortcomings before we get to the awesome judgement seat of Christ. We should be preparing at all times, because for many, death comes suddenly and without

20 In Christian history, people known as "apologists" were those who explained and defended the Faith. The word *apology* now has an entirely different meaning, one of expressing regret, rather than the "good defense" that was its primary meaning in the past.

warning. And when death is expected, we should take advantage of the opportunity to reconcile with the Lord through confession.

When a person prepares well for death, the circumstance may be painful for the family, but it can actually be peaceful, beautiful, and meaningful for the person who dies and ultimately for the family as well. I would argue that the most important day of a person's life is the day he or she dies. Because if one's death is a Christian ending, "blameless, peaceful, and ready for a good account at the awesome judgment seat," then it is the most glorious, joyful day of an individual's life.

Many times when someone is gravely ill, people pray for a miracle. And when the person dies, people are disappointed that their prayers were not answered. The greatest miracle, however, is not to cheat death through a medical cure. The greatest miracle is to have a good defense at the awesome judgment seat of Christ and for the gates of Paradise to open for someone who has lived in Christ and died in faith. And this ultimate victory is available to every person. As life ebbs away and the hope to extend earthly life fades, we have the hope of the spiritual miracle, which extends earthly life to eternal life.

This petition, in my humble opinion, is the most important one in the Liturgy, the most important prayer of one's life—that when life is over, we will pass painlessly, blamelessly, and peacefully from this life into everlasting life.

> When I ponder in my wretchedness on the many terrible things that I have done, I tremble for that fearful day, the Day of Judgment. But trusting in the mercy of Your compassion, like David I cry to You, "Have mercy on me, O God, according to Your great mercy."
>
> —Idiomelon Hymn from the Triodion[21]

21 In memory of +Anastasia Garcia, someone who died too young but who I believe embodied this petition. May her memory be eternal!

Commemorating our most holy, pure, blessed, and glorious Lady, the Theotokos and ever-virgin Mary, with all the saints, let us commend ourselves and one another and our whole life to Christ our God.

> And Mary said, "Behold I am the handmaid of the Lord; let it be to me according to your word."
>
> —Luke 1:38

For the fourth and final time in the Divine Liturgy, a petition commemorates the Theotokos. In reflecting on her life, would any of us really want to be her? Her parents were elderly and died when she was very young. She was raised in the temple by priests she didn't know. When she left the temple at about age thirteen, she had no family to return to. She was entrusted to the care of a man much older than she was, who would become her husband, except that he would die when she was still quite young, leaving her widowed. And her only Son would grow up to be killed in a horrific manner. Is this the kind of life we'd wish for ourselves, our children, or anyone else?

Let's look at some of the other saints we encounter in the Bible. Joseph, husband of Mary, went through the pain of being a widower. He then was betrothed to Mary, who had a child that was not his. Joseph followed the orders of an angel and moved to Bethlehem, then to Egypt, and eventually returned to Nazareth. He didn't live to see Jesus grow up. How about Joachim and Anna, parents of the Theotokos? They suffered the stigma of being unable to have children. Then, finally blessed with a daughter in old age, they didn't live to see her grow up. Eleven of the twelve disciples were murdered. A man sat paralyzed by the pool of Bethesda for thirty-eight years (John 5:1–15). A blind man was finally healed as a young adult but was rejected by his parents and kicked out of the temple after this miracle (John 9:1–38).

These holy people have two common denominators: First, they all had difficult lives. We don't think about that because we are reading about them in the pages of a book. Second, and most importantly, they all saw God's glory in some way. This is what draws us—their experiences of the glory of God, which overshadows their suffering.

The lesson for us is that we need to focus on God's glory. Our lives are less than ideal. Some of us will suffer illness, others will lose a job or a house, others will lose loved ones, and some will die too young. In the end, all that matters is that we see God's glory for eternal life. This petition honoring the Theotokos, coming after the petition about a Christian end and a good defense, is a great reminder that eternal life does not require us to live long but to live well—to live in unity with God, as did the Theotokos and all the saints.

When the archangel Gabriel visited the Virgin Mary and told her the news that she would bear the Christ, as well as the other things that would happen, she said, "Let it be to me according to your word" (Luke 1:38). In other words, "Let God be glorified in this." Her response should be our prayer as well, whether we are confronted with something very good or very challenging in life. Let whatever happens to us be according to His will, and let Him be glorified.

Through the mercies of Your only begotten Son, with Whom You are blessed, together with Your all-holy, good, and life-creating Spirit, now and forever and to the ages of ages. Amen.

> Blessed be the God and Father of our Lord Jesus Christ, the Father of mercies and God of all comfort, who comforts us in all our affliction, so that we may be able to comfort those who

> are in any affliction, with the comfort with which we ourselves are comforted by God.
>
> —2 Corinthians 1:3–4

We are now finishing the set of petitions called the Completion Litany, named so because it begins with, "Let us complete our prayer unto the Lord." We should hear these petitions in a personal way. An angel of peace, forgiveness of sins, the completion of our lives in peace and repentance, and a Christian end to our lives with a good defense at the awesome judgment seat of Christ—these are all things that impact each of us in a deeply personal way.

As with all litanies, the conclusion includes the ekphonesis glorifying the Holy Trinity. This doxological statement emphasizes that it is through the mercies (or perhaps a more accurate translation, "compassion") of the Lord that we will be able to receive *any* of these things for which we have prayed, most especially the last request—a good account at the awesome judgment seat of Christ.

And as with most litanies, the celebrant offers a prayer that is usually inaudible to the congregation (printed below). This prayer is called the Prayer of the Proskomide. The Proskomide, as you will recall, is the service before the Divine Liturgy where the Holy Gifts are prepared.

This priest's prayer here is not part of the actual Proskomide service but in a sense completes it. The bread and the wine on the altar are now about to be consecrated, and this prayer serves as an epilogue to the earlier preparations, asking God to receive the Gifts we are offering as we get ready to ask Him to consecrate them.

The prayer asks the Lord to hear our prayer, acknowledging that we are sinners and that no prayer and no gesture on our behalf make us worthy of His blessings. The prayer asks the Lord to accept our offering. In the Old Testament, people brought all kinds of animals to be sacrificed on the altar, and through these sacrifices, people atoned for their sins. Our offering of the Holy Eucharist is without shedding blood—Christ already has made the sacrifice for us. So, we ask that this sacrifice may be pleasing to God and that, as a result, the Holy Spirit will descend on us and the Gifts we are presenting.

> Lord God Almighty, You alone are holy. You accept the sacrifice of praise from those who call upon You with their whole heart, even so, accept from us sinners our supplication, and bring it to Your holy Altar of sacrifice. Enable us to offer You gifts and spiritual sacrifices for our sins and for the failings of Your people. Deem us worthy to find grace in Your sight, that our sacrifice may be well pleasing to You, and that the good Spirit of Your grace may rest upon us and upon these Gifts presented and upon all Your people. Through the mercies of Your only begotten Son, with whom You are blessed, together with Your all-holy, good, and life-creating Spirit, now and forever and to the ages of ages. Amen.

Peace be with all. And with your spirit.

> So if you are offering your gift at the altar, and there remember that your brother has something against you, leave your gift there before the altar and go; first be reconciled to your brother, and then come and offer your gift.
>
> —Matthew 5:23–24

How many days do I have to fast in order to receive Holy Communion? Is peanut oil considered to be oil?

I am often asked these kinds of questions, especially right before Pascha, when those who rarely receive Holy Communion want to make sure that they are meeting all the requirements. While fasting is an important part of our Orthodox Tradition, truth be told, the only fasting required for Holy Communion is abstaining from all food and drink on the morning you are receiving the Gifts. There are certain weeks when we are not required to fast on Wednesdays and Fridays, including the week after the Nativity (until January 5) and the week after Pascha, the week after Pentecost and the week following the Sunday of the Publican and the Pharisee. But even during a fast-free week, we are to abstain from food and drink the morning before receiving Holy Communion.

However, fasting from food and drink is not the most important thing we need to do to prepare. First and foremost, we must believe in God. This is why we confess our faith during the Divine Liturgy by reciting the Creed. We also need to have a relationship with God through our prayer life. Moral living is high on the list. It doesn't do any good to fast without praying or while living in habitual sin. And also on the list, if you will, is reconciliation with our fellow humans. We don't want to approach the chalice with an angry heart.

Set between the petitions and the Creed are two lines of the Divine Liturgy meant to facilitate our reconciliation. Why are they placed here? Because this follows the biblical commandment given by the Lord—that when we are offering a gift at the altar, if we remember that there is a rift between us and our brother, we ought to go and be reconciled to our brother and then offer the gift (Matt. 5:23–24). So, we bring our gifts to the altar (the Great Entrance), then we go to be reconciled to our brother before we offer the gifts for consecration. This is another example of how the Divine Liturgy comes directly from the Scriptures.

First the priest wishes us to have peace with God and with one another. Then we will be directed to love one another, to make the reconciliation needed so that we can confess the Faith with one mind and a spirit of unity, having been reconciled to one another in the peace of Christ.

What is needed to receive Holy Communion?

1. Faith in God.
2. A relationship with God.
3. Moral living.
4. Reconciliation with our fellow humans.
5. Praying the Divine Liturgy.
6. Fasting.

Let's take a closer look at the final two. It is important and necessary to pray at the Divine Liturgy before receiving Communion. This point is often overlooked. Ideally, we should be present in church from the first line of the service, because the Divine Liturgy is a journey that culminates in Holy Communion. How can one receive if one arrives after the Creed, without the opportunity to confess the Faith? How can one arrive after the giving of peace right before the Creed, with no opportunity to think about reconciling with a brother or sister? How can one arrive after the Great Entrance, missing the offering of the Gifts? How can one arrive after the Scripture readings, without hearing God's Word? Praying the Divine Liturgy is essential for receiving Holy Communion.

But what about fasting? Yes, fasting is on the list, but I wouldn't rank it as the highest necessity. It is certainly not more critical than the previous five items. However, it is important to fast because by fasting we gain control of our passions—the inclinations to attitudes and behaviors such as ego, lust, power, control, and anger—that take us away from God. When we tame our passion for eating by abstaining from certain foods—after all, we can go a day without an angry thought, but we can't go more than a few hours without a hungry thought—we will hopefully gain more control of our minds to abstain from the evil thoughts and deeds that constantly tempt us. Fasting is important because by disciplining our bodies, we discipline our minds and feed our souls. But it is not the only important preparation.

Receiving Holy Communion is not only the highlight of the Divine Liturgy but the pinnacle of experiencing intimacy with Christ in our life on earth. The entire service points us to both the joy and the reverence with which we are to approach. Peaceful existence with God requires peaceful existence with our neighbors. Thus before we receive Holy Communion, the Divine Liturgy once again reminds us of the importance of peace. The giving of peace immediately precedes a commandment to love one another, the topic of our next reflection. Peace and love lead to reconciliation, and these are all necessary to receive Holy Communion.

The Creed

Let us love one another, that with oneness of mind we may confess.

> Therefore confess your sins to one another, and pray for one another, that you may be healed.
>
> —James 5:16

When St. Paul lists the fruit of the Spirit in Galatians 5:22, the first one is love. In John 13:34–35, Jesus tells us, "A new commandment I give to you, that you love one another; even as I have loved you, that you also love one another. By this all men will know that you are my disciples, if you have love for one another." Saint John tells us that the motivating factor in Jesus Christ coming to the world to save us was that "God so loved the world" (John 3:16). God is love, and imitating God's love is what brings us closer to Him.

It is an act of love that the Lord sends the Holy Spirit upon our gifts of bread and wine, to consecrate them to become the Body and Blood of Christ. It is an act of love that through Holy Communion we are allowed to touch the Divine God. So, before experiencing God's love, the Church calls upon us to love one another and also to love God. Soon we will confess our Faith in reciting the Creed. But how can we confess our Faith together if we are at odds with one another? That's why we stop, leave our gifts at the altar, and seek reconciliation first with our brothers and sisters.

In the ancient Church, confession was a public act that occurred at this point of the service. People would go to one another and confess their sins. This is hard to comprehend, so let me say it in this way: Imagine that you live with twenty of your closest friends in a very close community. You have no interaction with anyone else. You eat your meals together, and you work side by side each day. Of course, you live in different houses, and each may have a spouse and a child, but basically you spend lots of time with these people. Then each Sunday, you celebrate the Divine Liturgy with them. In the span of a week, in this small, close group of people, there are bound to be arguments and misunderstandings that build enmity. So, once a week at the Divine Liturgy, you have an opportunity to go person to person and ask for forgiveness. Every week, the relationship would return to a pristine state.

The Church no longer functions like this; the communities are too big and too widespread for a public confession to be effective or even needed. We don't know many of our fellow parishioners. We don't live or work with them constantly either. But confession still occurs in a public context because we confess to a priest who represents the Body of the Church. This practice retains the ancient custom of public confession.

There are various practices regarding the Sacrament of Confession among the different Orthodox jurisdictions. Some Orthodox require frequent confession in the form of a quick listing of sins on the evening or the morning prior to the Liturgy, or confessing on a monthly basis. Some people go two or three times per year. Of course, confession of our sins should be part of our regular, daily prayer life. But the Sacrament of Confession should be formalized on a regular basis.

In the early Church, after people asked for forgiveness from one another, they would embrace and say "Christ is in our midst" with the response of "He was, He is, and He always shall be." This is called the kiss of peace. It is an embrace of love and peace between two people when they would first embrace and then kiss each other's hands as a sign of humility and forgiveness. In most churches, this practice has been discontinued, although when two or more priests or bishops concelebrate the Divine Liturgy, they exchange the kiss of peace in the altar, using the same greeting.

Regardless of differences in custom, an element of reconciliation with our fellow humans is necessary to receive Holy Communion. This command in the Liturgy is a reminder that we are called to love one another. We may come from different backgrounds and different life experiences, but in the eyes of the Lord, we are equal. So, we are to strive to be of one mind, focused on salvation.

The goal of life on earth is to prepare for eternal life, for salvation; therefore, the ultimate goal of every marriage and every friendship—and indeed every relationship—should be to help one another attain salvation. This is made possible when we love one another, when we share the same mindset, and when we come together to confess our faith as well as our desire to grow in that Faith.

Father, Son, and Holy Spirit, Trinity, one in essence and undivided.

> I love thee, O Lord, my strength. / The Lord is my rock, and my fortress and my deliverer.
>
> —Psalm 17/18:1–2

We have been invited to "love one another so that with oneness of mind we may confess." As we discussed in the previous reflection, the ancient Church included a confession or reconciliation between the members of the congregation followed by an embrace with the kiss of peace. This sequence then leads into the confession of our Faith. And even though we will confess our Faith personally—the Creed is one of the few corporate acts of worship in which we say "I believe" and not "we believe"—we will recite the words together.

So, when we are invited "with one mind" to confess, we respond with a statement of glory to the Holy Trinity by singing, "Father, Son, and Holy Spirit: Trinity, one in essence and undivided."

Imagine this dialogue:

Priest: Let us love one another so that with one mind we may confess.

People: Confess what?

Priest: Confess your shortcomings to one another.

People: (Confess their sins to each other, embrace in kiss of peace.) And now what?

Priest: Confess the basic thing we believe.

People: Yes. Father, Son, and Holy Spirit: the Trinity, one in essence and undivided.

Priest: Can you explain this further?

People: I believe (and then we recite the Creed).

So, we move from the *most* basic—we believe in the Holy Trinity—to the more specific in the Creed: what we believe about the Holy Trinity.

While this hymn is being chanted, the priest, who has faced the congregation, blessed them, then invited them to confess their faith, now turns back toward the altar and venerates the aer (cloth) that is covering the gifts. As he does this, he prays the words of Psalm 17/18:1–2, "I love thee, O LORD, my strength. / The LORD is my rock, and my fortress, and my deliverer."

Even though the priest's words are offered inaudibly, they are significant words indeed. Try this exercise. Take a piece of paper and write "The Lord is my ______________" and fill in the blank. How do you answer that question? Hopefully, you put something like "The Lord is my hope" or "The Lord is my destination."

Years ago, I met a man[22] who was coming to the end of his life. In one of our conversations, he told me about his relationship with the Lord. Since this was in the context of confession, he was addressing the Lord, and he was looking up at an icon of Christ as he was speaking. He confessed his sins and shortcomings, and he ended with a confession of his faith. He looked at the Lord and with tears in his eyes said, "Lord, you are my everything."

I have never heard anyone say something like this. It was powerful. Many years later, I can still hear him saying those words. Not a Divine Liturgy goes by that don't remember him or his faith as I venerate the Gifts and offer the prayer from Psalm 17/18. Indeed, this psalm verse sets a high bar. We are supposed to see the Lord as our rock, our fortress, and our deliverer; our beginning, our end, and everything in between. To be in heaven is to be every moment in the presence of God. He will be our everything whether we like it or not. Because life on earth is preparation for heaven, we should feel the same urgency and indeed the same joy. As the Divine Liturgy frequently reminds us, God should be the center of our lives.

The doors! The doors! In wisdom, let us be attentive.

> Set a guard over my mouth, O Lord, / keep watch over the door of my lips!
>
> —Psalm 140/141:3

22 In memory of my friend, +John Palios.

Christ's intention when He instituted the Holy Eucharist was for us to partake of it often. It is the sign of our unity with Him and our unity with one another. We know that *Communion* and *community* and *common* all share the same root word in English. *Koinonia* (communion) can also be translated as "fellowship," the kind of relationship we enjoy in the context of *koinotita* (community). The center of the church community is the Holy Eucharist, received by everyone who professes a common and unified Faith.

If one hundred people gathered for the Divine Liturgy and no one received, we would be left to wonder, "What was the point of offering the Liturgy?" People could have gotten together for a Matins or Paraklesis service (a service of supplication where no Holy Communion is offered). But when people gather for the Divine Liturgy, its purpose and central act is the receiving of Holy Communion by the faithful.

In the early Church, those who were not members of the community were dismissed from the Divine Liturgy before Holy Communion. They were allowed to be present at the beginning of the service for the prayer and the hymns, and they were allowed to be present for the reading of the Scriptures and the homily, which was traditionally offered after the Gospel reading. They could be present for the teaching portion of the service. But those who were catechumens or not members of the church were excluded from the confession of faith, the Creed, the Anaphora (where the Holy Gifts are consecrated), and from receiving Holy Communion. The intention was for *all* who were left—the members of the community—to confess their faith together in reciting the Creed and then together receive Holy Communion. The intention of our Lord was for us to receive the Eucharist as often as we can be prepared.

In our modern context, we do not ask people to leave the church if they are not Orthodox. They can stay through the entire service, though non-Orthodox are not invited to Holy Communion. So, why preserve this line about the doors in the Divine Liturgy? What purpose does it serve? Is it merely some historical vestige, or does it have any value now?

Here is a thought that comes to my mind when I reflect on this part of the service. Saint Paul writes in his Epistle to the Corinthians, "Do you not know that your body is a temple of the Holy Spirit within you, which you have from God? You are not your own; you were bought for a price. So glorify God in your body" (1 Cor. 6:19–20). If our bodies are the temples of the Holy Spirit, we need to guard the doors of our temples. We need to guard our eyes and what they see. We need to guard our ears and what they hear. We need to guard our mouths and what they say, our hands and what they do, our minds and what they think. And we need to guard our hearts and what they believe. The call to guard the doors of the church, from a historical perspective, has little meaning in the modern church. But a call to guard ourselves is still very much appropriate.

The historical call to guard the doors was to prevent those who were not yet initiated into the Faith from receiving the Holy Mysteries as the Christian faithful were about to do. The call to guard the doors of our bodies is a reminder to us to be mindful of the things that go against the Faith we are about to confess and to guard our lives from them. After all, how can we come to confess our faith if our bodies are tainted by the things we allow to come into "our doors"? We should guard the doors of our life so that the Faith we are about to confess in the Creed remains pure and without stain.

We are also reminded that through the Creed, we learn more about God and become more convinced in our belief. The words also remind us to be attentive—not to merely recite the Creed but to regard our Faith as the basis for our entire lives. We say the Creed so often, we can repeat it mindlessly. The command to "let us be attentive" is an admonishment not to be cavalier in reciting these words but to be truthful, honest, and sincere in confessing what we believe.

The Nicene Creed

I believe in:

One God, Father Almighty, Creator of heaven and earth, and of all things visible and invisible.

And in one Lord Jesus Christ, the only begotten Son of God, begotten of the Father before all ages;

Light of Light, true God of true God, begotten, not created, of one essence with the Father, through whom all things were made.

Who for us men and for our salvation came down from heaven and was incarnate of the Holy Spirit and the Virgin Mary and became man.

He was crucified for us under Pontius Pilate and suffered and was buried;

And He rose on the third day, according to the Scriptures.

And He ascended into heaven and is seated at the right hand of the Father;

He will come again with glory to judge the living and dead. His Kingdom shall have no end.

And in the Holy Spirit, the Lord, the Creator of life, who proceeds from the Father, who together with the Father

and the Son is worshiped and glorified, who spoke through the prophets.

In one, holy, catholic, and apostolic church, I confess one baptism for the forgiveness of sins.

I look for the resurrection of the dead and the life of the age to come. Amen.

> Immediately the father of the child cried out and said, "I believe; help my unbelief!"
>
> —Mark 9:24

A creed is something you believe in—something that defines you in relationship to something else. For instance, I believe in hard work, in doing the best with what I have on a given day, in being honest, and in being present. I try to center my life around these values. Notice, I didn't put "I like" in front of these phrases. Because a creed is about more than just what we like. It is about principles we are not willing to give up. I like ice cream, but if you told me I couldn't ever have ice cream again, I could still have a full life. However, if you told me I couldn't work hard, then a basic part of who I am would disappear.

The Nicene Creed is a statement of faith just over two hundred words long that defines *what* we believe as Orthodox Christians. The Creed is in four parts:

- what we believe about God the Father
- what we believe about Jesus Christ, His Son
- what we believe about the Holy Spirit, and
- what we believe about the purpose of the Church.

Take any of these elements out of the Creed, and our whole Faith would fall apart.

Entire books have been written about the Creed, its historical development, and its meaning. In this short reflection, allow me to give you a few highlights. The Creed was drafted at the First Ecumenical Council in Nicaea in the year AD 325. It was edited into its final and present form in AD 381 at the Second Ecumenical Council in Constantinople. That is why it is sometimes called the Nicene-Constantinopolitan Creed, or the Nicene Creed. Up until AD 313, the Church was an underground movement under persecution by the Roman Empire. Then in the Edict of Milan, Emperor Constantine effectively stopped the persecution of Christians by the Roman Empire. When the Church emerged after three centuries underground, many schisms and scandals occurred, as many churches were not in agreement about the basic tenets of the Faith. So, Emperor Constantine convened the First Ecumenical Council, meaning it included 318 bishops of the various church communities, and over the course of the council, the bishops put together a statement of faith that became the centerpiece for Orthodox theology and doctrine.

The Creed acknowledges God the Father as the Creator and Jesus Christ as one with the Father, both God and man. It speaks of the Incarnation through the Holy Spirit and the Virgin Mary. It affirms Jesus' Crucifixion, Resurrection, and Ascension and points to the Second Coming. The Creed speaks of the Holy Spirit, who is also Lord and Giver of Life and who proceeds from the Father.[23]

---

23 Later on, the Church of Rome would add the words "and the Son" (*Filioque* in Latin) to say that the Holy Spirit proceeds from the Father and the Son. This was one of the primary reasons for the Great Schism in AD 1054, when the Church of Rome and the Church of Constantinople excommunicated each other.

The Creed also speaks of the Church as being one, holy, catholic (meaning universal, not Roman Catholic), and apostolic—from the time of the apostles, with the ordination of bishops traced back to them in something we call "apostolic succession," with a continuity of apostolic doctrine. It also affirms our belief in the resurrection of the dead and eternal life.

If someone asks you, "What do you believe?" the answer is, "The Nicene Creed." It is important that each Orthodox Christian be able to recite it from memory so that at any moment, when we are challenged to articulate what we believe, we can do so. And more important, it is essential to understand what the Creed means, so that we can not only say the words but say them with understanding and belief.

The Creed is personal because we say "I believe," not "we believe," yet we recite it in a corporate context. The first requirement to receive Communion is faith, so we confess our Faith at each Divine Liturgy before receiving the Gifts. The Nicene Creed is also recited at each baptism by the godparents of a young child or baby who cannot say the words. It always makes me sad when those who vow to take responsibility for the spiritual upbringing of a child cannot even *read* the Creed properly, let alone say it from memory, understand what it means, or defend it with conviction.

In order to give witness for Christ, we need to say not only what we believe but also *why* we believe. So, recite the Creed often. Study and learn what each part means so that you can say it with knowledge and conviction.

The Anaphora

Let us stand aright! Let us stand in awe! Let us be attentive, that we may present the Holy Offering in peace.

> You who fear the Lord, praise him! / all you sons of Jacob, glorify him, / and stand in awe of him, all you sons of Israel!
>
> —Psalm 21/22:23

The Divine Liturgy is divided into chapters. We've experienced the opening chapters with petitions and hymns, listened to the reading of scriptures, stood for the Great Entrance of the Gifts and their presentation on the holy altar, and confessed our faith in the reciting of the Nicene Creed. The next chapter of the Divine Liturgy is called the *Anaphora*, the offering of the Gifts—the period of the service where we will call on the Holy Spirit to consecrate the bread and wine into the Body and Blood of Christ. The Anaphora begins with the words "Let us stand aright!" and will end after the consecration with a blessing: "And the mercies of our Great God and Savior, Jesus Christ, be with all."

The priestly prayers of the Anaphora of the Divine Liturgy of St. Basil the Great are significantly longer than those of the Divine Liturgy of St. John Chrysostom. However, the audible parts of the service are virtually the same.

The Anaphora announces that a new act of the Divine Liturgy is about to begin. We are called to "Stand aright!" to "Stand in awe!" and to "Be attentive." So far, we've prayed, we've sung, and we've learned. But now, the first of two miracles is about to occur: The Holy Spirit shortly will descend "on us and on the gifts here presented," and later we will have the chance to commune with the Divine Lord. So, as we are about to receive this miracle, we must "stand aright!" At this point, we are standing in church and should be doing so with rapt attention. In standing aright, we must not stand with anger, bitterness, envy, frustration, distraction, or doubt. We must stand eagerly and with enthusiasm, with faith and with hope.

We must stand "in awe," because what is about to happen is truly awesome. We should be as attentive as the fans whose team is about to win during the last minute of a football game or a hockey game, or when the last batter in a baseball game steps up to home plate. The fans rise from their seats for this final, climactic moment. In church we are to stand with awe and joy because we are about to experience a victory greater than any athletic triumph. We are about to experience again the descent of the Holy Spirit on Pentecost, and shortly after that, we will receive Holy Communion in a foretaste of the ultimate victory of eternal life.

The command to "be attentive" is heard before the readings of the Scriptures and now at the beginning of the Anaphora. The Church signals us not merely to hear what is about to happen or merely to be present. This is a time to open our hearts and our minds so that the words penetrate our ears and joy penetrates our hearts and souls. And along with that joy, we should experience serious and sober reflection, humility, and repentance as well.

The Holy Spirit is about to descend on us.

The Holy Spirit is about to consecrate ordinary offerings of bread and wine into the Body and the Blood of Christ.

The Body and Blood of Christ will be offered to us through Holy Communion.

These events demand our attention, our contrition, our awe.

Remember that before the Creed, the priest said "Peace be with all" and then called on us to love one another. The word *peace* also ushers us into the Anaphora by calling on us to present the offering in peace, to continue to hold ourselves in a state of reconciliation with one another and harmony with God.

The people's response confirms the spiritual disposition each worshiper should have at this climactic moment of the service. To the directive to "stand aright," "stand in awe," and "be attentive so that we may present the Holy Offering in peace," the people confirm that what is being presented is being offered with peace and praise—"a mercy of peace, a sacrifice of praise." It is not a halfhearted response, not an "Okay, let's get on with it." It is a contrite "Yes, I must offer mercy. The goal is to seek peace and reconciliation with God and with one another, and this sacrifice we are now offering, we offer with praise, with joy, and with a thankful heart."

The grace of our Lord Jesus Christ, and the love of God the Father, and the communion of the Holy Spirit be with you all.

> The grace of the Lord Jesus Christ and the love of God and the fellowship of the Holy Spirit be with you all.
>
> —2 Corinthians 13:14

While reading through these reflections, I hope you are beginning to understand that virtually every line of the Divine Liturgy is taken directly from Scripture—in this benediction, almost verbatim. Ironically, the Orthodox Church is often accused of favoring Tradition over Scripture. Yet as you can see, our "tradition" of the Divine Liturgy is replete with scriptural references.

This line from the Divine Liturgy appears in the Second Letter of St. Paul to the Corinthians. It is used as a benediction to prayers in many Christian denominations. It almost seems odd to find it in the middle of the Divine Liturgy, as opposed to the end. As already noted, we are embarking on the most awesome part of the service, and these words are a way of wishing us a good trip. We are called to stand well, to stand in awe, and to be attentive, and we are also immediately given the gifts of grace, love, and fellowship. God does not ask us to give to Him and expect nothing in return. For our attentiveness, He grants us His gifts.

Grace is a term normally connected to the Holy Spirit. In this case, it is connected to Christ. If grace is the Godlike quality that completes what is lacking and heals that which is infirm,[24] then grace is what takes bread and wine and elevates them into something so much greater. The love of God the Father makes it all possible, for the Son was begotten of the Father, and incarnated in the flesh "that whoever believes in him should not perish but have eternal life." (John 3:16). God's love continues to embrace us, even in our sinful state—to offer to us over and over again the opportunity to repent, to grow closer to Him, and to be one with Him in Holy Communion.

The word *koinonia* is translated "fellowship of the Holy Spirit" in the Bible and "communion of the Holy Spirit" in the Divine Liturgy. In the Greek language, koinonia by itself usually refers to fellowship, in a social sense. *Theia Koinonia,* or "Holy Fellowship," is how we refer to Holy Communion. So, let's look at koinonia from the fellowship sense. Imagine sitting down with your best friend and having an intimate conversation where deep thoughts are shared, burdens are lifted, fears are discussed, both of you lay your cards on the table, and there is a real sense of intimacy. You are both on the same page.

---

24 Wording taken from the Sacrament of Ordination.

When I think of fellowship with the Holy Spirit, I think of a sense of surrender and a similar sense of spiritual intimacy. I pour out my joys, my fears, my sorrows. I pour out everything, and immediately I am enveloped with a sense of warmth, comfort, and security. And in return, I receive the fullness of grace, which completes what I am lacking and heals my spiritual infirmities.

In offering us grace, God wants our empty spaces to be filled. In offering us love, He wants us to be one with Him and one with one another. He gives His love to us in so many ways, and He asks us to love Him and to love one another in the same way He loves us. In offering us fellowship, He is promising to comfort us. He invites us to share ourselves with one another fully, as He does with us.

This blessing of God is offered through the voice of the priest, who is God's representative in His Church. This in itself is a weighty thing. This blessing reminds me, *Who am I, to offer this on God's behalf?* And as with all blessings in the divine services, the people are called upon to offer a response. In this case, they respond to the priest, "And with your spirit," meaning that they pray for the priest to have divine grace, love, and fellowship as well.

As I study the Divine Liturgy I'm continually amazed at the poignancy of each line and how the service builds to an amazing climax. We are now entering into the most sacred moments of the service, but we do not enter them with trepidation; rather, we enter them assured of God's grace and love for us and His desire to share fellowship with us.

Let us lift up our hearts. We lift them up to the Lord.

> Let us lift up our hearts and hands / to God in heaven.
>
> —Lamentations 3:41

It is a tradition in the Orthodox Church to build a large dome over the center of a church sanctuary. In the dome is painted an icon of Christ, called the *Pantocrator,* which essentially means "ruler of all." Looking up toward His icon in the dome, we see an overarching embrace of all of us. We see the Lord as almighty and also as all-merciful.

After blessing the congregation with "the grace of our Lord Jesus Christ, the love of God the Father, and the communion of the Holy Spirit," the priest invites the congregation to "lift up our hearts." The priest then raises his arms to heaven. At every Divine Liturgy, when I raise my arms toward the dome, three thoughts go through my mind: First, I look up to Christ, and I thank Him that I have lived another week to offer another Divine Liturgy. Secondly, I see Him as the Almighty God. Third, I raise my hands to Him in heaven in a gesture of joy that He is God, and also with desperation because I so greatly need His mercies on my life. The raising of my arms is actually one of the most liberating experiences of the Divine Liturgy—a release from all inhibition, a total surrender. It is one of the few moments in the service when I forget that I am in front of a church full of people. It is a private moment between the Lord and me.

The people respond to this directive to "let us lift up our hearts" by saying, "We lift them up to the Lord." In some churches, people are also encouraged to raise their arms to the heavens, imitating the gesture of the priest. Lifting hands to heaven is a regular part of worship in Protestant churches, but it is foreign in many Orthodox churches. Yet the call to lift up our hearts allows us to imitate the priest's actions and to also lift up our own hands to heaven. In the parish where I serve, I encourage people to use this moment to feel a sense of liberation as well. I often tell people that the lifting up of hands was part of Orthodox liturgical tradition long before there was a Protestant church.

Along with lifting up our hands, we also lift up our hearts to the Lord. In this moment of freedom and surrender, we lift up our whole being to Him—our hopes, our dreams, our struggles, our successes. We send all of them up to the Lord.

I am somewhat perturbed when I offer this line of the Divine Liturgy, and instead of lifting up hands and hearts to the Lord, some people instead stare at the floor. This response in some ways symbolizes how many people receive the Good News of the gospel. Instead of lifting their hearts to Christ, they respond in confusion and, occasionally, indifference.

The Divine Liturgy is not only a dialogue of petitions and responses; in this part of the service, we are called to both a physical response—the lifting up of hands—and a spiritual response—the lifting up of hearts. As we hear these words, we should ask ourselves, *Am I lifting up my heart to the Lord? Or am I lifting up my heart to something else? Does God have my heart, my soul, and my life? Is the Lord relegated to fitting into the corners of my life, or does my life fit around the joy of the Lord?*

Giving ourselves to the Lord is the most liberating experience we can have because it sets us with direction and focus on a course to Paradise. We know where we are going. Lifting up our hearts, our hands, our souls, and our lives to the Lord sets us on the path to the everlasting freedom that will come in everlasting life.

Let us give thanks to the Lord. It is proper and right.

> O give thanks to the Lord, for he is good; / for his steadfast love endures forever.
>
> —Psalm 117/118:29

When God created the world, He created humankind in His image and likeness. His intention was that we experience an everlasting life and love, just as the Persons of the Holy Trinity share. God created a Paradise for humankind to reside in. He gave the Garden of Eden to humanity so that we could live in a state of bliss, in union with Him. Because God loved us so much, He didn't make our stay in Paradise a compulsory requirement. At any moment, humankind could choose to leave. In Genesis 2:16–17, we read that "the LORD God commanded the man, saying 'You may freely eat of every tree of the garden; but of the tree of the knowledge of good and evil you shall not eat, for in the day that you eat of it you shall die.'" This gave humankind the choice to stay with God or to go away from Him.

The first sin of humankind was not Adam and Eve's partaking of the forbidden fruit. The first sin was ingratitude. In Genesis 3:6, we read that when the serpent tempted Eve to eat the fruit, she "saw that the tree was good for food, and that it was a delight to the eyes, and that the tree was desired to make one wise." Instead of being grateful for all the things at their disposal, instead of thanking God for all the things He had given them, humankind essentially said to God, "We want the tree too." This first sin of ingratitude was followed by the disobedience of partaking of the tree, and then failure to repent. I've often wondered if the Fall could have been redeemed if Adam and Eve had simply repented.

So, after we lift up our hearts to the Lord, and before asking the Holy Spirit to come and consecrate the Gifts, we are reminded of the need to be grateful. We are reminded to give thanks to the Lord and to give thanks for all His gifts, especially in anticipation of the ones we are about to receive.

The response to this command to give thanks to the Lord is one of agreement: "It is proper and right." The words in Greek are *Axion ke dikaion. Axion* can be translated as "worthy," and *dikaion* can be translated as "right," "righteous," or "honorable." It is both worthy and proper, righteous and honorable, to come to the Lord with a sense of thanksgiving. Every time we thank Him, we are doing the very thing that Adam and Eve failed to do; we are acknowledging the gifts of the Lord with gratitude. In giving thanks to Him, we show that we are grateful and not greedy when we lift up our hearts to the Lord.

The priestly prayer below speaks of the need to give thanks to God and describes His majesty and magnitude. It acknowledges the Fall of Adam and how Christ raised us up again from our fallen state. It takes us through the entire spectrum of human history, from the Creation to the Fall to the Kingdom to come. Of course, many blessings from God are unseen, so we acknowledge even the blessings that we cannot see and do not know. We also thank God for the Divine Liturgy we are offering, understanding that the angels in heaven are present among us, worshiping with us.

> It is proper and right to hymn You, to bless You, to praise You, to give thanks to You, and to worship You in every place of Your dominion. For You, O God, are ineffable, inconceivable, invisible, incomprehensible, existing forever, forever the same, You and Your only begotten Son and Your Holy Spirit. You brought us out of nothing into being, and when we had fallen away, You raised us up again. You left nothing undone until you had led us up to heaven and granted us Your Kingdom, which is to come. For all these things, we thank You and Your only begotten Son and Your Holy Spirit: for all things we know and do not know, for blessings manifest and hidden that have been bestowed on us. We thank You also for this Liturgy, which You have deigned to receive from our hands, even though thousands of archangels and tens of thousands

> of angels stand around You, the Cherubim and Seraphim, six-winged, many-eyed, soaring aloft upon their wings.[25]

Singing the triumphal hymn, exclaiming, proclaiming, and saying . . .

> But be filled with the Spirit, addressing one another in psalms and hymns and spiritual songs, singing and making melody to the Lord with all your heart, always and for everything giving thanks in the name of our Lord Jesus Christ to God the Father.
>
> —Ephesians 5:18–20

In an earlier reflection, I discussed the enthusiasm of college football fans. Each school has a fight song, which the band leads while students join in, cheering their team to victory. When the band plays, people jump up without a prompt and sing at the top of their lungs, performing their college's hand gestures. At these games, people do not sit silently during the fight song. Everyone gets involved.

Worship in the Orthodox Church is a far cry from the exuberance of college football games. When people habitually come late and don't participate in the worship, leaving the singing of responses to the chanters and the choir, it appears that we lack joy in worshiping the Lord.

More significant, however, than the joy we bring to worship is the joy of our Christian life on the other days of the week as well. Is

25 Inaudible prayer from the Anaphora of the *Divine Liturgy of St. John Chrysostom.*

the song we sing in our Christian life a hymn of triumph or a hymn of complacency?

Each time I intone this line of the Divine Liturgy, I proclaim it with greater volume. This line is the rallying cry, if you will, that a significant moment of the service is about to occur. We have thanked the Lord for His many seen and unseen blessings, and we have acknowledged that we are standing in the presence of myriads of angels and archangels.

Now is the time for a triumphal hymn; it proclaims the glory and the majesty of God. The use of the word *triumph* implies that there is a fight to be won—a fight between good and evil, between God and the devil, between sin and salvation, between eternal life and eternal condemnation, between joy and despair. The struggle of the Christian life is the fight for this triumph.

The Good News of Christ must be proclaimed, not merely said. It is to be shared, not held in. Our Christian journey begins with our personal understanding of the Faith. But its end point is the proclaiming of that Faith to all nations. We should sing the Faith not only in our own hearts but proclaim it to the whole world.

When people exclaim or cry out, they are expressing either joy or desperation. We do both as we cry out to the Lord. We cry out with joy to our Savior, who is our hope for salvation. And we cry out in desperation for mercies that we don't deserve—but so greatly need.

Our cry of the triumphal hymn needs to be with the passion of fans at a football game. We are members of the Church, Christ's team, and we must sing with passion, both in the Divine Liturgy and throughout the week.

When the priest intones this line, the asterisk (star) that covers the bread on the diskos is removed. The offering of bread and wine is now ready to be consecrated.

Holy, holy, holy, Lord Sabaoth, heaven and earth are filled with Your glory. Hosanna in the highest. Blessed is He Who comes in the name of the Lord. Hosanna in the highest.

> In the year that King Uzziah died I saw the Lord sitting upon a throne, high and lifted up; and His train filled the temple. Above him stood the seraphim; each had six wings: with two he covered his face, and with two he covered his feet, and with two he flew. And one called to another and said:
>
> "Holy, holy, holy is the LORD of hosts;
> the whole earth is full of his glory."
>
> —Isaiah 6:1–3

> And those who went before and those who followed cried out, "Hosanna! Blessed is he who comes in the name of the Lord!"
>
> —Mark 11:9

As we approach the moment of the Consecration of the Holy Gifts, we hear a hymn that is a combination of two scripture passages—two events that reveal the Lord to us. The first reveals the Lord in a vision of the prophet Isaiah: the Lord is seen sitting on a throne, seated in glory among the seraphim. In the second event, we recount Palm Sunday, when Jesus entered Jerusalem on a donkey in a sign of humility. Taken together, this hymn reflects both the glory and the humility of the Lord.

The glory of the Lord is something we cannot comprehend. A human being can fill a room with love or joy. God can fill not only one room but also all the rooms on earth with His glory at the same time. Heaven and earth are filled with His glory. As the Holy Spirit is about to descend on the Gifts we have presented to make ordinary substances—bread and wine—into extraordinary substances—the Body and Blood of Christ—we acknowledge that this is indeed an act of glory. After all, it is difficult to comprehend that the Lord of Glory will descend from heaven and again stand with His people wherever the Divine Liturgy is offered.

The Lord is not only the Lord of glory but also the Lord of humility. For His glory is not used for conquest but for service. God's glory is experienced in acts of service, not necessarily acts of victory. On Palm Sunday, Christ entered Jerusalem on a donkey rather than a chariot. He did not arrive with armies of soldiers but with twelve disciples. And His message was not one of military overthrow but one of peace. His Kingdom would not be a kingdom of brute strength but one of service.

In this hymn, we hear the words of Palm Sunday, "Hosanna in the highest," the hymn the children sang for Jesus as He rode by them. They ran to Him, placing palm branches on the road before Him. We are reminded that we are also to become like the children, waving symbols of victory and crying out to Jesus with childlike innocence.

Something profound is about to happen in the Divine Liturgy. A moment of God's glory will happen in our midst. God will humble Himself and come and stand among us. We will offer to Him not grandiose gifts but ordinary ones. We will get on our knees, putting aside our lofty achievements in order to receive a measure of His grace and glory.

So, we see that glory and humility go hand in hand. We experience God's glory through a humble offering. God shares His glory by humbly standing with us. We experience God's glory when we set aside ourselves to be filled with Him.

Indeed, heaven and earth are filled with His glory. The church is about to be filled with it as well.

Blessed art thou, O Lord, God of our fathers, and to be praised and highly exalted for ever;

And blessed is thy glorious, holy name and to be highly praised and highly exalted forever;

Blessed art thou in the temple of thy holy glory and to be extolled and highly glorified forever.

Blessed art thou, who sittest upon cherubim and lookest upon the deeps, and to be praised and highly exalted forever.

Blessed art thou upon the throne of thy kingdom and to be extolled and highly exalted forever.

Blessed art thou in the firmament of heaven and to be sung and glorified forever.

(Song of the Three Young Men 1:29–34)[26]

The Divine Plan: Holy Are You and Most Holy

Together with these blessed powers, Master, who loves mankind, we also exclaim and say: Holy are You and most holy, You and Your only begotten Son and Your Holy Spirit. Holy are You and most holy, and sublime is Your glory. You so loved Your world that You gave Your only begotten Son so that everyone who believes in Him should not perish, but have eternal life. When He had come and fulfilled for our sake the entire plan of salvation, on the night in which He was delivered up, or rather when He delivered Himself up for the life of the world, He took bread in His holy, pure, and blameless hands,

26 In the Orthodox Old Testament, the Hymn of the Three Young Men is part of Daniel 3:25–90. This quote would be Daniel 3:52–56 in the Revised Standard Version. The "Song of the Three Youths" is an independent book in the RSV, part of the LXX.

and, giving thanks and blessing, He hallowed and broke it, and gave it to His holy disciples and apostles, saying . . .

> For God so loved the world that He gave His only Son, that whoever believes in Him should not perish but have eternal life.
>
> —John 3:16

Today's reflection is based on an inaudible prayer offered by the priest as the people sing the Thrice-Holy Hymn. Although the people usually do not hear this brief prayer during the service, I want to comment on it because it highlights God's divine plan for us.

In a previous reflection, we examined the prayer that takes us back to the Creation and the Fall: "You brought us into being out of nothing, and when we fell You raised us up again." God created us to experience a oneness with Him, just as God exists in Trinity—Father, Son, and Holy Spirit—in a perfect oneness before the Creation of the world. In trying to explain the story of Creation to some young people at summer camp, I said to them,

> Imagine if only three of us were at this camp and had access to the beautiful facilities. The three people would desire to share the experience with more people, so imagine that the three of us created more people. We wouldn't create slaves or robots but would create people just like us to experience the camp. Of course, we would give these people the freedom to leave if they wished.

This is why God created us. He created us to be like Him, to enjoy a oneness of purpose and love as He enjoys it. He created a Paradise for us to live in with Him. And He gave us the freedom to leave by putting a tree in the Garden of Eden that we were told not to touch. The divine plan was for us to choose to live with God forever. He didn't make us His slaves. He made us like Him, with the ability to live in eternal bliss, in His image and likeness. This prayer affirms God as Trinity, confirming the eternal divinity of the Father, the Son, and the Holy Spirit.

The Fall of humankind was not in God's divine plan. Instead, humanity chose to go away from God. God, out of His love and mercy, created a new plan so that fallen humanity could again be united with Him in Paradise. The plan involved sending His only begotten Son, Jesus Christ, into the world, not only to die for our sins but to show us how to live in unity with God. Christ personifies love, obedience, service, and all the Godlike qualities we are to practice in order to make it back to Paradise.

When someone asks me, "What do I have to believe in order to be a Christian?" I point them to three chapters of the Bible: The first is Genesis 1, that God created us in His image and likeness. One who is greater than we are made us, and He made us perfect. The second is Genesis 3, where humankind decided to go away from God, which we call the Fall. The world is no longer perfect, and we—not God—are the cause. The consequences of the Fall are sin, hardship, and ultimately physical death. The third is John 3, specifically John 3:16, which tells us that salvation is possible through the saving work of Jesus Christ. Humanity can be saved through Him. We all still will die an earthly death, but we can be resurrected with Christ and live again eternally with Him in Paradise, as humankind did before the Fall. This is why this prayer from the Divine Liturgy references John 3:16: "You so loved Your world that You gave Your only begotten Son so that whoever believes in Him should not perish, but have eternal life."

Christ fulfilled the divine plan when He gave Himself up for the life of the world by dying on the Cross. He suffered the physical death that every human being suffers because of the Fall, even though He is

God and never committed a sin. And He rose from the dead, showing us that by dying with faith, the resurrection is possible.

However, it is not merely dying with faith that gets us into Paradise. And it is not only through death that we can share a oneness with God. The divine plan tells us that we also are to live with faith and that we can experience a oneness with God in this life, right here and now. This oneness is possible through prayer, through service to others, and most especially in a physical and tangible way, in the Holy Eucharist. This prayer sets the scene for the Consecration of the Holy Gifts, which is about to happen next.

A Vision of Heaven: Holy, Holy, Holy, Lord Sabaoth

Priest: (in a low voice) We thank You also for this Liturgy, which You have deigned to receive from our hands, even though thousands of archangels and tens of thousands of angels stand around You, the Cherubim and Seraphim, six-winged, many-eyed, soaring aloft upon their wings,

Priest: Singing the triumphal hymn, exclaiming, proclaiming, and saying . . .

People: Holy, holy, holy, Lord Sabaoth, heaven and earth are filled with Your glory. Hosanna in the highest. Blessed is He who comes in the name of the Lord. Hosanna in the highest.

Priest: (in a low voice) Together with these blessed powers, Master, who loves mankind, we also exclaim and say: Holy are You and most holy, You and Your only begotten Son and

Your Holy Spirit. Holy are You and most holy, and sublime is Your glory.

> At once I was in the Spirit, and lo, a throne stood in heaven, with one seated on the throne!
>
> —Revelation 4:2

The Anaphora is the part of the service where the Consecration of the Holy Gifts takes place. And while we have been exploring each line, hymn, and prayer of the Anaphora and the rest of the Divine Liturgy, something profound, in my opinion, occurs when we take the above-quoted section and read it together, beginning from the middle of one prayer, including a hymn, and ending in the middle of another prayer. In my opinion, this body of words taken together paints a picture of heaven.

We know very little of what heaven will be like. It is incomprehensible to the mind that knows only the things of earth. We know that we won't have our earthly bodies with us in heaven. They will die and decay here on earth. The soul will continue on with a perfected body, but what does that look like? We do not know.

Many people think of heaven in secular terms. They imagine their best day on earth—golf courses, beaches, bars, and hanging out with friends—and they ascribe these things to heaven. I don't know how many times at a funeral I have heard people say things like, "I bet Uncle Bill is up there playing cards" or "I bet Uncle Pete and his friends are making trouble." I'm not sure if I should evaluate these comments as silly or sad, because we describe God with words like *majesty* and *glory*—terms that transcend and blow away "fun."

To be in heaven is to stand forever in the presence of God. In the prayers quoted above, we thank God for accepting our Liturgy that is offered in the presence of sinful people in a man-made building, because the Divine Liturgy of heaven is so much more powerful than any of us can imagine. Our earthly worship services are almost nothing in comparison to worship in heaven. So we thank God for accepting our earthly Divine Liturgy, simple as it may be, because in the heavenly Divine Liturgy, He is surrounded by "thousands of archangels and tens of thousands of angels." We are familiar with the sound of thousands of fans cheering at a football game. But what if 100,000 angels were all singing in perfect rhythm, in perfect pitch? Can you imagine what that would sound like? I actually can't. That is the kind of majesty that awaits us.

We've seen the cherubim and the six-winged seraphim—the angels without bodies, the ones who stand closest to God's throne—depicted in icons. What do they look like in real life? I can't imagine. Again, more majesty awaits us.

Can you imagine what it would be like if you were asked to join the heavenly choir, and your voice sounded beautiful? Then imagine that we are all in that choir—not a choir of tens of thousands of angels but of billions of voices singing as one the praises of God. The mind can't conceive what a billion voices sound like, but in heaven, we'll find out. That joy is unfathomable.

Finally, when we examine the phrase "sublime is Your glory," here are two words we cannot explain, and they are used together. To be sublime is to exceed "exceeding goodness." Take the greatest goodness and the greatest strength we know and multiply that out to infinity. That's what "sublime" means to me. We throw the word *glory* around the sports world: in high school, the team achieves "gridiron glory"—greatness that will always be remembered, even years and decades later. Take greatness and fame and multiply that to infinity, and that's what "glory" means to me. We know that infinity multiplied by infinity is an impossibility, because the number is so great it cannot be identified. Put "sublime" and "glory" into the same sentence, and we realize that we cannot comprehend them, alone or together.

We should speak of heaven more often than we do, because our end goals guide our days and our future as much as our present reality. It's easy to lose sight of this end goal because where in the world, other than in the Divine Liturgy, are we reminded of the majesty of heaven? Thankfully, St. John Chrysostom included a God-inspired vision of God's Kingdom here in the Liturgy as a way to remind, encourage, and inspire us for the life that is to come.

Take, Eat, This Is My Body . . . This Is My Blood

Take, eat, this is My Body, which is broken for you for the remission of sins. Amen.

Likewise, after partaking of the supper, He took the cup, saying,

Drink of this, all of you; this is My Blood of the new covenant, which is shed for you and for many for the remission of sins. Amen.

> Now as they were eating, Jesus took bread, and blessed, and broke it, and gave it to the disciples and said "Take, eat; this is my body." And he took a cup, and when he had given thanks he gave it to them, saying "Drink of it, all of you; for this is my blood of the covenant, which is poured out for many for the forgiveness of sins.
>
> —Matthew 26:26–28

In a previous reflection, we spoke of God's divine plan, which included the creation of the world and our freely choosing to live in a state of unity with God in Paradise, or heaven. The Fall caused humanity to be removed from Paradise, but the Crucifixion and Resurrection of Jesus Christ opened the path back to Paradise.

We affirm this truth in the opening line of the Divine Liturgy when we hear "Blessed is the Kingdom . . . now and forever and to the ages of ages." As I noted in our first reflection, the most important word of the service is *now,* because God's Kingdom is not just a far-off reality but is present in the here and now. He gives us the opportunity in this life to become one with Him in a physical and tangible way in the Holy Eucharist, which He instituted to sustain us and to strengthen our union with Him.

During the forty years in which the children of Israel slowly were making their way to the Promised Land, they complained that they had no food. So the Lord caused manna to fall from heaven (Exodus 16). Manna was a substance similar to bread; it was, in essence, "the bread of life," because it sustained the Israelites during their wanderings. Jesus taught of Himself,

> I am the bread of life. Your fathers ate the manna in the wilderness and they died. This is the bread which comes down from heaven, that a man may eat of it and not die. I am the living bread which came down from heaven; if any one eats of this bread, he will live forever; and the bread which I shall give for the life of the world is my flesh. . . . Truly, truly I say to you, unless you eat the flesh of the Son of man and drink his blood, you have no life in you; he who eats my flesh and drinks my blood has eternal life, and I will raise him up at the last day. For my flesh is food indeed, and my blood is drink indeed.

> He who eats my flesh and drinks my blood abides in me, and I in him. As the living Father sent me, and I live because of the Father, so he who eats me will live because of me. This is the bread which came down from heaven, not such as the fathers ate and died; he who eats this bread will live forever. (John 6:48–51, 53–58)

The Body and Blood of Christ are like the manna that fell from heaven and fed God's children in the wilderness. We are on our way to the Promised Land, and we need sustenance on our journey as well. The Holy Eucharist provides that. However, the Eucharist is different from manna. The people of Israel ate the manna, and eventually they died. But by partaking of the Holy Eucharist, we will live eternally with God.

Unlike the manna, which fell from heaven, we present our gifts to God, who sends the Holy Spirit to consecrate the ordinary elements of bread and wine and make them into the extraordinary elements of the Body and Blood of Christ. Unlike the sacrifices of the Old Testament, which required the blood of animals that were sacrificed, our sacrifice is without the shedding of blood. Christ told us to partake of His Body and Blood in the form of bread and wine, consecrated by Him, to establish the Holy Eucharist. As we are about to consecrate the Gifts, we are taken back to the Upper Room at the Last Supper, and we hear again Christ's words of institution.

On days we attend the Divine Liturgy, we partake of the Holy Eucharist, which should be the center of our lives. Afterward, we should carry ourselves with gratitude. And on other days, we should be preparing ourselves to receive them again. The Holy Eucharist should be on our minds on a daily basis.

Remembering, therefore, this saving commandment and all that has been done for our sake: the Cross, the tomb, the Resurrection on the third day, the Ascension into heaven, the enthronement at the right hand, and the second and glorious coming again.

> For I received from the Lord what I also delivered to you, that the Lord Jesus on the night when he was betrayed took bread, and when he had given thanks, he broke it and said, "This is my body which is for you. Do this in remembrance of me." In the same way also the cup, after supper, saying, "This cup is the new covenant in my blood. Do this, as often as you drink it, in remembrance of me." For as often as you eat this bread and drink the cup, you proclaim the Lord's death until he comes.
>
> —1 Corinthians 11:23–26

The same questions keep returning. Even if we don't speak them aloud, we might think them: *Why is it important to attend the Divine Liturgy every Sunday? It's just the same. Why not just attend once in a while?*

I can give you at least three good reasons why you should attend the Divine Liturgy every Sunday, and more often if possible.

1. *We go to the Divine Liturgy to touch God.*
   Only in the Holy Eucharist can we touch the Living God, and only in the Holy Eucharist can God touch us in a physical way. This is why receiving Communion is central to our participation in the Divine Liturgy. If we attend the Liturgy but do not receive, we are not experiencing its main purpose—touching God. The Divine Liturgy is the venue that makes this possible on a continual basis.

2. *Every Divine Liturgy is like a little Pentecost.*
   The Holy Spirit comes down to make the ordinary become extraordinary. This happens not only with the bread and wine that become the Body and Blood of Christ but also with the people in attendance, who are given a measure of grace just as the disciples were given grace on Pentecost. (We will go into more depth on this topic in a future reflection.)

3. *We celebrate the Divine Liturgy to remember what God has done for us.*
   We take in a lot of sensory stimuli in a given week. We watch TV, we browse the internet, we peruse Facebook and Instagram and the latest social media craze. We see billboards, we peruse magazines at the store, we enjoy conversations with friends, and we eat, drink, gossip, work, work out, relax, and sometimes we do nothing. In the middle of our frenzied lives, sometimes we lose God. We forget to pray. We forget how to love one another. We forget that God loves us. Going to the Divine Liturgy is a corrective—a necessary reminder of what God has done for us. It is an important reminder that God loves us. It is a frequent reminder of where we've come from and where we're going.

The prayer quoted today is offered by the celebrant inaudibly. It provides an important message: it calls on us to remember all the things that Christ has done for us. He instituted the Holy Eucharist, which He commanded us to do in His memory. Christ did not merely suggest that we receive the Holy Eucharist; He commanded us to do so. The prayer calls on us to remember the Cross, the Tomb, the Resurrection on the third day, the Ascension into heaven, and the enthronement at the right hand of the Father. All these things have happened in order to reopen the door to Paradise for us.

What has not happened yet is the second, glorious coming of Christ, outlined in Matthew 25:31–46, where He will come again in glory to judge all the peoples of all the nations, deciding who will receive eternal reward or eternal punishment. Right now we live in a time of expectation. The works of salvation have already happened. We live in this world, working toward the Kingdom of God, building a case for ourselves so that when we stand before the Lord, He will be merciful and judge us worthy of His Kingdom.

If we have no goals in life, it is hard to find purpose and meaning. A student's goal is to finish school. So every day, even on days he or she doesn't want to attend, learning is the main focus because doing well in school helps achieve the goal, which is to finish. A worker's goal is to provide financial means for his or her family. This serves as motivation even when one doesn't feel like going to work. In the same way, the goal of the Christian life is not just belonging to a church or saying prayers or being nice. The goal of the Christian life is to be judged worthy by Christ to inherit eternal life. Each day should include some effort toward that goal. And each Sunday should be a regular check-in to meditate on that goal and how we are doing on our journey toward it this week.

The Divine Liturgy is a reminder of this overarching goal of the Christian life as well as the means to achieve that eternal goal of unity with the Lord forever in Paradise. The means to this goal is becoming one with the Lord in the Holy Eucharist. Returning to the words of St. Paul in his First Letter to the Corinthians, "for as often as you eat this bread and drink the cup, you proclaim the Lord's death until he comes" (11:26). Saint Basil the Great added another phrase to this verse in his Divine Liturgy when he wrote, "Do this in remembrance of Me, for as often as you eat this bread and drink this cup, you proclaim My death, and you confess My Resurrection."

We say "I love you" often to those we love. They need to hear those words, and we need to hear those words. We need to say those words, and they need to say those words to us. Why? Because the words *I love you* give us confidence in ourselves and in others. They reassure us on the worst of days that someone cares about us. No one gets tired of hearing they are loved. No one complains that this phrase is redundant.

In the Divine Liturgy, we hear again that God loves us. We affirm again that we love Him. We remember what He did for us. We remember where we are going.

Your own of Your own we offer to You, in all and for all. (Part 1)

> "But who am I, and what is my people, that we should be able thus to offer willingly? For all things come from thee, and of thy own have we given thee."
>
> —1 Chronicles 29:14

This line of the Divine Liturgy offers us two thoughts that are so profound we will examine them over the course of two reflections.

The first profound thought is that we have nothing to offer to God of our own. Whatever we have that is good came first from Him. God created wheat, and we fashion it into bread. God created grapes, and we make them into wine. So, even though we offer these gifts in the context of the Divine Liturgy—someone bakes the bread, and someone makes the wine—the ingredients of these gifts were made by God. We are offering back to Him what He first gave us.

Every good thing we have can be traced back to the Lord. I own a nice home, which I purchased with money that I earned from a job, that I received because of education, which was fostered by a mind that was created by God. If we take every positive thing we possess and trace its origin, we discover that "every good endowment and every perfect gift is from above" (James 1:17)—its origin is in God.

As we hear the priest speak this sentence, three liturgical actions are taking place. First, he elevates the Gifts toward heaven. In most churches, over the altar where he stands is an icon of the Virgin Mary holding Christ—the Platytera. When I elevate the Gifts at each Divine Liturgy, I look up at Christ and feel a connection, that we are offering these Gifts to Him. This is one reason for icons in our churches. They tell stories and reveal theology to us, giving us reference points to the characteristics and virtues of the holy people depicted in them. And they place us in heaven. When we are in church, we are surrounded by the angels and saints, as we will be in heaven. But they also give us a way to connect what we are doing with the angels, the saints, and the Lord. Elevating the Gifts while looking up at Christ helps me remember what we are doing: we are offering the Gifts to Him, from the gifts that He first gave us.

Second, the celebrant crosses his hands, right over left. Like every other liturgical action, this gesture is intentional: it is a reminder of the Cross. In crossing the hands, we remember that the greatest gift we have ever received is Christ's death on the Cross for us and His Resurrection from the dead. We are not merely offering gifts of bread and wine, we are also remembering and celebrating what Christ did for us. The priest's cuffs—worn over the wrists of all deacons, priests, and bishops—represent the bound hands of Christ during His Passion. They remind the clergy, and in turn the people, that our hands are supposed to be bound in the sense that they should be prohibited from certain actions. If we are God's people, we should act appropriately at all times. Our hands should not be raised in anger or used for dishonest work; rather, they should be used for helping our fellow human beings and giving glory to God.

The third liturgical action is that we kneel as the Gifts are about to be offered. There has been controversy over the centuries as to whether we should kneel or not kneel at the Divine Liturgy, and a good argument can be made for either side. We stand in honor of the Resurrection. Holy Communion represents the hope of our personal resurrection, and that is why we stand to receive. But we kneel in honor of Pentecost. And because the Consecration of the Gifts is another Pentecost, we kneel as we anticipate the grace of the Holy Spirit.[27]

If we attended the Divine Liturgy on a daily basis, we would most likely not kneel on Sundays because Sunday is the day of the Resurrection. However, because we do not attend the Divine Liturgy every day, the prevailing custom in the Church is that we kneel on Sundays (outside the paschal season).

As the priest elevates the Gifts and says, "Your own of Your own we offer to You, in all and for all," let us remember that every good gift comes from God. Let us look up to the icon of the Lord in the dome of the church or above the altar and connect with Him at this most important moment. Let us look to the hands of the priest and remember the sacrifice of Christ on the Cross, as well as the personal sacrifices we should and must make in order to be faithful Christians.

And as we bow our heads and bend our knees, let us do so in awe. When in our lives do we kneel? Only to our Creator and our Savior. Let us remember that He is God, and we are His children—a thought that is both awesome and joyful. If worship is meant to be

27 During the paschal season, from Pascha through Pentecost, it is the tradition of the Church that we do not kneel at the consecration; we merely bow our heads. If one feels compelled not to kneel on a Sunday in honor of the Resurrection (and not in militant protest), then standing and bowing the head is sufficient. If one feels compelled to kneel out of reverence and deep respect for the descent of the Holy Spirit, that cannot be considered wrong either, even on a Sunday. As more than one priest has said to me, it is never wrong to kneel. In the liturgical rubrics of the Church, kneeling is required on three occasions: during the special prayers offered on Pentecost, during the Sacrament of Ordination (except for the ordaining bishop or bishops), and in the Sacrament of Confession, when the prayer of absolution is offered.

the work of the people, this line of the Divine Liturgy provides us an opportunity to do some really important spiritual work.

Your own of Your own we offer to You, in all and for all. (Part 2)

> But we would not have you ignorant, brethren, concerning those who are asleep, that you may not grieve as others do who have no hope. For since we believe that Jesus died and rose again, even so, through Jesus, God will bring with him those who have fallen asleep.
>
> —1 Thessalonians 4:13–14

In our previous reflection we considered the profound thought that we have nothing to offer to God of our own. The second profound thought in this line of the Divine Liturgy is that the Holy Gifts are offered for all: the Church Militant and the Church Triumphant. The Church Militant refers to the segment of the Church that is alive on earth—the fighting Church, which includes you and me. The Church Triumphant refers to the segment of the Church no longer on the earth—the saints and others who have passed away.

Before the Divine Liturgy begins, the priest prepares the Gifts behind the icon screen in the altar in a service called the Proskomide, usually during the Matins service that precedes the Divine Liturgy.[28] The bread is placed on the diskos, a stemmed plate. The plate represents the world, because centuries ago, when the Divine Liturgy was written, people thought that the world was round and flat.

28 While Greek practice prepares the Gifts during Matins (Orthros), in Slavic churches the Proskomide occurs as a separate service before the Liturgy, since Matins usually is celebrated as part of Vigil the previous evening.

Several pieces of bread[29] are placed on the diskos, and a square cube is cut and placed in the center—the "Lamb." This piece will become the Body of Christ in the consecration. A triangular piece is placed to the right of the Lamb in honor of the Theotokos. Next, nine small triangles are cut and placed on the left side of the Lamb, representing the nine categories of saints—angels, prophets, apostles, hierarchs, martyrs, ascetic fathers, unmercenary healers, the ancestors of Christ and saints of the day, and the saint whose Divine Liturgy we are celebrating. Beneath the pieces for Christ, the Theotokos, and the saints, the priest places two piles of bread crumbs to represent the people.

The particles in the bottom left pile are for members of the Church Militant, and the priest prays for his bishop and the people of his parish by name. This process can take anywhere from a few minutes to a few hours, depending on how many people the priest is praying for. On the bottom right side of the diskos, the particles represent members of the Church Triumphant, and the priest prays for those who have passed away. The Church constantly is praying for those who have fallen asleep in the Lord—in the Proskomide, in memorial services, and so on. Just because a person has died and no longer is physically present does not mean they have left the Church. They have simply moved from the Church Militant to the Church Triumphant. They are still part of the Church. This is a very comforting thought.

Throughout all the years I have served as a priest, I have prayed for my family in the Proskomide. A particle of bread has been present for each of them on the diskos at every Divine Liturgy. When my father passed away a couple of years ago, I placed a particle of bread for him in the section where the Church Triumphant is commemorated. So,

29 The bread used is called *prosphoro*, a leavened bread that is usually baked by members of the parish as an offering and is used for Holy Communion.

at the Divine Liturgy, my entire family still stands together. It is the only place where we can all be together anymore. I take a lot of comfort from this, that while my father may not share the dinner table with me again, he is sharing in the Divine Liturgy with me every time it is celebrated.

When you want to feel close to your loved ones, ask your priest to pray for them in the Proskomide, and remember that at the Divine Liturgy you stand together as one family. I tell people who are in grief that, rather than going to the cemetery to mourn, they should come to the church, look up at the diskos as the priest elevates it, and know that their loved ones are remembered there. And even if their specific names haven't been submitted, they are included in the prayer for "every righteous spirit made perfect in the faith," which is offered during the consecration and which we will discuss in a future reflection.

On a practical note, when you submit names to the priest and ask him to pray for you and your loved ones, it is important that you list for him their segment of the Church. In other words, if you hand the priest a list of names and ask him to pray for them, his natural question will be whether they are part of the Church Militant or the Church Triumphant. So that he doesn't have to guess, write "for the health of" and list people of the Church Militant you wish to pray for, and then write "in memory of" and list the people in the Church Triumphant you wish to pray for.

One last comment regarding the Church: The stole that the priest or bishop wears for every liturgical act always has two rows of fringe at the hem. One row is for the Church Militant, and the other is for the Church Triumphant. The purpose of this is twofold: First, it is a visual reminder for us to remember always those who have passed on. Second, it is a reminder that when we gather to pray—where even two or three are gathered in His name—both the Church Militant and Church Triumphant are with us.

So, when you gather with others for the Divine Liturgy, the Sacrament of Confession, a wedding, or a prayer in a hospital, remember that the saints, the angels, the Church Militant, and the Church Triumphant are united with you in prayer.

> O God of spirits and of all flesh, You who trampled down death and abolished the power of the devil, and gave life to Your world, give rest to the soul of Your servant(s) (Name) who has (have) fallen asleep in a place of light, in a place of repose, in a place of refreshment, where there is no pain, sorrow, and suffering. Gracious and loving God, forgive every sin he (she/they) has (have) committed in word, deed, or thought, for there is no one who lives and is without sin. You alone are without sin. Your righteousness is an everlasting righteousness, and Your Word is truth.
>
> For You are the Resurrection, the Life and the repose of Your departed servant(s) (Name), O Christ our God, and to You we send up glory, with Your Father who is from everlasting and Your all holy, good and life-creating Spirit, now and forever and to the ages of ages. Amen.[30]

We praise You, we bless You, we give thanks to You, and we pray to You, Lord our God.

> Enter his gates with thanksgiving, / and his courts with praise! / Give thanks to him, bless his name!
>
> —Psalm 99/100:4

30 From the *Memorial Service, Divine Liturgy of St. John Chrysostom* (Brookline, MA: Holy Cross Orthodox Press, 1984), 161–162.

The moment of consecration is about to happen. This is a Consecration of the Gifts, bread and wine, that we have presented to God from His own gifts. It is also a moment of reconsecration of ourselves. We also are gifts that He has created. Why do I say reconsecration of ourselves? Because as we kneel, the priest prays in the altar, "Send down Your Holy Spirit upon us, and upon the Gifts here presented." The Holy Spirit makes holy and sets apart ordinary things—bread and wine—into extraordinary things, the Body and Blood of Christ. And at the same time, He reconsecrates us ordinary, sinful people into extraordinary people—children of God. So, as we kneel at each Divine Liturgy, we should kneel with hearts that are open to receiving the Holy Spirit yet again. We should bring to mind our imperfections that need healing. We should recommit ourselves to Christ, to our marriages, to our children, to our jobs, to all the positive roles we hold in life. As the Holy Spirit comes down on the Holy Gifts, we should allow His grace to wash over us—the way the water washed over us at baptism, the way forgiveness washes over us in confession, the way grace washed over us at our weddings. We should be open to the same grace at this moment of the Divine Liturgy.

The hymn that is sung during the consecration is a simple hymn of praise and thanksgiving. The words call us to humility.

We praise You. To praise someone means to acknowledge that something great has happened. However, we are not praising a good test score or an athletic achievement when we praise God. We are praising our Creator, who has done something remarkable in creating us. We are praising our Creator, who has done something wonderful in saving us from our sins. We are praising our Creator, who continually makes the ordinary into the extraordinary by His divine grace that He sends so freely upon us.

We bless You. In past centuries—we see this multiple times in the Old Testament—a father on his deathbed would give his blessing to his son. In modern times, a father gives a blessing in some cultures for his daughter to get married. To bless someone is to give them both honor and freedom. Usually, we speak of God's blessings on us. It seems odd that we would "bless" God. Yet that is what the hymnographer wrote: we bless You! When I think of this phrase, I think of us giving God permission to be Lord of our life. As He reconsecrates us as His children at each Divine Liturgy, we, too, play a role in this action as we reconsecrate ourselves to Him. We give Him control of our lives. We reaffirm that He is our God and our Lord. He is the Savior and the director.

We give thanks to You. We are supposed to thank God in all circumstances. In this important moment of the Divine Liturgy, we offer thanks for the great gift that we are about to receive—the Holy Spirit coming upon us to heal what it is infirm and complete what is lacking in each of us, as well as coming down to consecrate the Holy Gifts. These Gifts then become the spiritual medicine we all need for the sustaining, healing, and perfecting of our souls. This moment of awe should fill us with thanksgiving.

And we pray to You. In Psalm 24/25:21, we read, "May integrity and uprightness preserve me, for I wait for thee." I never pray for wealth or power. I pray for things like integrity, wisdom, patience, and stamina. Prayer is a statement that our hope rests in God. This is why we pray so often. Prayer connects us with God and is possible at any moment when we want or need it. So, we kneel before God in faith during the beautiful prayer that is about to be offered on our behalf.

Lord our God. The hymn does not actually say "Lord our God" in its original Greek. It says only "our God." Many people think of God as a trinket; they wear a cross as a good-luck charm. Some people think of God as a friend, someone to go to for help and to lean on. God is our Lord, our Savior, and our hope. He cannot be fully comprehended. This is why we kneel before Him. I don't kneel at any other time in my life except in prayer and worship. I don't kneel before friends—even good friends. I kneel only before God as a sign of deep respect and humility. He is God. I am His servant. The acknowledgment, on our knees before God as Lord, should impact us after we get up from our knees. As we leave church after each Divine Liturgy and resume our lives, our roles, and our worldly stresses, we should remember that we have knelt before God and have placed our faith and our hope in Him again.

I am fortunate to have served in the altar with many good liturgists during my formative years. One of them would actually say the words of the hymn before beginning the prayer of consecration as we knelt in the altar. Perhaps that is because priests don't hear this hymn as we are offering the prayer. I'd like to think that he saw himself as a child of God and wanted to reaffirm his faith before invoking the Holy Spirit on the Gifts. I have heard many priests and bishops do this. And in my priesthood, I have followed the same practice.

Once again we offer to You this spiritual worship without the shedding of blood, and we beseech and pray and entreat You:

Send down Your Holy Spirit upon us and upon the Gifts here presented.

And make this bread the precious Body of Your Christ. Amen.

And that which is in this Cup, the precious Blood of Your Christ. Amen.

Changing them by Your Holy Spirit. Amen. Amen. Amen.

> Indeed, under the Law almost everything is purified with blood, and without the shedding of blood there is no

> forgiveness of sins. Thus it was necessary for the copies of the heavenly things to be purified with these rites, but the heavenly things themselves with better sacrifices than these. For Christ has entered, not into a sanctuary made with hands, a copy of the true one, but into heaven itself, now to appear in the presence of God on our behalf. Nor was it to offer himself repeatedly, as the high priest enters the Holy Place yearly with blood not his own; for then he would have had to suffer repeatedly since the foundation of the world. But as it is, he has appeared once for all at the end of the age to put away sin by the sacrifice of himself.
>
> —Hebrews 9:22–26

As the choir sings the hymn of thanksgiving ("We praise You, we bless You . . ."), the people are kneeling while the priest offers the prayer of consecration. As with everything in the Divine Liturgy, these words have a scriptural basis as well.

In the Old Testament, the Jewish Law required the people to make sacrifices to God for various things—for sins, for thanksgiving, even for joy. Many sacrifices required the shedding of blood. The 613 tenets of the Mosaic Law gave explicit instructions on what sacrifices were needed and how they were to be conducted. So, from the Old Testament, we get the tradition of the blood sacrifice.

One example requirement for the shedding of blood is the first Passover, recounted in Exodus 12. When the Israelites were held as slaves in Egypt, the Lord sent Moses to Pharaoh and through Moses ordered Pharaoh to let the people go. Pharaoh refused. So, the Lord inflicted ten plagues upon the Egyptians. After each plague, Pharaoh said that he would let the people go, only he didn't. The tenth plague was the death of the firstborn son of each house in Egypt.

The Lord warned the people of Israel that the angel of death would pass over each home and kill the firstborn son. The only way to avoid this was to shed the blood of an unblemished lamb and place it over the doorway of each home. Seeing the blood of the lamb, the angel would pass over the house. Hence the origin of the Feast of Passover.

The lambs were slaughtered on the eve of Passover at midafternoon outside the city wall,[31] at the same hour that centuries later Christ, the Lamb of God, would be crucified and die for us on a Friday afternoon outside the city wall of Jerusalem. By partaking of His blood, the angel of death will pass over us, and we can enter into eternal life.

Because Christ shed His blood for us, it is no longer necessary to offer a blood sacrifice to God. We offer bread and wine, because that is how Christ instituted the Holy Eucharist—the ritual He taught us to do until His Second Coming, to remember what He did for us.

We ask the Lord to send down His Holy Spirit on us and on our Gifts. In asking Him to send the Holy Spirit upon us, we are living another Pentecost, when the Holy Spirit came down on the apostles and allowed simple fishermen to become leaders and heralds of the gospel (Acts 2). In other words, God took ordinary men and made them extraordinary.

Likewise, we ask the Holy Spirit to come down on us in the same manner, to make us extraordinary people. We ask for His grace, which is imparted through our mere presence at this moment of the Divine Liturgy. Many priests, including me, spread their hands wide before the prayer of consecration, gesturing toward the people and asking the Lord to reconsecrate *us*—to again send down His grace upon us through the Holy Spirit.

We then ask for the Holy Spirit to make the bread into the Body of Christ. We ask Him to make the wine in the cup to be the Blood of Christ. And we "crown" this request by asking that they be changed by the power of the Holy Spirit.

31 www.jewishencyclopedia.com/articles/11934-passover-sacrifice.

In the Orthodox Church, we do not have a theological term for what happens at this moment. I remember as a child looking up, hoping to see the Holy Spirit coming down as a bright light or something. And He never did—at least not in a way I could see it. He consecrates the Gifts invisibly, and they retain their chemical properties; they still look and taste like bread, they still look and taste like wine. Yet they are different. How this happens is a mystery. This is why in the Greek language we use the word *mysteria*, or "mysteries," as opposed to the word *sacrament*. How bread and wine become the Body and Blood of Christ is a mystery, in the same way it is a mystery how our sins can be lifted away in the Sacrament of Confession, or how a man and woman can be united into a family.

In Luke 8:10, Jesus says to His disciples, "To you it has been given to know the secrets of the Kingdom of God; but for others they are in parables, so that seeing they may not see, and hearing they may not understand." For one who looks at the Divine Liturgy in a casual or cynical way, the consecration is just another prayer while the choir sings a hymn. But for those who truly have given their heart and soul to the Lord, this moment is the loftiest moment of the Divine Liturgy. We are present for a miracle as the Holy Spirit comes down upon us and upon our Gifts, and what we receive is a reconsecration of ourselves and the Body and Blood of Christ now in our midst.

Six Reasons to Receive Holy Communion

So that they may be for those who partake of them for vigilance of soul, remission of sins, communion of Your Holy

Spirit, fullness of the Kingdom of heaven, boldness before You, not for judgment or condemnation.

> You yourselves are our letter of recommendation, written on your hearts, to be known and read by all men; and you show that you are a letter from Christ delivered by us, written not with ink but with the Spirit of the living God, not on tablets of stone but on tablets of human hearts.
>
> —2 Corinthians 3:2–3

Holy Communion is the centerpiece of the Orthodox Christian Church. The Divine Liturgy points us to the Eucharist not only as the climax of the service but our very reason for worshiping. We worship in a corporate context so that we can receive Holy Communion—so that we can touch the divine God.

The study of Orthodox theology generates questions that often are answered in the text of the Divine Liturgy. Such is the case with this reflection. After the Holy Gifts have been consecrated, the priest kneels before the altar and continues the prayer of consecration with a list of six reasons to receive Holy Communion. Because in most churches this prayer is inaudible, I want to share with you not only its words but also their rich meaning.

1. *So that they may be for those who partake of them for vigilance of soul.*
   Holy Communion is like food for the soul—the godlike part of each of us. The soul came from God and desires to be filled with Him. It is constantly wounded by the cares of life and the stresses of the world. It is filled through receiving Christ in the Eucharist. Holy Communion, when received with proper spiritual disposition, awakens the soul, encourages the soul, and

keeps the soul vigilant. When we are not receiving Holy Communion regularly, the soul more easily falls into despair. Just as the hungry person needs food to function correctly, we need the Body and Blood of Christ to function at our best.

2. *Remission of sins.*
   The Greek word used here is *afesin*, which means "remission" or "wiping out." Holy Communion, in concert with our personal repentance—which includes the Sacrament of Confession—helps to wipe out our sins on a continual basis so that we can work toward oneness with the Lord. Prayer, fasting, moral living, reconciliation, worship—all these things are prerequisites to receiving Holy Communion, and they help us live in Christ in this life as we prepare to live with Him in the next.

3. *Communion of Your Holy Spirit.*
   In this instance, "communion," or *koinonia*, means "fellowship." When we share fellowship with the Holy Spirit, we receive His grace, and He heals and strengthens the things that are infirm and lacking in us. Having prayed for the Holy Spirit to come down upon us as He comes down on the Gifts we present, we now pray that He would come into each of us.

4. *Fullness of the Kingdom of heaven.*
   Christ promised that we who believe will one day inherit His Kingdom. We live in the period of time between this promise and the day Christ comes again to judge the living and the dead and to grant His eternal Kingdom to those who are righteous. So, we pray that the promise of Christ will be fulfilled in our lives and in the lives of our fellow worshipers. Holy Communion is a necessary step in this journey, as it gives us the spiritual sustenance to pass through this life on the way to

eternal life. Holy Communion helps bring the promise to its eventual fulfillment.

5. *Boldness before You.*
   Many of us lack boldness or confidence. We lack confidence in material things, in ourselves, in others, and sometimes in spiritual things. We wonder if the promises of Christ are really true, or we worry whether we will be worthy of the promised Kingdom. Holy Communion helps us to have spiritual confidence in both areas. By receiving often, we are strengthened to live our Christianity in a secular world, which often challenges and ridicules what we believe. By receiving often, with proper preparation, we have confidence that indeed God does love us and desires us to be with Him. Staying away from this eucharistic encounter with Christ for long periods of time will attack our confidence so that we are afraid to approach or are made to feel indifferent. Receiving often is a spiritual confidence builder.

6. *Not for judgment or condemnation.*
   As if to reassure us that it is okay to receive, these words are added to the prayer. Of course, no one is ever worthy to receive the Body and Blood of Christ; we receive them through His divine mercy. We can prepare ourselves, but we cannot proclaim ourselves worthy. So, we ask the Lord to deem us worthy to receive and for this act not to lead to our condemnation. To receive the Eucharist without preparation, to receive in anger, or to receive when engaged in an immoral lifestyle leads to condemnation. Yet we all sin, and we all need God's mercies each time we receive Holy Communion. For how else can a sinful human being—even one who strives not to sin—be able to touch the Divine God?

There are many reasons to receive Holy Communion, and St. John Chrysostom highlighted six of them in this prayer: a heightened sense of vigilance in our souls, the remission of our sins, fellowship and grace with the Holy Spirit, a precursor to inheriting the Kingdom of heaven, confidence and encouragement in our faith, and the avoidance of judgment and condemnation.

And with these blessings, we will approach not only with fear of God, faith, and love—as we will soon be invited—but we will come with purpose as we prepare to touch God.

Again, we offer You this spiritual worship for those who have reposed in the faith: forefathers, fathers, patriarchs, prophets, apostles, preachers, evangelists, martyrs, confessors, ascetics, and for every righteous spirit made perfect in faith.

> But you have come to Mount Zion, and to the city of the living God, the heavenly Jerusalem, and to innumerable angels in festal gathering, and to the assembly of the first-born who are enrolled in heaven, and to a judge who is God of all, and to the spirits of just men made perfect, and to Jesus, the mediator of a new covenant.
>
> —Hebrews 12:22–24

This sentence concludes the Prayer of Consecration. Again, this entire prayer is said quietly by many priests, so you'll have to listen carefully or follow along in the Divine Liturgy book to discover it. These prayers, even the ones we don't hear out loud, are so important to the celebration of the Liturgy that I continue to comment on them.

Two things come to my mind as I offer these prayers every week. The first is our connection with the Church Triumphant. As I have already commented, when we offer the Gifts "for all," that means all are represented—those who are alive (Church Militant) and those who have passed away (Church Triumphant). After the Gifts have been consecrated, we affirm that we are offering them not only for ourselves but also for those who have gone before us—on behalf of and in concert with all the saints. We name the Church Triumphant in several categories—forefathers, fathers, prophets, apostles, preachers, evangelists, martyrs, confessors, and ascetics. When I pray for these groups, I think not only of specific saints, like the evangelists Matthew, Mark, Luke, and John; I think of "evangelists" in the sense of people who have worked to spread the gospel, such as former Sunday school teachers who have passed away.

Our "forefathers" include grandparents and ancestors. Our "fathers" include our parents, including my own father. When I think of "patriarchs," I think of all the clergy who have served. "Prophets" include the prophets of the Old Testament, but I also think of those who have spoken with a prophetic voice about the mighty works of God. "Apostles" remind us of those who have invited others to the Faith. When I hear "preachers," I think of teachers—those who have taught me and others the Faith. "Evangelists" reminds me of those who have spread the Word with enthusiasm. "Martyrs" are those who have died for Christ and also those who have lived for Him. *Martyr* means "witness," so everyone who gives witness in Christ, whether they are killed for their faith or not, is called to be a martyr. "Confessors" are spiritual fathers who act as guides for the faithful and have suffered for the faith, without necessarily dying. "Ascetics" are those who have lived secluded in monasteries, where they have devoted their lives to prayer, as well as those in the world who have lived lives of sacrifice and self-denial.

The list brings us to the final category: *every righteous spirit made perfect in the faith*. This accounts for everyone we can think of—our parents, friends, coworkers—everyone we can remember who has lived as a Christian.

My second thought as I offer this prayer is that of all the lists in life, the most important list is *every righteous spirit made perfect in faith*. When we are students, we are concerned with being on the honor roll. We love being recognized for awards and promotions. Later in life, many people are obsessed with being remembered when they are gone. Someone once said to me, "See my name on that building, Father? No one will remember you when you are gone, but they will remember me." To which I replied, "I don't care if anyone remembers me when I'm gone, as long as the Lord remembers me in His Kingdom. Because if I'm not on His list, what good is all the other stuff that I've done? However, if I'm on His list, I really don't need to be on any other." Think about this statement: "I (your name) want to be on the list of people made perfect in faith." Hold it up to other accomplishments and goals of your life, and you may find your priorities shifting. Becoming a person who is a "righteous spirit made perfect in faith" should be at the top of your list.

Especially for our most holy, pure, blessed, and glorious Lady, the Theotokos and ever-virgin Mary.

It is truly right to bless you, Theotokos, ever blessed, most pure, and Mother of our God. More honorable than the Cherubim, and beyond compare more glorious than the Seraphim,

without corruption you gave birth to God the Logos. We magnify you, the true Theotokos.

> All this took place to fulfill what the Lord had spoken by the prophet: "Behold a virgin shall conceive and bear a son, and his name shall be called Emmanuel" (which means, God with us).
> —Matthew 1:22–23

If you read through the Divine Liturgy by yourself, each word receiving the same emphasis, you would finish the Prayer of Consecration, where we remember "forefathers, fathers, patriarchs, prophets" and so on, and then you'd read "and for every righteous spirit made perfect in faith, especially for our most holy, pure, blessed and glorious Lady, the Theotokos and ever-virgin Mary." Because the celebrant offers the Prayer of Consecration silently in most parishes, it seems like a hard segue to go from singing, "We praise You, we bless You, we give thanks to You and we pray to You, Lord our God" right to "Especially for our most holy, pure, blessed and glorious Lady." Again, in the context of the Prayer of Consecration and the text of the entire Divine Liturgy, this fits much more easily.

Let's reflect for a moment on where we have just been. We offered the Gifts on behalf of all and for all. The celebrant then asked the Holy Spirit to come down on those present, which covers everyone in the church. He continued the prayer, remembering those who have fallen asleep in the Faith. And now the service remembers specifically the Virgin Mary.

The Theotokos is mentioned several times in the Divine Liturgy. She is commemorated four times at the end of a litany: "Commemorating our most holy, pure, blessed, and glorious Lady, the Theotokos and ever-virgin Mary, with all the saints, let us commend ourselves and one another and our whole life to Christ our God." One of the antiphons at the beginning of the Liturgy is dedicated to her: "Through the intercessions of the Theotokos, Savior, save us." And in Greek and Antiochian practice, following the Consecration of the Gifts, we again pause to remember and to praise the Theotokos.[32]

After the priest says aloud, "Especially for our most holy, pure blessed and glorious Lady, the Theotokos and ever-virgin Mary," the people respond by singing a hymn in her honor, printed at the beginning of this reflection ("It is truly right to bless you, Theotokos . . .").

The Church's veneration of the Virgin Mary is found throughout Orthodox liturgical services. The Matins service includes a set of hymns called "The Magnificat" (also called "The Meglynarion" or simply the Ninth Ode of the canon). This set of hymns is based on Luke 1:46–55:

> My soul magnifies the Lord, and my spirit rejoices in God my Savior;
>
> For He has regarded the low estate of His handmaiden. For behold, henceforth all generations will call me blessed;
>
> For He who is mighty has done great things for me, and holy is His Name, and His mercy is on those who fear Him from generation to generation.
>
> He has shown strength with His arm, He has scattered the proud in the imagination of their hearts;
>
> He has put down the mighty from their thrones and exalted those of low degree; He has filled the hungry with good things, and the rich he has sent empty away.
>
> He has helped his servant Israel, in remembrance of His mercy, as He spoke to our fathers, to Abraham and to his posterity forever.

---

32 This is Slavic practice only on certain feast days.

These verses are broken up into six parts, as I have divided them above. And after each set of verses is the refrain "More honorable than the Cherubim and beyond compare more glorious than the Seraphim, without corruption you gave birth to God the Logos. We magnify you, the true Theotokos."

But in the case of the hymn after the consecration, we offer a different verse to begin—"It is truly right to bless you"—and conclude with the same refrain from Matins. On feast days of Christ, feast days of the Virgin Mary, and during the paschal season, the hymns of the Ninth Ode of Orthros are replaced with hymns dedicated to the Virgin Mary but are more specific to the feast we are celebrating. The last hymn (*Katavasia*) of the Ninth Ode replaces this hymn of the Divine Liturgy. This is why there is sometimes a substitution.

As we conclude the Prayer of Consecration for "every righteous spirit made perfect in the faith," we invoke the name of the Virgin Mary specifically. Why does the Church honor her so frequently? She is considered the greatest of all human beings because she bore Christ in her womb. Our salvation is a result of Christ coming into the world, but her acquiescence to bear Him is an integral part of the equation. So, while we worship Christ for saving us, we honor the Theotokos—the "God bearer"—for bearing Him on our behalf. In this instance, unlike the others where she is commemorated "with all the saints," she is remembered and honored alone, above them, above all the angels, above all except the Lord Himself.

> Beneath your tender compassion we take refuge, O Theotokos. Despise not our supplications in distress, but deliver us from all peril. You alone are pure; you alone are blessed. (From *Lenten Vespers*[33])

33 Translated by Fr. Seraphim Dedes.

From the Church Triumphant Back to the Church Militant

For Saint John the prophet, forerunner, and Baptist; for the holy, glorious, and most praiseworthy apostles; for Saint(s) *[Name]*, whose memory we celebrate; and for all Your saints, through whose supplications, visit us, O God. And remember all who have fallen asleep in the hope of the resurrection to life eternal. [*Here the Priest commemorates by name those departed whom he wishes.*] Grant them rest, O our God, where the light of Your countenance keeps watch. Again we beseech You, Lord, remember all Orthodox bishops who rightly teach the word of Your truth, the presbyterate, the diaconate in Christ, and every priestly and monastic order.

Again we offer You this spiritual worship for the whole world, for the holy, catholic, and apostolic Church, and for those living pure and reverent lives. For civil authorities and our armed forces, grant that they may govern in peace, Lord, so that in their tranquility we, too, may live calm and serene lives, in all piety and virtue.

Strive for peace with all men, and for the holiness without which no one will see the Lord.

—Hebrews 12:14

While the hymn to the Virgin Mary is being sung, three important things take place. The first is that the priest offers incense over the Gifts that have just been consecrated. Incense, as you will recall, is associated with prayer. The first psalm asks for our prayers to rise as incense before the Lord (Ps. 140/141:2). And in the midst of the Anaphora, having just consecrated the Holy Gifts, this is a very appropriate occasion to offer incense together with our prayers to the Lord.

The second event occurs when the priest blesses the *antidoron* ("instead of the gifts"), which is blessed bread offered to the faithful at the time of Holy Communion. It is offered both to break the pre-Communion fast, giving sustenance to the body, as well as to cleanse the palate of any remnants of the Eucharist so that if one coughs or sneezes, no particles are expelled. It is also offered at the end of the service, especially for those who didn't receive Holy Communion. In large parishes, it is not uncommon to see the priest bless several bowls of bread at this time.

The Virgin Mary is the "mother of us all," so as we sing her hymn, the priest offers a prayer and begins to pray for us. He first invokes the names of saints: We commemorate St. John the Baptist, who in the iconostasis is placed near Christ's left hand.[34] (The Virgin Mary is at His right hand.) We commemorate also the apostles, the saint(s) of that particular day, and "all the saints." We ask God to bless us, and we ask for the intercessions of the saints to bring about that blessing.

The priest already has commemorated by name those who have passed on to the Church Triumphant in the service of the Proskomide (before the Divine Liturgy) and in the memorial service. However, there is a place in the Divine Liturgy where specific names of our deceased loved ones can be mentioned, and it is during this prayer, which follows the consecration. We remember "every righteous spirit made perfect in faith" along with the Theotokos and the

34 In Slavic tradition sometimes St. Nicholas replaces the Forerunner at Christ's left.

saints, and we also remember our loved ones by name. As the priest is remembering those who have passed on, it is also appropriate for the faithful in the church to remember their loved ones at this moment.

The prayer then transitions into prayers for the Church Militant. First, we pray for those who are leading the Church—the bishops, the priests, the deacons, and everyone in holy orders. Since we are offering this Divine Liturgy "for all," we also pray for the entire world. We pray for the "holy, catholic, and apostolic church," quoting from the Creed. In doing so, we pray for the gospel of Christ to be spread throughout the world. We pray for those who are striving for pure and holy lives. This includes not only monks and nuns and people who have dedicated their entire lives to Christ; it also includes those of us who sit in the pews, working toward holiness in our own unique walks of life.

We pray for those who are in public service, that the light of Christ will shine through their efforts. Whether our civil authorities are Christian or not, they are the leaders who set the course of life in our country and throughout the world. We pray for those in public service to work for peace and that all people who live in every nation will have peaceful lives, striving for piety and holiness, regardless of their beliefs.

In the Anaphora of the Divine Liturgy of St. Basil the Great, the prayer offered here is significantly longer. I would like to offer a portion of it below, as it includes other specific groups of people.

> Remember, Lord, those who bear fruit and do good works in Your holy churches, and those who remember the poor. Reward them with Your rich and heavenly Gifts. Grant them in return for earthly things, heavenly Gifts; for temporal, eternal; for corruptible, incorruptible.
>
> Remember, Lord, those who are in the deserts, on mountains, in caverns, and in the chambers of the earth. Remember,

Lord, those living in chastity and godliness, in asceticism and holiness of life.

Remember, Lord, this country and all those in public service whom you have allowed to govern on earth. Grant them profound and lasting peace. Speak to their hearts good things concerning your Church and all your people that through the faithful conduct of their duties we may live peaceful and serene lives in all piety and holiness. Sustain the good in their goodness; make the wicked good through Your goodness.

Remember, Lord, the people here presented and those who are absent with good cause. Have mercy on them and on us according to the multitude of Your mercy. Fill their treasuries with every good thing; preserve their marriages in peace and harmony; nurture the infants; instruct the youth; strengthen the aged; give courage to the faint hearted; reunite those separated; bring back those in error and unite them to Your holy, catholic, and apostolic Church. Free those who are held captive by unclean spirits; sail with those who sail; travel with those who travel; defend the widows; protect the orphans; liberate the captives; heal the sick.

Remember, Lord, those who are in mines, in exile, in harsh labor, and those in every kind of affliction, necessity, or distress; those who entreat your loving kindness; those who love us and those who hate us; those who have asked us to pray for them, unworthy though we may be.

Remember, Lord our God, all Your people, and pour out Your rich mercy upon them, granting them their petitions for salvation.

Remember, O God, all those whom we have not remembered through ignorance, forgetfulness or because of their multitude since You know the name and age of each, even from their mother's womb. For You, Lord, are the helper of the helpless, the hope of the hopeless, the savior of the afflicted, the haven of the voyager, and the physician of the sick.

Be all things to all, You who know each person, his requests, his household, and his need. Deliver this community and city, O Lord, and every city and town, from famine, plague, earthquake, flood, fire, sword, invasion of foreign enemies, and civil war. Amen.

Among the first remember, Lord, our Archbishop *[Name]*; grant him to Your holy churches in peace, safety, honor, and health, unto length of days, rightly teaching the word of Your truth.

> Remember your leaders, those who spoke to you the word of God; consider the outcome of their life, and imitate their faith.
>
> —Hebrews 13:7

Christ chose twelve men to be His disciples. After His Resurrection, He commissioned them as apostles. In John 20:21–22, we see the first ordination when Jesus said to His disciples, "'Peace be with you. As the Father has sent me, even so I send you.' And when he had said this, he breathed on them, and said to them, 'Receive the Holy Spirit.'"

The apostles are considered the first bishops of the Church. A bishop is defined as the spiritual leader of a geographic area. Saint Peter was the bishop of Rome; St. Thomas went to India. The apostles eventually ordained their successors as well as additional bishops to go to more cities and start more churches. To this day the bishops continue to ordain their successor bishops through the laying on of hands and the giving of the Holy Spirit.

Each bishop can trace his lineage to the time of the apostles in something called apostolic succession. This is one of the things that sets the Orthodox Church apart from the rest of Christendom.[35] Our bishops are linked via apostolic succession to the time of Christ Himself, having preserved the apostolic Faith without change. And no one can become a bishop on his own. At least three bishops ordain a new bishop, and a synod (or large group) of bishops approves each ordination.

Not only is the bishop a tie to the time of Christ, but in our theology, we call the bishop the *Typos Christou*, or "type of Christ." He models Christ for us. Orthodox parishes feature a liturgical piece of furniture called the bishop's throne, which sits on the right side of the church outside the altar. In some churches, it is behind the altar table. And in Slavic Churches, the "throne" is a raised platform in the middle of the nave, adorned with an icon of Christ dressed as a bishop in vestments. When there is no bishop present, the throne remains empty. When the bishop is present, he stands at the throne "in the place of Christ."

The primary job of the bishop is that of teacher, while the primary job of the priest is celebrant of the sacraments. That is why, in many circumstances, the bishop stands at the bishop's throne during the service rather than serving in the altar. However, at the time of the sermon, the bishop will preach.

The bishop also has the title *poimenarhis*, or "shepherd." This is why he carries a staff. This tradition comes from the Gospel of St. John when Jesus says, "I am the good shepherd. The good shepherd lays down his life for the sheep" (John 10:11). The shepherd's staff was used both to guide the sheep as well as to protect them from those who would do them harm.

---

35 Although the Roman Catholic Church also claims apostolic succession, only the Orthodox Church has retained the ancient teachings without addition and change.

The role of the bishop is critical in the life of the Church, because the apostolic nature of the Church is expressed through his office. Obviously, bishops are human beings, subject to temptations just as we are. They make mistakes, just as we do. The difference is that when a bishop, who has the role of Typos Christou, makes a mistake, it is magnified because he is representing Christ and the Church. When a layperson sins, they may scandalize another person. When the bishop sins, he potentially scandalizes the whole Church. Whether this is fair or not, it is his reality and burden.

This is why we pause in our prayers to remember our bishop. Earlier in the Divine Liturgy, we prayed for him by name, and we also prayed for all the clergy and laity. We prayed for everyone in the Church, but we prayed first for the bishop. This petition is offered specifically for our local bishop and no one else. It asks God to keep him safe, honorable, and healthy. It prays for him to serve in peace. And most especially, it prays for him to rightly teach the truth of the Word of God.

And remember those whom each one of us has in mind, and all the people.

> First of all, then, I urge that supplications, prayers, intercessions, and thanksgivings be made for all men, for kings and all who are in high positions, that we may lead a quiet and peaceable life, godly and respectful in every way. This is good, and it is acceptable in the sight of God our Savior.
>
> —1 Timothy 2:1–3

The last three lines of the Anaphora ask God to remember everyone, to call everyone to unity, and to bestow the mercies of Christ on us all. In this reflection we will examine the call to remember everyone.

The word *intimacy* means to establish a sense of unity with someone else. Intimacy involves trust and vulnerability. Most people connect intimacy with sexual relations, but intimacy is not limited to sexuality. That's probably one of the reasons our world is as messed up as it is, because we've lost the true meaning of intimacy.

A conversation can be intimate in the sense that the talk is deep, and vulnerability is shared. Confession is an example of such a conversation. The most intimate thing we can do in life, however, is share a deep conversation with the Lord. This is called prayer. And the most intimate moment of prayer is Holy Communion because it includes physical as well as spiritual intimacy with the Lord.

The most intimate thing we can share with another person is also prayer. To bring someone to mind in prayer is the greatest gift we can give to that person. For what could be greater or more intimate than bringing someone else's name to God?

This petition serves two purposes. First, it calls us to remember specific people in our own lives. In the Divine Liturgy, we have prayed "for all." We have prayed in generalities for civic leaders and spiritual leaders. We've prayed for those striving to live in purity and holiness. We've prayed for peace for the entire world.

But at this moment of the service, we are encouraged to call to mind individual people and their needs. If three hundred people are in church, and each calls to mind three others, then nine hundred souls are lifted up in prayer at once. So, while this line of the Divine Liturgy is not one of the most well-known, well remembered, or well heeded, it is actually one of the most intimate.

Second, this petition serves as a reminder to us to pray for one another. We are not just to pray for ourselves and our own needs. We are not just to pray in generalities. But we are to pray specifically and to pray for individual people—to join the names and needs of others with our own. We are reminded that spiritual unity is always possible through prayer. And through spiritual unity comes the ability to form deep, lasting friendships and healthy working relationships. Forgiveness becomes easier, patience more likely, and peace more prevalent because we are praying for one another. After all, how can I pray for someone and still hate him? It doesn't seem possible. Prayer unifies and bring us closer together.

Outside the confines of the Divine Liturgy, among the greatest gifts you can offer someone is to pray *with* them. I'm not sure why in the Orthodox Church we do not have a strong tradition of doing this. In many Protestant churches, it is common for two or more people to hold hands or stand in a circle, with everyone taking a turn to offer a prayer. I believe this is something we've missed out on. It is very powerful to stand with another person (handholding is not important) and to pray for them in their presence. It is very powerful to stand with another person and listen to them pray for you.

In the corporate context of the Orthodox Church, only the bishop commemorates the name of the priest. When the priest serves alone, he says his own name when receiving Holy Communion. No one else speaks it in the service. I remember years ago when a member of my congregation asked to say a prayer for me while I stood next to him. It was one of the greatest gifts I have received—to hear someone else pray for me by name. I know that this is a gift I enjoy both receiving and giving. And I encourage you to pray with others too.

As we participate in church, if each of us remembers even three people during this petition, we will be lifting up a lot of souls. That's a pretty amazing opportunity we have at each Divine Liturgy!

And grant that with one voice and one heart we may glorify and praise Your most honorable and majestic name, of the

Father and of the Son and of the Holy Spirit, now and forever and to the ages of ages. Amen.

> May the God of steadfastness and encouragement grant you to live in such harmony with one another, in accord with Christ Jesus, that together you may with one voice glorify the God and Father of our Lord Jesus Christ.
>
> —Romans 15:5–6

As we move toward the conclusion of the Anaphora, we hear a call to unity as we glorify and praise the Lord. Unity is expressed in several ways in the Divine Liturgy.

First, it is the tradition in the Orthodox Church that only one Divine Liturgy is celebrated in a parish on a given day. There is no tradition of several Liturgies being celebrated throughout the day. This is because the intention of the service is to bring all the faithful together in one holy, eucharistic assembly.[36]

Second, we all are called to worship. At the Divine Liturgy, especially on Sundays, the intention is for the whole body of the church to be present so that all may glorify God as one. If you miss the Liturgy, your voice is absent from the "one voice" of the community.

Third, we are called to unity of heart. Our body has many parts but only one heart. The heart unifies the body by pumping blood through the entire organism. And in order to have a healthy church, the congregation should seek to move as one, to have a collective heart that beats in unity. When there are factions, antagonists, and

36 In some large communities, where the church is too small to hold the entire congregation, more than one Divine Liturgy is held, but an additional Liturgy requires an additional priest to celebrate it and an additional altar. An individual priest may only celebrate the Divine Liturgy and commune once per day.

agitators in the church, the heart of the church is damaged because unity is stifled.

So, what are the things that allow us to come together in unity? The last prayer, offered quietly by the priest, gives us the answers.

Remember, Lord, this city in which we live, and every city and land, and the faithful who live in them. We all share the same space. Even though we each may have a private home or apartment, we share the same city with everyone who lives in it. We share the same roads, the same schools, the same parks, and the same air. We are all part of a greater whole. And it is incumbent on us to see ourselves not only as private citizens but also as members of our cities and nations. We have a duty not only to our families and ourselves but to society, to the greater whole. In remembering our city and our country, we seek to work together so that all may enjoy freedom and blessings.

Remember, Lord, those who travel by land, sea, and air; the sick; the suffering; the captives; and their salvation. Years ago, I served as the deacon to the metropolitan of Boston. I will always remember one prayer that he often offered: "Lord, remember those who are suffering because we are indifferent to them." When I offer this prayer at the Divine Liturgy, praying for the sick, the suffering, and the captives, I often think of the "forgotten"—those who are not on anyone's mind. Indeed, if the Divine Liturgy is offered on behalf of all, we must also include those who are unknown to us—but known to God. Unity can only be achieved when all are accounted for.

Remember those who bear fruit and do good works in Your holy churches and those who are mindful of the poor, and upon us all send forth Your mercies. The final line of the prayer asks for the Lord to remember those who minister to the forgotten—in our churches and among the poor. Many people who help those in need are doing so as volunteers or in very low-paying positions. They have a great love for the work they do and for those for whom they do it. They sacrifice their own sustenance in many instances. So, we pray for their strength.

Most people who work in our churches do so as volunteers. If the church is the spiritual hospital, working to heal those who have been wounded, then each person who labors in the church has the potential to be a part of that healing. We are praying for everyone who works for the church, that their efforts may glorify God—greeters, ushers, altar servers, the parish council, members of Philoptochos (a philanthropic organization for women in the GOC; other jurisdictions have similar organizations), Sunday school teachers, and others who volunteer their time. I purposely use the caveat *that their efforts may glorify God.* Unfortunately, some in parish leadership do not belong there. Sometimes their efforts actually harm the flock rather than help it. So, in praying for those who serve in the church, we ask that their efforts will be Christ-centered, seeking in all things to glorify God. And we also pray that others will be inspired to step forward and work in the church. Unity is only possible when we all are working toward the same goal, with focus, purpose, and harmony.

And grant that with one voice and one heart we may glorify and praise Your most honorable and majestic name, of the Father and of the Son and of the Holy Spirit, now and forever and to the ages of ages. Amen. Having mentioned all the faithful, those remembered, those forgotten, and those who labor, we pray that all can come together with "one voice and one heart," praying in unity, with hearts that beat together in unison. We pray that we may glorify God as we travel through the Divine Liturgy to its climax of unity in Holy Communion.

> Remember, Lord, this city in which we live, and every city and land, and the faithful who live in them. Remember, Lord, those who travel by land, sea, and air; the sick; the suffering; the captives; and their salvation. Remember those who bear fruit and

do good works in Your holy churches and those who are mindful of the poor, and upon us all send forth Your mercies. And grant that with one voice and one heart we may glorify and praise Your most honorable and majestic name, of the Father and of the Son and of the Holy Spirit, now and forever and to the ages of ages. Amen.

And the mercies of our great God and Savior, Jesus Christ, be with you all.

> Grace, mercy, and peace will be with us, from God the Father and from Jesus Christ the Father's Son, in truth and love.
>
> —2 John 1:3

The portion of the Divine Liturgy called the Anaphora is now coming to an end. The bread and wine that were offered on the altar are now the Body and Blood of Christ. In prayer, we've stated the purpose of receiving them. We have sung a hymn of praise to the Virgin Mary. We've remembered our leaders, both civil authorities and our hierarch. We've called to mind our families and friends and anyone in need of prayer. And we've asked God to give us grace to come together with one voice and with one heart to glorify and praise Him.

As we close off this section of the Divine Liturgy and begin to transition to the time when we receive the Gifts that have been consecrated, the final liturgical act in the Anaphora is a blessing. "Be with you all" can pertain to two groups of people. Obviously, all the people present at the service receive the blessing. And "you all" pertains to all the people we called to mind throughout this section of the Divine Liturgy. As we turn the corner toward our personal encounter with Christ at Holy Communion, we do so in a sense of unity that the mercy of our great God and savior Jesus Christ will be with all.

Let us look more closely now at what we are being blessed with. In Greek, the phrase is *ta elei,* meaning "the mercies." *Mercy* means the bestowing of something we don't deserve. So, God gives us mercy that we haven't earned. The use of this word in the plural—mercies—is a recognition that we need a lot of mercy from God, and we need His mercies in many ways, individually and collectively.

Since we've called to mind many different people who all need different kinds of mercy, we ask for mercies in the plural. We need God to forgive our shortcomings. We need His grace to endure setbacks. We need His wisdom to make good decisions. We need His help in many ways for the many complex things that happen in our lives.

Of course, God in His infinite goodness bestows mercy upon all. Everyone has an opportunity to receive mercy from Him. In spiritual terms, all have infinite value in God's eyes. Thus, His mercy is bestowed on all because He infinitely values each of us.

The response of the people to this blessing from the priest is twofold: We bow our heads in recognition of and respect for God's mercies. And we offer the response "And with your spirit" to the celebrating priest, recognizing that he also is in need of God's mercies. We pray that the same mercy that will come upon us may come down on him as well.

Do not put us to shame,
    but deal with us in thy forbearance
    and in thy abundant mercy.
Deliver us in accordance with thy marvelous works,
    and give glory to thy name, O Lord!

Let all who do harm to thy servants be put to shame;
 let them be disgraced and deprived of all power and dominion,
 and let their strength be broken.
Let them know that thou art the Lord, the only God,
 glorious over all the world.
(Song of the Three Young Men 1:19–22)[37]

37 In the Orthodox Old Testament, the "Hymn of the Three Young Men" is part of Daniel 3:25–90. This quote is from Daniel 3:42–45. In the RSV, the "Song of the Three Youths" is an independent book, part of the LXX.

The Lord's Prayer

Having commemorated all the saints, again and again, in peace, let us pray to the Lord.

> Pray at all times in the Spirit, with all prayer and supplication. To that end keep alert with all perseverance, making supplication for all the saints.
>
> —Ephesians 6:18

The petition for today is a very special one to every member of the clergy. That is because when a person is ordained as a deacon—the first order of the clergy—the ordination takes place immediately prior to this petition. And once the ordination has concluded, the first liturgical line the newly ordained deacon offers is this petition.

While the words may seem mundane to many—"*Again* we're praying in peace"—when I offer this petition I think of a military jet lighting its afterburners. For those who don't know what I'm talking about, you've probably seen a military plane in a movie: the two engines in the back of the plane light up and increase the thrust and speed when taking off and in combat situations. A normal flight becomes a supersonic flight. The afterburners rapidly increase altitude, and they are used in combat situations in order to provide extra speed in hostile territory.

Even though I do not increase the pace of the service at this point of the Divine Liturgy, my spirit kicks into a higher gear. The Gifts are no longer waiting to be consecrated; they are ready to be received. Only a few petitions and prayers stand between us and the reason we came to church—to touch Christ and for Christ to touch us.

This prayer "in peace" is different from the initial petitions at the beginning of the Divine Liturgy. When we begin the Liturgy, we often come to church frazzled by the stresses of the world. We begin our worship with prayers for peace, and part of that peace is peace for our minds that are filled with stress and worry. Having now been in worship for some time—if we've attended from the beginning of Matins, we have been in worship for nearly two hours, and if we've attended from the beginning of the Divine Liturgy, we have been in worship for nearly an hour—hopefully our minds are relaxed, and we have truly been able to "lay aside every worldly care." After all the work we've done so far in the service, we want to keep our posture of peace as we turn to the main event.

If the word *agios* means "set apart," and the saints are those who have set themselves apart because of their pursuit of holiness, we now invoke them in this petition to remind ourselves that we are not alone. We are standing in the presence of holy people, and we have joined our prayers with the intercessions of "all the saints." Now we offer one final set of petitions before Holy Communion, beginning them in the same way as the other litanies began: praying in peace to the Lord but praying in greater number and with greater strength.

In military jets, the afterburners can be used only for short periods, as they burn up a lot of fuel. They give an already powerful fighter jet a little extra thrust. In our daily lives, we can't live as if we have afterburners going constantly. The spiritual life is a steady and methodical one. Like the fighter jet, we are built in a powerful way. We are created in the image and likeness of God. However, the extra boost we get at the Divine Liturgy from Holy Communion creates even greater strength to carry into the battle of the week. It lets us reach new spiritual heights—higher altitude—and gives us added strength to combat the storms and stresses we all face.

Having reached this high altitude in the service, since we have called down the Holy Spirit on ourselves and on the Gifts, the Divine Liturgy now kicks into high gear as we race toward its glorious conclusion.

> Give thanks to the Lord, for he is good, / for his mercy endures for ever. / Bless him, all who worship the Lord, the God of gods, / sing praise to him and give thanks to him, / for his mercy endures for ever. (Song of the Three Young Men 1:67–68)[38]

For the precious Gifts here presented and consecrated, let us pray to the Lord.

> For everything created by God is good, and nothing is to be rejected if it is received with thanksgiving; for then it is consecrated by the word of God and prayer.
>
> —1 Timothy 4:4–5

These reflections are not meant to be academic. There are many scholars much more educated than I who have written theological and learned commentaries on the Divine Liturgy. I intentionally leave out scholarship for the most part in order to give us practical thoughts for our minds and hearts as we experience the Liturgy each time it is celebrated.

38 In the Orthodox Old Testament, this quote can be found in Daniel 3:89–90.

At first glance, this petition is kind of odd. The Gifts have already been consecrated, so why are we praying for them? Some theorize that this petition was connected to the one that follows it at some point in history.

Leaving the subject of its historical placement, allow me to focus on what this petition means to me as I offer it. The purpose of the Divine Liturgy is twofold: First, we offer and consecrate Gifts of bread and wine, which become the Body and Blood of Christ. And second, we ourselves are consecrated by partaking of them. As I offer this petition, we are now quickly heading to the receiving of Holy Communion, and I reflect on the second purpose: our own readiness to offer ourselves to be consecrated by God.

To consecrate something means to set it apart. We have taken ordinary things—bread and wine—and by the grace of God, they have become extraordinary things—the Body and Blood of Christ. In preparing now for Holy Communion, ordinary people can become extraordinary, too.

For the Consecration of the Gifts to happen, something had to be offered—the bread and the wine. So, in approaching Holy Communion and asking the Lord to consecrate us and to bless us, we should offer something to Him in return. Ask yourself these questions each time you approach to receive: *What am I prepared to offer God in return for the extraordinary blessing He is about to give me? Am I ready to give a greater effort in prayer? in Scripture reading? in being patient with someone? in forgiving someone?*

As you approach the chalice, come with a concrete offering in mind—something that you plan to do *this* week that will bring you closer to Christ. Then in receiving Holy Communion, pray that the Lord will not only consecrate you, but that He will bless and consecrate the goal you've set for the week.

This practice keeps the Divine Liturgy living and active in our lives. It is very easy to attend each Sunday in a mechanical way and to become complacent in the midst of the repetition. It is easy to walk up to the chalice almost on autopilot. So, in order to bring more purpose to our experience, we have to come with a willingness to do some of the work, remembering that the Divine Liturgy is "the work of the people." Part of that work is worshiping, offering responses, and listening attentively to the prayers. However, most of the work occurs *after* the service has concluded—in how we apply the Divine Liturgy to our life this week, living out the Liturgy after the Liturgy.

As you hear this petition, hear it with ears that interpret it as, "What can I offer to God so that I can be consecrated through the experience of receiving Holy Communion?" Hear it with a heart that is committed to growing closer to Christ, even if that means stretching the boundaries of your comfort zone. No growth occurs without stretching. And no stretching occurs without vulnerability. If you've gotten to this point of the Divine Liturgy and still haven't tuned in, it is not too late. Your personal encounter with Christ is only a few minutes away. Approach with a plan to offer something of yourself so that you can be consecrated with something from Him.

> For thy name's sake do not give us up utterly, and do not break thy covenant, and do not withdraw thy mercy from us, for the sake of Abraham thy beloved and for the sake of Isaac thy servant and Israel thy holy one, to whom thou didst promise to make their descendants as many as the stars of heaven and as the sand on the shore of the sea. For we, O Lord, have become fewer than any nation, and are brought low this day in all the world because of our sins. And at this time there is no prince, or prophet, or leader, no burnt offering, or sacrifice, or oblation, or incense, no place to make an offering before thee or to find mercy. Yet with a contrite heart and a humble spirit may we be accepted, as though it were with burnt offerings of rams and bulls, and with tens of thousands of fat lambs; such may

> our sacrifice be in thy sight this day, and may we wholly follow thee, for there will be no shame for those who trust in thee. And now with all our heart we follow thee, we fear thee, and seek thy face. (Song of the Three Young Men 1:11–18)[39]

That our God who loves mankind, having accepted them at His holy and celestial and mystical altar as an offering of spiritual fragrance, may in return send down upon us the divine grace and the Gift of the Holy Spirit, let us pray.

> For on my holy mountain, the mountain height of Israel, says the Lord God, there all the house of Israel, all of them, shall serve me in the land; there I will accept them, and there I will require your contributions and the choicest of your Gifts, with all your sacred offerings.
>
> —Ezekiel 20:40

What benefits do we hope to take away from Holy Communion? First, "divine grace," and second, "the gift of the Holy Spirit." As we have already mentioned, grace is a gift from God that completes what is lacking and heals what is infirm in each of us. We all are lacking something. And we are all infirm in the sense that we are less than 100 percent healthy physically, emotionally, and spiritually—probably at all moments of our lives. So, as we prepare to receive the Gifts that have been offered and consecrated, we pray that our loving God, who has received them, may send down upon us divine grace to heal the aspects of our lives that need healing.

39 In the Orthodox Old Testament, this quote can be found in Daniel 3:34–41.

In the Bible, we read of the fruit of the Holy Spirit as well as gifts (in Greek, *harismata*, meaning "graces"). Even though this petition uses the Greek word *dorean* for the "gift" of the Holy Spirit, when I hear it, I think about all the different things (gifts, graces, and fruits) we receive from the Holy Spirit. In 1 Corinthians 12, we read:

> Now there are varieties of Gifts, but the same Spirit; and there are varieties of service, but the same Lord; and there are varieties of working, but it is the same God who inspires them all in every one. To each is given the manifestation of the Spirit for the common good. To one is given through the Spirit the utterance of wisdom, and to another the utterance of knowledge according to the same Spirit, to another faith by the same Spirit, to another Gifts of healing by the one Spirit, to another the working of miracles, to another prophecy, to another the ability to distinguish between spirits, to another various kinds of tongues, to another the interpretation of tongues. All these are inspired by one and the same Spirit, who apportions to each one individually as he wills. (vv. 4–11)

This means that each of us has been given a different gift by the Holy Spirit, a different talent, and a different grace. We could continue the list to say some are teachers, some are priests, some are architects, and so on. Each of our gifts is inspired by the same Spirit, and none are to be valued more than others. Yes, certain vocations bring an individual a higher income, but we can glorify God equally in any vocation. God sees each person as having infinite value. And when each person uses a talent to glorify God, He places infinite value on that offering.

In Galatians 5:22–23 we read, "But the fruit of the Spirit is love, joy, peace, patience, kindness, goodness, faithfulness, gentleness, self-control." This fruit is accessible to everyone. We all have the same potential to grow this fruit in ourselves and to offer it to the world, regardless of our vocations.

In the last reflection, we discussed how in approaching the chalice, we again offer ourselves to God to be reconsecrated by Him. Our part is the offering of ourselves; we come to church with faith, having prepared for Holy Communion. And God consecrates us, just as He consecrated the Gifts by sending down on us His divine grace and the gift of the Holy Spirit. He reinfuses in us the fruits of the Spirit to reinvigorate and reenergize our own gifts. If someone is a teacher, after receiving Holy Communion she becomes a more committed and focused teacher, honoring and glorifying God with her talent to teach.

Receiving Communion should strengthen each person who approaches. We offer. God consecrates. He does this through grace, which heals what is infirm, completes what is lacking, reinfuses us with the fruits, and strengthens the gifts. As you hear this petition, listen with joy. It should comfort your soul, because you are preparing to receive divine grace and the gift of the Holy Spirit yet again. We do not experience the Divine Liturgy just to "come to be counted" or go through the motions. The Liturgy is a reinvigorating of the soul and a reenergizing of our lives.

Having asked for the unity of the faith and for the communion of the Holy Spirit, let us commend ourselves and one another and our whole life to Christ our God.

> And his Gifts were that some should be apostles, some prophets, some evangelists, some pastors and teachers, to equip the saints for the work of ministry, for building up the body of Christ, until we all attain to the unity of the faith and of the

> knowledge of the Son of God, to mature manhood, to the measure of the stature of the fulness of Christ.
>
> —Ephesians 4:11–13

The last petition before Holy Communion summarizes two themes of the Divine Liturgy. The theme of "unity of the faith" echoes the early part of the service where we prayed "for the stability of the holy churches of God and for the unity of all." The first sense of unity we desire is with those who are close to us—our families and our friends. The second type of unity refers to our communities, beginning with our parish community. How can we expect to have unity in our neighborhoods and in our workplaces if we don't have unity in our church? Third, there should be harmony between parish communities. After all, we should all be striving toward the same goal.

Modeling Christian behavior in the workplace, on the athletic field, in our children's schools, in our neighborhoods, and when driving promotes unity among people. If we are supposed to love God and love our neighbor, then unity with our neighbor is as important as our personal unity with the Lord. The ultimate level of unity is the unity of all people. However, since we can't even wrap our minds around this idea of all people united, we must strive for unity in as big a circle as possible. Certainly unity is possible in families, among friends, and in an individual church community.

The second theme we recall is "the communion of the Holy Spirit." The first prayer of Matins, as well as a silent prayer offered by the priest before celebrating the Divine Liturgy, is directed to the Holy Spirit:

> Heavenly King, Comforter, the Spirit of Truth, present in all places and filling all things, treasury of blessings and Giver of Life, come and abide in us, cleanse us from every stain and save our souls, O Gracious One.

If the Holy Spirit is the bestower of grace, the source of our talents, the "Heavenly King," the "Comforter," and the "Spirit of Truth," then we want Him to "abide in us," "to cleanse us from every stain," and to "save our souls." We want the experience of Pentecost, where the Holy Spirit empowered the apostles to preach the gospel in all languages. We want His grace to help change us from ordinary to extraordinary people.

We want to combine these two themes of unity of the Faith and communion of the Holy Spirit. We want to commend not only ourselves but one another to these ideas. And we need one another to lean on for encouragement. We commend ourselves and one another and also rely on others to work at commending us.

The Christian life is not compartmentalized into a neat package that we unwrap only on Sunday mornings. The Christian life is supposed to be a continuous growth in Christ and glorification of Him. Ultimately, we pray that our whole life becomes an extension of the Divine Liturgy. The themes that are repeated continually throughout the Liturgy—peace, safety, commitment, intercession of the saints, the call to be attentive, grace, gratitude—are to be applied to life every day if we are to reach the Kingdom of God. Then we can live with a joy and a confidence that we are indeed well on our journey to everlasting life. Committing our whole life unto Christ our God in this life is the necessary preparation for living in His presence for eternity.

The priest offers a response to this petition: "To You, O Lord." It is a confirmation that we are supposed to commend ourselves and one another and our whole life to Him. Our whole life is not supposed to be about advancement of career or increasing our financial gains. It is supposed to be about the Lord, our commitment to Him, and our preparation to be with Him forever in His Kingdom.

And grant us, Master, with boldness and without condemnation, to dare call You, the heavenly God, Father, and to say:

> Let us then with confidence draw near to the throne of grace, that we may receive mercy and find grace to help in time of need.
>
> —Hebrews 4:16

Two of the boldest statements of the Divine Liturgy are found in a prayer that precedes the Lord's Prayer and also in the Lord's Prayer itself. When the priest prays before the Lord's Prayer (usually inaudibly), the first words are: "We entrust to You, loving Master, our whole life and hope."

This is a bold statement indeed. Because if we entrust our whole life to God, it means that we remain calm when stuck in rush hour, we forgive the person who has really hurt us, we don't fly off the handle when we are wronged, and we gently correct someone who has done something wrong rather than embarrass him. It means that at every juncture in life, we make the godly decision rather than the human one.

To entrust the Lord our "whole hope" means to be able to trust God in all circumstances. So, if someone loses a job, or has been diagnosed with a serious illness, or has a child with a severe handicap, he goes to God with perfect trust and does not allow discouragement and disappointment to creep in.

If I really think about this phrase, "I entrust to You, loving Master, my whole life and my whole hope," I feel like a total hypocrite. I do get annoyed in rush hour, I sometimes have a hard time forgiving others, I sometimes get angry when I am wronged, and I sometimes correct others in a way that is unnecessarily harsh. I'd like to think I'd maintain hope in God under very serious circumstances, but so far, I haven't had anything very serious happen to me.

This prayer is not discouraging to me, however, nor is it meant to be. This prayer sets out the ideal for us as a goal. The ideal is to be like God—loving, forgiving, without sin. This is why we pray for a "perfect, holy, peaceful, and sinless" day rather than ask "for a somewhat perfect, partly holy, mostly peaceful, and relatively sinless" day—which is probably the more realistic statement. We pray for the ideal. We state the ideal. We strive for the ideal. And when we fall short of it, we try again the next day. Our judgment before God will be based on our *pursuit* of the ideal, not on our failure to achieve it. God is going to judge us on what we did, not on what we didn't do.

After this prayer, we offer the Lord's Prayer, where we also make a bold statement: "Forgive us our trespasses as we forgive those who trespass against us." This means that we can expect from the Lord whatever measure of forgiveness we have offered others. This also is a bold request.

Between these two prayers we hear the priest's supplication to the Lord: "And grant us, Master, with boldness and without condemnation, to dare call You, the heavenly God, Father, and to say . . ." This means: Lord, allow us to offer these bold requests, although we are going to fail at them again and again. Allow us to offer them with confidence, rather than feeling like hypocrites, and allow us to offer them without fear of condemnation.

Most of us are familiar with this inspirational saying:

> Watch your thoughts; they become words. Watch your words; they become actions. Watch your actions; they become habits. Watch your habits; they become character. Watch your character; it becomes your destiny.

If our destiny—God's intention for our lives—is for us to attain the Kingdom of heaven, then working backward, our journey starts with our thoughts and our words. These hopefully evolve into actions and habits, which shape our character and allow us to fulfill God's intention for us. So, it is good that we make these bold statements about entrusting our lives and our hopes to God. We are asking God not to condemn us but to allow us to say these words as a springboard to actions and habits, which shape our character and lead us to everlasting life.

It is amazing that the Divine Liturgy was written centuries before this famous quote, and yet these thoughts essentially are stated in this line. The following prayer is offered by the priest immediately before this line:

> We entrust to You, loving Master, our whole life and hope, and we beseech, pray, and implore You: Grant us to partake of Your heavenly and awesome Mysteries from this sacred and spiritual table with a clear conscience for the remission of sins, the forgiveness of transgressions, the communion of the Holy Spirit, the inheritance of the Kingdom of heaven, and boldness before You, not unto judgment or condemnation.

Pray Like This

Our Father, who art in heaven, Hallowed be Thy name. Thy kingdom come. Thy will be done, on earth as it is in heaven. Give us this day our daily bread; and forgive us our trespasses, as we forgive those who trespass against us; and lead us not into temptation but deliver us from evil.

> And in praying do not heap up empty phrases as the Gentiles do; for they think that they will be heard for their many

words. Do not be like them, for your Father knows what you need before you ask him. Pray then like this:

Our Father who art in heaven,
Hallowed be thy name.
Thy kingdom come,
Thy will be done,
On earth as it is in heaven.
Give us this day our daily bread;
And forgive us our debts,
As we also have forgiven our debtors;
And lead us not into temptation,
But deliver us from evil.

—Matthew 6:7–13

The greatest and most well-known of all prayers is the Lord's Prayer. It covers the entirety of human history—we remember the past, we pray for the present, and we hope for the future. We also pray for the entire human race. Immediately before introducing us to this prayer in the Gospels, Jesus warns His followers about praying with empty phrases. Our prayers need to not be long, but they should be purposeful. Each word of this prayer is packed with meaning, so much so that entire books have been written about it. Allow me to share a few of my own thoughts about it with you.

Our Father. In these two words alone, we encapsulate the two greatest commandments of loving God and loving our neighbor. We identify God as Father, as Creator, as the Almighty. And this prayer, even offered privately, is always said in an inclusive way. God is *our* Father, not just mine. He is Father to all of us. This is a reminder that we are to be brother or sister to our fellow humans.

Who art in heaven. This covers past, present, and future. It speaks to the origin of the Creation as well our destination. It speaks of the eternity and infiniteness of God.

Hallowed be Thy name. The name of God is holy, and we are to glorify His name in our words and actions.

Thy Kingdom come. We are to look forward to the coming of God's Kingdom, and we are to prepare with joyful anticipation as well as a sense of urgency.

Thy will be done. This phrase has two meanings: First, God has articulated His will for us, and we are to follow Him by following His commandments. But He has not revealed certain things about our individual lives—who we will marry, how many children we will have, how long we will live, and whether we will move from one place to another. These words remind us not only to be obedient to God but to trust Him with the unknown.

On earth as it is in heaven. We are to make our life on earth a practice for life in heaven. Our life here should mirror the life we hope to have in the Kingdom. If heaven is centered around the peace and love of God and continuous union with Him, then our life on earth should reflect that as well.

Give us this day our daily bread. Very simply put, this phrase asks God to give us the things we need today. In Exodus 16, we read about the manna[40] that God sent from heaven every day to sustain the people of Israel as they wandered in the wilderness for forty years. The Lord caused an adequate amount of manna to fall from heaven each day to feed all the people. On Fridays, double the amount would fall so that they could save some for the Sabbath, when they couldn't work. People were not to hoard more than their share. They were to come out each day trusting that God would provide "the daily bread," which is where this phrase comes from.

"Daily bread" refers to much more than bread, however. It asks God to give us the things we need today and to help us to trust that

40 See previous reflection on "Take, Eat, This is My Body," p. 190.

other things will be provided when we need them. Often when I pray the Lord's Prayer, I bring other people to mind with this phrase. I think of people who are sick or who are in need, and I ask God to provide for them on this particular day. And sometimes what is needed simply may be comfort or a good day. I remember years ago praying for a man who was very sick with cancer. On his daughter's wedding day, I remember praying with him not to be cured from cancer but to have the strength to walk her down the aisle, because *that* was the need of that particular day.

Forgive us our trespasses as we forgive those who trespass against us. We need God's forgiveness for our sins, and we need to forgive others as well. The previous reflection on granting us "confidence . . . without fear of condemnation" specifically refers to this phrase. It is really a bold request for God to forgive us our sins according to the measure that we use to forgive the sins of others.

And lead us not into temptation but deliver us from evil. This reminds us to avoid temptations and tempting situations, and it also reminds us that we need God's continual help to stay away from evil. We must give effort. And we must lean on Him for help in this effort.

In lieu of the prayer that is either quoted from the Divine Liturgy or from the Book of Psalms, I am including the Lord's Prayer again as a reminder that we should say it every day.

> Our Father, who art in heaven, hallowed be Thy name. Thy kingdom come. Thy will be done, on earth as it is in heaven. Give us this day our daily bread; and forgive us our trespasses, as we forgive those who trespass against us; and lead us not into temptation but deliver us from evil.

For Thine is the Kingdom and the power and the glory, of the Father and of the Son and of the Holy Spirit, now and forever and to the ages of ages. Amen.

> For thine is the kingdom and the power and the glory, for ever. Amen.
>
> —Matthew 6:13[41]

When the Lord's Prayer is offered in the context of worship, traditionally it is followed by the ekphonesis—the ending "For Thine is the Kingdom"—which is offered only by the priest, not by the people. When we offer the Lord's Prayer outside of worship, it generally ends with "lead us not into temptation but deliver us from evil." The ekphonesis is not said.

It is interesting that the Lord's Prayer is stated in both the Gospel of Matthew and the Gospel of Luke. Luke 11 does not include "for thine is the kingdom," which only appears in Matthew's account (sometimes as a footnote). The Liturgy ends the Lord's Prayer with this phrase because the Church traditionally incorporates a statement of glory to the Holy Trinity at the end of every prayer, both in the Divine Liturgy and outside of it. All prayer is offered to God, and God has revealed Himself as Trinity.

We obsess a lot in life with the concept of *kingdom*. We continually seek material gain so that we can build up our kingdoms. We buy homes, cars, furniture, and clothes, and then when we get more money, we buy more and more things. But we are supposed to see the place we live as an extension of God's Kingdom and to see life as a preparation to live in His Kingdom on a permanent basis.

---

41 Included as a footnote in some Bible translations.

The Divine Liturgy gives us a glimpse into the Kingdom. The Liturgy is a metaphor for how we are to live life on earth—with love, purpose, focus, charity, and thanksgiving. God's Kingdom is present in the Divine Liturgy. His Kingdom is our ultimate goal. And in between these two realities of the present and the eternal future, we are supposed to live our lives with a Kingdom focus.

When many people think of power, they think of the power of nature, or the power of money, or the power of corporations. However, the greatest power on earth is the power of God. He grants us the power to love, to forgive, and to repent. God is the one who brings us the miracles of marriage, of children, of intelligence. It is God who has given us the sunlight to warm us, the water that sustains life, and the means, in terms of our talents and abilities, to make sure all aspects of life are covered. Think for a minute: Which things are the greatest—the things we create or the things He creates? He is the ultimate power.

We use the word *glory* and equate it with fame and accomplishment. However, all human glory and fame is temporary. Sure, a person may be remembered long after death. But what glory is there in being remembered? The permanent glory is the glory of God; to share in His eternal glory is the greatest thing a human being can do and should be the number-one goal in each human life.

God has no beginning and no ending. His Kingdom, power, and glory also are without beginning and without end; they are *forever.* The greatest gift we can receive in our lives is the entrance into God's heavenly Kingdom, because once we have gone to heaven, its glory and majesty will never end. It will be forever.

Nothing in this earthly life is forever; even suffering ends at death. Riches and power also end at death. The only thing we take with us when we leave this world is our souls—the Godlike part of us that was given to us at conception. God will judge each soul and then will assign it to a place of repose, peace, and refreshment, or to a place of pain and suffering. This judgment will be permanent. So, in this prayer, as we remember God's Kingdom, power, and glory, we pray that our souls will be prepared for the awesome judgment seat of Christ and will be assigned a place in God's heavenly Kingdom.

Peace be with all. And with your spirit.

> On the evening of that day, the first day of the week, the doors being shut where the disciples were, for fear of the Jews, Jesus came and stood among them and said to them, "Peace be with you."
>
> —John 20:19

We are about to become one with the Lord in the receiving of Holy Communion—the entire purpose for which we have come. In two other instances the priest says to the people, "Peace be with all": before the Gospel reading and before the recitation of the Creed. That is because we want to come to these events in peace. We want to be at peace to hear the Word of the Lord through the Gospel. We want to be at peace as we confess our Faith. And now we want to be at peace as we receive Holy Communion.

A response is required, as with all petitions and prayers of the service. And this response belongs to the entire congregation, not just the choir or the chanter. Never is this response more appropriate than with this benediction. The Lord, through the hand of the priest, offers us a blessing of peace—much like when someone says "Good morning," meaning that they wish for us to have a good morning. And we wish for them the same good morning in return.

When the priest says *"Peace be with all,"* he is praying to God and desiring that we will have peace—absence of conflict, the peace of

God, and the kind of peace that is beyond our understanding (Phil. 4:7). And this blessing demands two responses: First, an immediate reply from the people to the priest, "And with your spirit," which means that the people wish for the priest to have peace as well. Second, in our lives we should spread peace to all, so that all will live in peace. This exchange of peace should be implied in all our interactions; we should be people who encourage peace, and others should bring peace to us as well.

Once again, the Divine Liturgy is work for all the people. It is not a production where the priest, choir, and chanter are the cast and the congregation is the audience. Once in church, in a sermon about congregational singing, I noted that the priest doesn't say, "Peace be with the choir, since they are the only ones who will answer." He says, "Peace be with *all*." He doesn't say "Peace be with me" or "Peace be with you and me," but with humility and love wishes peace for us all. With the same humility and love, let us respond back, "And with your spirit," so that the spirit of the priest or bishop who is offering the blessing also receives the peace of God, which surpasses all understanding.

Let us bow our heads to the Lord.

> So he came to a city of Samaria, called Sychar, near the field that Jacob gave to his son Joseph. Jacob's well was there, and so Jesus, wearied as he was with his journey, sat down beside the well. It was about the sixth hour. There came a woman of Samaria to draw water. Jesus said to her, "Give me a drink." For his disciples had gone away into the city to buy food. The Samaritan woman said to him, "How is it that you, a Jew, ask a drink of me, a woman of Samaria?" For Jews have no

> dealings with Samaritans. Jesus answered her, "If you knew the gift of God, and who it is that is saying to you, 'Give me a drink,' you would have asked him, and he would have given you living water."
>
> —John 4:5–10

In the story of the woman at the well in John 4, the Gospel shows us that Jesus was fully human, as He arrived in the middle of the day, thirsty from His journey. Jews and Samaritans were enemies, and men didn't associate freely with women, so when Jesus asked the Samaritan woman for a drink, He was breaking two social norms of the time. Naturally, the woman was somewhat suspect and cynical in her response to His request. After all, why would a Jewish man ask for a drink from *her?*

Jesus' answer disarmed her and opened a dialogue between them. As a result, she became the first person to share the gospel with others. She told all the people in her town about Jesus, saying, "Come, see a man who told me all that I ever did. Can this be the Christ?" (John 4:29).

If, as Jesus said, we truly "knew the gift of God"—if we really understood the Lord and the Divine Liturgy—when the priest or deacon says, "Let us bow our heads to the Lord," we would not only bow our heads, we would lay down prostrate before Him. After all, who is worthy to stand in the Lord's presence? Who is worthy of His forgiveness? Who is worthy to receive Him in the Holy Eucharist? No one.

And if we really knew the gift of salvation and the power of Jesus Christ to save souls and change lives, we wouldn't want to leave the church at the end of the service. We certainly would not arrive late for worship. We wouldn't want to miss a Sunday. If we really knew the gift offered to us in Holy Communion, then our behavior, our focus, and our entire lives would change.

So, why doesn't it work that way? Why isn't the Divine Liturgy life-changing for us every time we participate? Why can't we sustain our focus? The simple answer is that we are human, and we live in a fallen world where we battle between the spiritual and the material. This battle is evident in the entire account of the Samaritan Woman (John 4:5–42). When Jesus tells her about the gift of "living water" (4:10), she returns a material response, asking where she can get it.

Jesus tells her that "every one who drinks of this water will thirst again, but whoever drinks of the water that I shall give him will never thirst" (vv. 13–14). Once again she thinks of her material convenience and asks Jesus for this water that will quench her thirst. With this living water in hand, she will no longer have to trudge to the well to draw (v. 15).

Eventually the dialogue moves from the material to the spiritual as she perceives that Jesus is a prophet, telling Him that the Messiah will come and "show us all things" (vv. 19, 25). At last Jesus reveals Himself to her: "I who speak to you am He" (v. 26). After this encounter, the woman becomes the first evangelist as she spreads the Good News.

This line of the Divine Liturgy, instructing us to bow our heads to the Lord, reminds me of the Samaritan woman. The words remind us to bow our heads, our bodies, and our lives to Him. We learn so much about the gifts of God throughout the Divine Liturgy so that we are ready to partake of the "living water"—the Holy Eucharist—and experience its life-changing power so that it becomes for us "a spring of water welling up to eternal life" (v. 14).

Like the Samaritan woman, we don't completely know the gift of God. This is why it is important to stay in the dialogue—to continue praying, to continue worshiping, to continue learning—so that like her, our hearts can be completely converted to Christ, to living for Him, to sharing Him with others in our words and deeds.

According to the Need of Each

We give thanks to You, invisible King, who by Your boundless power fashioned the universe, and in the multitude of Your mercy brought all things from nothing into being. Look down from heaven, O Master, upon those who have bowed their heads before You; for they have not bowed before flesh and blood, but before You, the awesome God. Therefore, O Master, make smooth and beneficial for us all, whatever lies ahead, according to the need of each: Sail with those who sail; travel with those who travel; heal the sick, Physician of our souls and bodies.

> To the King of ages, immortal, invisible, the only God, be honor and glory for ever and ever. Amen.
>
> —1 Timothy 1:17

Having been directed to bow our heads to the Lord while everyone sings "To You, O Lord," the priest offers this beautiful prayer. This is one of my favorite prayers in the Divine Liturgy because it is all encompassing and inclusive.

First, it recognizes God as King, with infinite power that brought all things from nothing into being. Think of the power of that statement. Boundless power. Creator of all things.

The image of the Master looking down from heaven upon our bowed heads projects power and grace, might and comfort. We do not bow to the sacred images in the icons or to the people around us. We bow down to God Himself.

Then we ask God to look upon each of us and our unique, individual needs. Yet we do not ask Him to meet each need. After all, some of our "needs" are really desires. And some of our desires may not be best for us or our salvation. Rather, we ask God to guide our lives according to our benefit. We are asking that He guide us to follow after His commandments and grant us forward momentum in our journey to salvation.

In Matthew 6:34 we read, "Therefore do not be anxious about tomorrow, for tomorrow will be anxious for itself. Let the day's own trouble be sufficient for the day." This is a reminder that we need to focus on today's needs. That doesn't mean that we don't make plans; it means that we should ask God to help us meet the challenges of today. And then tomorrow, we ask Him to do the same.

Specific needs are then listed—for God to "sail with those who sail, travel with those who travel, and heal the sick." I often think of additional needs when I pray this prayer:

Comfort those who are grieving.
Make joyful those who are sad.
Lead back those who are lost.
Help correct those in error.
Inspire those who lack direction.
Strengthen the one who has doubt.

The prayer concludes with a reference to the Lord as "Physician of our souls and bodies." The Holy Fathers often write of the metaphor of the Church as a hospital. We are all patients who to some degree are wounded in both soul and body. The chief Physician of the hospital is the Lord, assisted by priests and laypeople who, while wounded in their own ways, assume the role of assistant healers to the Lord. Priests work as the physicians of the soul, while doctors and medical personnel work as physicians of the body. Both work as vessels of the Lord to provide healing to those entrusted to their care.

The human being is one entity composed of soul and body, linked together. God places the soul, our spiritual component, in each person, and the body protects the soul in this life. The doctor is the physician of the body. The priest is the physician of the soul. The Lord is the architect of both. And, as the author of each life, He is the ultimate physician of our souls.

Through the grace, compassion, and love for mankind of Your only-begotten Son, with whom You are blessed, together with Your all-holy, good, and life-creating Spirit, now and forever and to the ages of ages. Amen.

> Grace, mercy, and peace from God the Father and Christ Jesus our Lord.
>
> —1 Timothy 1:2

In the previous prayer we asked God to provide for each of our needs and to be the Physician of our souls and bodies. He provides for these needs "through the grace, compassion, and love for mankind" of our Lord Jesus Christ. Grace, as we have noted, is the gift from God that heals what is infirm and completes what is lacking in each of us. Compassion is the abundance of mercy shown to us, especially when we do not deserve it. And love is the gift of God, who sacrificed His own life for us.

All things are possible through God. And miracles, large or small, that God bestows on us come through His compassion, His grace, and His love.

Even though we cannot become God, we can become like God. We can receive grace from God, and we can be filled with His grace.

And we can act gracefully to one another, in the sense of building up one another and overlooking shortcomings, which is an act of grace.

We can show compassion to one another. We can bestow forgiveness. We can overlook the faults of others, even when they don't "deserve" it. We don't have to insist on retribution when someone has wronged us.

And we can show love to one another. Love involves sacrifice, joy, and vulnerability. We can sacrifice for one another, and we can do so with joy, rather than out of guilt or in expectation of return. Love involves becoming vulnerable. So, in becoming vulnerable to others, we grow in love for them. And in showing vulnerability to the Lord, we grow closer to Him.

We can also show vulnerability in prayer. To pour out our sorrows as well as joys makes us vulnerable. We can be vulnerable in worship. The first time we open our mouths to sing or raise our hands to heaven, we may feel a bit exposed. However, it is precisely *this* kind of vulnerability that not only leads us closer to the Lord but makes for a more meaningful worship experience.

We are about to approach the chalice. It is only through God's grace that our ordinary elements of bread and wine have become the Body and Blood of Christ. It is only by God's mercy that we can partake of them. How can we touch Christ as sinful human beings? How can we touch Him without condemnation or punishment? Only through His great compassion for us.

As the people sing "Amen," the priest offers a prayer and prepares to elevate the Lamb and offer it for distribution to the faithful. The words of this prayer reveal Christ as enthroned in heaven and at the same time present among us. It asks for Him to sanctify us, to allow us to receive His Body and Blood, and—through the Church—that all will come to know and receive Him also.

Hearken, O Lord Jesus Christ our God, from Your holy dwelling place and from the throne of glory of Your Kingdom, and come to sanctify us, You who are enthroned with the Father on high and are present among us invisibly here. And with Your mighty hand, grant Communion of Your most pure Body and precious Blood to us, and through us to all the people.

Holy Communion

Let us be attentive! The Holy Gifts for the holy people of God.

> [God said] "Say to all the congregation of the people of Israel, You shall be holy; for I the Lord your God am holy."
>
> —Leviticus 19:2

For the first time since the Holy Gifts were consecrated, the priest touches the Body of Christ (also called the Lamb, or *Amnos*) with his hands. He elevates the Lamb above the diskos and intones these words. First, the people are called to attention with "Let us be attentive." This command, in Greek *Proskomen*, is given several times in the Divine Liturgy: before the readings of the Epistle and the Gospel, before the recitation of the Creed, and at the beginning of the Anaphora. It is now offered one final time before Holy Communion.

But what about the phrase, "The Holy Gifts for the holy people of God"? At face value, these words seem discouraging. After all, how many people consider themselves to be holy? If someone did consider himself holy, others might think of him as arrogant.

Let's look at this phrase in a different way. Holy means "set apart," so these words could be read as: "The *set apart* Gifts for the *set apart* people of God." The Gifts look like bread and wine, but they are no longer ordinary bread and wine. They are the Body and Blood of Christ. They have been set apart from all other things in the world, for these Gifts are now divine.

The people who will receive the Gifts also are set apart, for those who receive the Eucharist touch the Divine God; they are set apart from others. The experience of receiving Holy Communion should motivate us to be different—to be God-centered people rather than self-centered people.

A common question is, "Who is worthy to receive the Gifts?" After all, we are all self-centered people. Sin, by its definition, is glorification of self over glorification of God. A priest once commented to me that a barometer to use in determining whether we should receive Holy Communion is our answer to the question, *Am I struggling to be holy?* Few achieve holiness in this life—this is why we have a tradition of saints who have found holiness, as examples to motivate us—but we can struggle. We will experience steps forward as well as setbacks. The goal is to stay in the struggle.

Another frequent question is, "How often should I receive Holy Communion?" One answer I have given is to ask people to evaluate their struggle over the course of the past week in making this decision. If someone has struggled well, then she should receive Holy Communion. If someone else has not struggled at all in the past week, giving in to temptation without a fight, then he should consider abstaining from Holy Communion.

Let me give an example. If a person struggles with cussing and sets a goal not to use profanity for the week, let's say that on six of seven days he is successful, but on one day he fails. His overall struggle was pretty successful. He is engaged in the struggle, and that is positive. On the other hand, let's say that a person is swearing wantonly every day and doesn't fight the temptation at all. Then he is not struggling. And if there is no struggle, he is not working toward being set apart; he is not working toward holiness. And if someone is not working toward holiness, should he or she be receiving the Holy Gifts? Perhaps a week without struggle would be a week to abstain from Holy Communion.

One of the reasons why it is important to cultivate a relationship with a spiritual father (a priest who serves as one's confessor, mentor, and advisor) is to sort out the struggle for holiness as well as how often someone should receive Holy Communion. Each of us should engage with others, including a spiritual father, as we strive toward holiness.

The purpose of life is this struggle for holiness, with the life goal of attaining it in the Kingdom of God. The purpose of Holy Communion is to aid and to strengthen us in that struggle. And the purpose of the Divine Liturgy is to give us an opportunity to receive Holy Communion. So, each Orthodox Christian should worship at the Divine Liturgy as often as possible and receive Holy Communion as often as possible. Realizing that no one is ever worthy to receive—after all, who can say "I feel worthy today"?—the challenge comes in the preparation. And one barometer we can use to gauge our preparedness on a given day is, "Am I struggling, or am I giving in?"

If you are giving in, it is important to understand why. Someone who consistently is succumbing to temptation without a fight is not going to be successful in the journey to salvation. Again, there is a significant difference between "I'm struggling not to commit a certain sin" and "I'm habitually sinning without remorse."[42] If you are struggling, that's good. Keep struggling. Keep fighting. The battle for your soul is a real one. God wants your soul. So does the devil. God fights for you with His blessings. The devil fights for you with

42 Cohabitating before marriage is an example of this sin. Refraining from sexual relations before marriage is a struggle. When a couple decides to move in together and have sexual relations regularly with no concern about sin, they are not struggling. But those who struggle with this temptation, even if they occasionally fail, should continue receiving Holy Communion, though perhaps not during the week that they fail. Those who give in habitually and without repentance should not commune. Again, this is why the relationship with a spiritual father is important—to have someone to guide you toward holiness rather than taking that journey all by yourself.

temptations. This is a battle we fight every day, every week. Holy Communion is an aid in the fight for your soul. But it is not an aid we should take lightly.

No one is worthy to touch the Divine God in Holy Communion. However, it is not perfection that God expects. He knows we are not worthy. What He wants from us is our attempts—our struggle for holiness. He wants us to be set apart. He wants to set us apart through receiving Holy Communion. This is why we are reminded at each Divine Liturgy that the Holy Gifts are for the holy people. These Gifts are set apart from all other gifts, given to those who are striving to set themselves apart.

One is Holy, one is Lord, Jesus Christ, to the glory of God the Father. Amen.

> Therefore God has highly exalted him and bestowed on him the name which is above every name, that at the name of Jesus every knee should bow, in heaven and on earth and under the earth, and every tongue confess that Jesus Christ is Lord, to the glory of God the Father.
>
> —Philippians 2:9–11

We've all been to pep rallies. We've all cheered on a favorite team. When I was in high school at football games, our cheerleaders would yell out something, and those of us in the stands would yell something back. In one of the cheers, the cheerleaders yelled "Go!" and the fans responded by yelling, "Fight!"

The Divine Liturgy also includes many responses from the congregation. When the priest says, "The Holy Gifts for the holy people of God," this is a rallying cry, the "go" of the cheerleaders. Our response, "One is Holy, One is Lord, Jesus Christ," is our "fight." We have heard the message, and as the set-apart people of God about to receive the set-apart Gifts, we are now ready to fight for holiness.

This short hymn brings to mind some very important questions for the Christian life. If *holy* means "set apart," then in our lives, what do we set apart as special, as holy? As an example, those of us who are married should honor our spouses above all other people because we share a special bond unlike any other bond with any other person. For those who have children, we love and set apart our own children above all other children because they are ours. So, in saying "One is Holy," we need to consider what we value most in our lives. Does the Faith come before everything? Is it second? Third? Where is our pursuit of holiness on the list of priorities for our lives?

In medieval times, people would bow to the kings and queens, lords and ladies of society. They would address royalty as "my lord" and make the appropriate bow as a sign of respect and reverence. When a member of the royalty entered the room, everyone stood up and then bowed down. In contemporary life, what gets your attention above everything else? What do you run to, or bow down to, in life? Is it the television set, the smartphone, the refrigerator, or the Starbucks on the corner?

What attracts you and pulls you in? If Jesus is truly our Lord and Savior, then He should pull us to Himself above all other things. If we are spending more money on Starbucks than we offer to the church in our yearly stewardship, then Starbucks is of greater value to us. If we have hours to spend watching television but no time to pray or read the Bible, then the television is of greater value than faith. "One is Lord" reminds us that our relationship with the Lord should be above all the things we treasure in life.

And who is the Lord? Jesus Christ, our Savior, who came down to earth to be one of us, who conquered death by His death and who rose from the dead. Jesus is the One who shows us the road back to the Father. Jesus glorified the Father at all times, and we are called to do the same—believe in Jesus as the Christ, and glorify God in all things.

This is another barometer for our lives. Ask yourself these questions when you are faced with a decision: *Does this please God? Does this glorify God?*

Ask this the next time you want to cut someone off in traffic, the next time you want to start an argument or say something condescending to someone, the next time you are short with someone, or the next time you feel cranky.

"The Holy Gifts for the holy people of God" is our destination. "One is Holy, one is Lord, Jesus Christ, to the glory of God the Father" is the means by which we reach our destination. We will make great strides in our battle for holiness if we keep in mind that only one is holy, only one is the Lord, and that is Jesus Christ. And our goal is to be like Him, to worship Him, and to give glory to the Father. This is how we can strive for holiness. This is the *only* way to strive for holiness.

Praise the Lord from the heavens; praise Him in the highest. Alleluia.

> Praise the LORD! / Praise the LORD from the heavens, / praise him in the heights!
>
> —Psalm 148:1

After the short hymn "One is Holy," the people sing a Communion Hymn as they prepare for Holy Communion. In contemporary times, the hymn is usually offered by the choir or a chanter, and people are encouraged to sing along. The Communion Hymns vary depending on the day of the week and various feast days of the liturgical year.

The Communion Hymn is very short—usually only a single verse of Scripture—so it is sung in one of three ways. It may be elongated, so that it is only sung once, with each word being stretched out syllable by syllable. It can take five to ten minutes to sing "Praise the Lord from the heavens" with certain pieces of music. A second way the hymns are sung is by repeating the one verse of Scripture several times, for as long as it takes the clergy in the altar to commune and to prepare to distribute the Holy Gifts. The third way is to sing the hymns several times, with an additional verse of the psalms intoned, between each slow repetition.[43]

It is interesting to note that the Communion Hymns are based (with one exception) on verses from the psalms, which are part of the Old Testament and precede Jesus' earthly ministry. A remnant of the Old Testament and its Old Covenant is very present as we are about to partake of the New Covenant.

Here are some Communion Hymns that are derived from the psalms, as well as the feast day(s) they are chanted:

- Blessed is He who enters in the name of the Lord. . . . The Lord is God and He has given us light. (Psalm 117/118:25, Palm Sunday)
- O taste and see that the Lord is good. (Psalm 33/34:8, Pre-Sanctified Liturgies during Lent)
- I will lift up the cup of salvation and call on the name of the Lord. (Psalm 115/116:13, all feast days of the Theotokos)
- God has gone up with a shout, the Lord with the sound of a trumpet. (Psalm 46/47:5, Ascension)
- The Lord has sent redemption to His people. (Psalm 110/111:9, Nativity / Christmas)

---

43 This third example is rarely seen in parishes. Most use the first two ways.

- Their voice goes out through all the earth, and their words to the end of the world. (Psalm 18/19:4, feast days of the apostles)
- Let Thy good spirit lead me on a level path! (Psalm 142/143:10, Pentecost)

The only Communion Hymn that is based on New Testament Scripture is the Communion Hymn of the paschal (Resurrection) season: "Receive the Body of Christ. Taste from the eternal fount." The words are based on two passages in the Gospel of John: "Whoever drinks of the water I shall give him will never thirst; the water I shall give him will become in him a spring of water welling up to eternal life" (4:14) and "Jesus stood up and proclaimed 'If any one thirst, let him come to Me and drink. He who believes in Me, as the scripture has said, "Out of his heart shall flow rivers of living water"'" (7:37–38).

The Communion Hymns do two things for us. First, they are traditionally chanted very slowly, slowing the service and hopefully our thoughts as well, so that we are contemplative, meditative, and still as we prepare to receive Holy Communion. A hymn like the doxology is up-tempo and quick because it calls us at the beginning of the service to worship with enthusiasm. But the Communion Hymn is deliberately slow because it calls us to reverently consider the task that is at hand: our reception of the Body and Blood of Christ.

During the Communion Hymn, several things happen inside the altar as the clergy receive the Eucharist and prepare to distribute it to the faithful. (We will discuss this subject in the next reflections.) These hymns also provide a time for the faithful to pray the Holy Communion prayers as well.

Second, the Communion Hymns stick in our heads—at least, they do for me. Repeating the same hymn several times in a slow cadence in church allows us to hold these hymns in our minds and our hearts during the week. I can't tell you how many times I've found myself humming one of these slow hymns, which in turn slows down my busy thoughts and provides a calmness, a reverence, and a purposefulness in the middle of a busy week. Learning some of these hymns can do the same for you. Listen to the choir, hum along, and internalize the words and meaning. On almost every Sunday, the Communion Hymn reminds us of the importance of praising the Lord, both in deed and in word. *Is my life a praise to the Lord?* It's an appropriate question to ask every day, but especially so as we prepare to receive Holy Communion each Sunday.

Behind the Icon Screen

Broken but Undivided

> The cup of blessing which we bless, is it not a participation in the blood of Christ? The bread which we break, is it not a participation in the body of Christ? Because there is one bread, we who are many are one body, for we all partake of the one bread.
>
> —1 Corinthians 10:16–17

The next several reflections will center on what occurs in the altar before the people receive Holy Communion—specifically the clergy's reception of the Eucharist and its preparation for distribution to the faithful. These activities are generally unseen and unheard by the faithful in the nave. However, because priests who wear microphones often leave them on during this time of the service, if you listen carefully you will hear bits and pieces of the information that follows. It is not my intention to debunk or take the mystery out of what happens behind the altar but to explore the rich meaning in what is transpiring during this time.

After the priest elevates the Lamb (the piece of bread that is the Body of Christ) and intones, "The Holy Gifts for the holy people of God," he "fractures" the Lamb, meaning he breaks it into four pieces. As he does this, he offers the following words:

The Lamb of God is apportioned and distributed; apportioned, but not divided; ever eaten, yet never consumed; but sanctifying those who partake.

This is indeed a profound statement. In a practical way, the Body must be apportioned, or broken, in order to be distributed to the faithful. Yet Christ is not divided. When we attend a banquet, a finite amount of food is served. The supply is not inexhaustible. Yet we never run out of Christ. There is enough Christ for every Christian in every Orthodox parish throughout the world on every day, whenever a Divine Liturgy is celebrated. How many hundreds of thousands of Orthodox churches celebrate the Divine Liturgy each Sunday? Yet there is enough grace of the Holy Spirit to consecrate the Gifts offered in every one of them. We never run out of Christ.

We never even run out of Holy Communion. Yes, on a practical level, there are times when the chalice is nearly empty when I'm done distributing the Gifts, and after the Divine Liturgy, whatever is left is consumed by the priest so that the chalice is truly empty. Holy Communion remains, however, at all times in the tabernacle on the back edge of the altar. The quantity of Holy Communion that is kept there is a small amount, in human terms. However, in godly terms, to receive even the smallest amount of Christ is to receive a great amount of grace, holiness, power, and encouragement.

This short line of the service also reminds the celebrant, and anyone else who may hear it, that the Body and Blood of Christ sanctify all those who partake of them. They reconsecrate us. They refocus us. They renew us.

Next, one piece of the fractured Lamb is placed into the chalice as the priest offers these words:

The fullness of the Holy Spirit. Amen.

The Holy Spirit consecrated the Gifts into the Body and Blood of Christ, and now the Body and Blood have been combined in the chalice. The fullness of what the Holy Spirit has done is not visible and tangible. Body and Blood are now in the form in which we will receive them—together.

Hot water is now added to the chalice from a special vessel called the *zeon,* which one of the altar servers brings. The priest blesses the water with the following words:

Blessed is the fervor of Your saints, always, now and forever and to the ages of ages. Amen.

The words *warmth* and *fervor* are connected. A fervent heart is warm to certain ideas. The fervor—the excitement—of the saints who have spread the Word of God and who have lived and died for the Lord are an integral part of our Orthodox history and of the Divine Liturgy. Without the fervor of the saints, we would not have received the Faith from the generations who came before us. It is the fervor of the saints that kept the Church going through times of persecution and strife. Because the Divine Liturgy is a gathering of both Church Militant and Church Triumphant, we again acknowledge the importance of the saints and the Holy Spirit who poured His grace so richly upon them.

As the water is poured into the chalice, the priest says the following words:

The fervor of the Holy Spirit. Amen.

Again, who provides the warmth that encourages fervor? The grace of the Holy Spirit. The entire ministry of Christ is summarized and encapsulated in the Divine Liturgy. The Pentecost event is also part of the Divine Liturgy, as we discussed earlier at the Consecration. Following the Consecration, the warm water is added to the chalice in the same way that, following the Resurrection, the Holy Spirit added His warmth to the Church.

I believe, Lord, and confess . . .

> [Martha] said to [Jesus], "Yes, Lord; I believe that You are the Christ, the Son of God, He who is coming into the world."
>
> —John 11:27

Holy Communion is awesome! How ordinary substances of bread and wine can be transformed into the Body and Blood of Christ is mysterious, mystical, and profound. How an ordinary human being can touch *the* Body and *the* Blood of Christ and not be eviscerated by the experience is truly awesome. It is an experience that should fill us with awe and wonder.

Sometimes I fear that because we partake so often, Holy Communion becomes routine. I remember once confessing to my spiritual father that my mind wanders in church. He comforted me with the notion that every mind wanders in church. This is why it is good that the Divine Liturgy is long and complete, so that even if our minds are not engaged in the service 100 percent of the time, many powerful moments and powerful events will stir the heart and prepare it for its encounter with the Lord through the Gifts.

In an earlier reflection, I wrote on the requirements for receiving Holy Communion—faith, a relationship with Christ through a prayer life, moral living, reconciliation with others, worship at the Divine Liturgy, and fasting. The decision to receive Holy Communion is one that should be made well in advance of the worship service. Since I no longer make a choice whether to receive or not—a priest receives Holy Communion at every Divine Liturgy—I have to think back to my days as a layman to remember what it was like to make this choice.

It wasn't until I was in college that I began receiving Holy Communion on a regular basis. I also began fasting on a regular basis. I hadn't yet made the connection that I should fast on Wednesdays and Fridays, regardless of whether I was going to receive Holy Communion. So, I would plan on Tuesday whether I was going to receive the following Sunday. If so, I would keep the fast and try to prepare myself as best I could.

Now, in addition to all the other requirements one should meet in preparation for Holy Communion, we should offer Holy Communion prayers. Most people are not familiar with the fact that there is a canon of preparation for Holy Communion that should be prayed the night before receiving or in the morning before coming to church. This canon consists of dozens of prayers and hymns. The last eight of these prayers are offered by the celebrant before he receives Holy Communion. In some parishes, these prayers are read aloud by all the people; in others, the celebrant offers them loudly enough to be heard by all. And in still other churches, the celebrant offers them quietly, and the people do not hear them.

I've heard many debates over where and how these prayers should be offered. I also know that most people do not know about the Canon of Holy Communion and that most are not praying it. What

I do believe, however, is that these eight prayers prior to receiving the Eucharist are very important and personal. Each person receiving Communion should offer them. So, if you are in a church where the prayers are offered aloud, read along. If you are in a church where the celebrant is offering them so that you can hear them, listen attentively. And if you are in a church where you do not hear them, pray them yourself—either before you go to Divine Liturgy or while the priest is preparing to distribute Holy Communion.

These eight prayers appear below, with some brief commentary.

I believe and confess, Lord, that You are truly the Christ, the Son of the living God, Who came into the world to save sinners, of whom I am the first. I also believe that this is truly Your pure Body and that this is truly Your precious Blood. Therefore, I pray to You, have mercy upon me, and forgive my transgressions, voluntary and involuntary, in word and deed, in knowledge or in ignorance. And make me worthy, without condemnation, to partake of Your pure Mysteries for the remission of sins and for eternal life. Amen.

The first requirement for receiving Holy Communion is faith, so the first statements of these prayers are statements of faith—of belief in Christ and belief in the power of the Holy Spirit to consecrate ordinary Gifts of bread and wine into the Body and Blood of Christ. Coupled with these statements of faith are words of contrition: viewing oneself as the first among sinners; asking forgiveness for all sins, including even sins of ignorance—the unknown sins; and acknowledging that to receive Holy Communion is an act of mercy; we do not want the Lord to condemn us for what we are about to do.

Behold, I approach for Divine Communion. O Maker, burn me not as I partake. For You are fire consuming the unworthy. But cleanse me from every stain.

In Exodus 3, we read the account of Moses encountering the burning bush. In the second verse we read, "And the angel of the LORD appeared to him in a flame of fire out of the midst of a bush; and he looked, and lo, the bush was burning, yet it was not consumed." The prayer asks that we, like the burning bush, be allowed to touch the Divine God but not be burned.

O Son of God, receive me today as a partaker of Your mystical supper. For I will not speak of the mystery to Your enemies, nor will I give You a kiss, as did Judas. But like the thief, I confess to You: Remember me, Lord, in Your Kingdom.

There is a stark contrast between Judas and the repentant thief on the cross. Judas, the disciple, the member of Christ's inner circle, partook of fellowship with Christ and yet betrayed Him. And not only did he betray Christ, he did it with a kiss—a sign of affection. The thief, on the other hand, had lived an awful life and was crucified as punishment. In his dying moments, he asked Jesus to remember him. He found faith, repentance, forgiveness, and salvation at the end of his life. The lesson for us is that we cannot be like Judas, enjoying the divine fellowship of Holy Communion and then betraying the Lord with the way we live our lives. We need to be like the thief, continually seeking repentance.

Tremble, O man, as you behold the divine Blood. It is a burning coal that sears the unworthy. The Body of God both

deifies and nourishes me. It deifies the Spirit and wondrously nourishes the mind.

In Isaiah 6, we read about Isaiah's vision of God in the temple. He saw the Lord sitting on a throne and the seraphim standing above the throne. Then one of the seraphim flew to Isaiah and touched his mouth with a burning coal, which the angel had taken from the altar. And Isaiah was not harmed. (More on this vision in the next reflection.) So, we see the image of Christ as a fiery coal. Imagine putting a burning coal in your mouth! You would be burned, if not killed. So it is with the Body of Christ: it will burn the unworthy, but for the one who approaches with faith, the Body of God unites us with Him and gives sustenance to the spirit and the mind.

You have smitten me with yearning, O Christ, and by Your divine eros You have changed me. But burn up with spiritual fire my sins, and grant me to be filled with delight in You, so that, leaping for joy, I may magnify, O Good One, Your two comings.[44]

Our hope in receiving Holy Communion is that our sins will be burned up but not we ourselves. Holy Communion should bring not only awe but also joy to our spirits.

How shall I, who am unworthy, enter into the splendor of Your saints? If I should dare to enter into the bridal chamber, my vesture will condemn me, since it is not a wedding garment; and being bound up, I shall be cast out by the angels.

44 As for the "two comings," these refer to the Incarnation and the Second Coming. The idea of a third coming, a "rapture" in the middle, is a new Protestant teaching of the last few centuries. The Orthodox Church does not believe in the rapture.

Cleanse, O Lord, the filth of my soul, and save me, as You are the one who loves mankind. In Your love, Lord, cleanse my soul, and save me.

The parable of the great banquet is told both in the Gospels of Matthew (22:1–13) and Luke (14:16–24). A man was giving a marriage feast for his son and invites guests to come in. In each case, the invited guests decline and make excuses, and the man is angry with his guests who turned him down. He asks his servants to go out and find everyone to invite them to the banquet. In Matthew's account, the master giving the feast finds a man who had no wedding garment at the banquet and orders him to be cast out. The lesson of this parable is that all are invited to the banquet (salvation), and we should not make excuses or turn down the invitation. However, accepting the invitation comes with an expectation to dress appropriately, meaning to clothe our souls with faith and with the virtues of faith—repentance, humility, charity, and so on.

Master who loves mankind, Lord Jesus Christ, my God, let not these Holy Gifts be to my judgment because I am unworthy, but rather for the purification and sanctification of both soul and body and the pledge of the life and Kingdom to come. It is good for me to cleave unto God and to place in Him the hope of my salvation.

This prayer again acknowledges the majesty of God, that He is our Master and that He is the hope of our salvation. And it asks that even though we are unworthy, He allow us to partake of Him regardless, with words that again remind us of our future hope and life purpose in His coming Kingdom.

The last of the prayers is the third prayer, repeated in the Canon of Holy Communion for emphasis. This will serve as today's prayer:

O Son of God, receive me today as a partaker of Your mystical supper. For I will not speak of the mystery to Your enemies, nor will I give You a kiss, as did Judas. But like the thief, I confess to You: Remember me, Lord, in Your Kingdom.

Behold, I approach Christ, our king and God.

In the year that King Uzziah died I saw the Lord sitting upon a throne, high and lifted up; and his train filled the temple. Above him stood the seraphim; each had six wings: with two he covered his face, and with two he covered his feet, and with two he flew. And one called to another and said:

"Holy, holy, holy is the LORD of hosts; the whole earth is full of his glory."

And the foundations of the thresholds shook at the voice of him who called, and the house was filled with smoke. And I said: "Woe is me! For I am lost; for I am a man of unclean lips, and I dwell in the midst of a people of unclean lips; for my eyes have seen the King, the LORD of hosts!" Then flew one of the seraphim to me, having in his hand a burning coal which he had taken with tongs from the altar. And he touched my mouth, and said: "Behold, this has touched your lips; your guilt is taken away, and your sin forgiven."

—Isaiah 6:1–7

After offering the Communion Prayers, a series of events occurs as the priest receives Holy Communion. I share this behind-the-scenes action with you for three reasons: first, so you can better understand what is going on in the altar at this moment; second, because the faithful have an important role to play here; and third, because what is said as the priest receives Holy Communion pertains to the faithful as well as the clergy.

As the priest concludes the Communion prayers, he makes three bows before the holy altar, saying, "God be gracious to me a sinner and have mercy on me." This is a modification of the prayer of the Publican in Luke 18:13, "God be gracious to me a sinner," and the Jesus Prayer, "Lord, Jesus Christ, Son of God, have mercy on me a sinner." The priest makes these bows several times before significant moments during the Divine Liturgy: the Small Entrance, the Great Entrance, the Consecration, and now before he receives Holy Communion.

Next, the priest turns toward the people and asks for forgiveness. He says, "My brothers and sisters in Christ, please forgive me." At the moment that I am saying this, the choir or chanters are always singing, so I'm not sure that I'm even heard. I wish this could be done in the midst of silence. This plea for forgiveness is important because it is necessary for a priest to reconcile with his people before receiving Holy Communion, just as it is important for the people to reconcile with the priest and with one another. In an ideal world, the priest could ask each person individually for forgiveness, but obviously that is impractical. What is practical, though, is for everyone in the congregation to look up as the priest comes out from the altar and speaks. It is actually a humbling thing to stand in front of an entire church and ask for forgiveness. Sometimes I even try to make eye contact with people I have wronged. So, what should the people do at this moment? They should offer forgiveness in return by saying the words, "May God forgive both you and me" or "May God forgive the both of us."

The priest then turns toward the altar and says, "Behold, I approach Christ our immortal King and God." The priest—and soon the people—is not merely approaching a table and is not merely going through a ritual; he and all of us are approaching Christ Himself! This is profound and awesome.

The priest then communes from the Body of Christ, taking a portion of the Body in his left hand and then placing it in his right hand so that the right hand receives from the left. This is also significant, since no one "takes" Holy Communion of their own volition but receives it as a gift from God, through the hand of the priest, or in the case of the priest, through both of his hands. The priest says as he communes, "Behold, I approach Christ, our immortal King and God. Unto me, *[Name]*, the unworthy presbyter, is imparted the precious and all-holy Body of our Lord and God and Savior, Jesus Christ, for the remission of my sins and life eternal." What is significant here is that the priest says his own name, even though both he and the Lord know it. As we will learn shortly, everyone should offer his or her name when receiving Holy Communion.

The priest then wipes his hands on the sponge on the antimension to make sure that no particle of the Body remains on his skin. He next lifts the chalice and receives the Blood of Christ. There is no rubric indicating whether the priest should lift the chalice high before or after receiving. So, each priest does this a little bit differently. I had the great blessing to observe one of the best liturgists I've ever seen for many of my formative years as an altar boy. His name was Fr. John Zanetos (of blessed memory). Every Divine Liturgy, at this moment, he would lift the chalice high in the air over his head. As a young boy of ten, I thought this was powerful, like the Lord was towering over every head in the church. This awe-inspiring moment is one of the things that kindled my desire to follow God's call to the priesthood. So, I raise the chalice in the same way that Fr. John did, and I say the words that every priest says: "Again, I approach Christ, our immortal King and God. Unto me, *[Name]*, the unworthy presbyter, is imparted the precious and all-holy Blood of our Lord and God and Savior, Jesus Christ, for the remission of my sins and life eternal." The priest then drinks from the chalice.

After receiving Holy Communion, the priest wipes his lips with a red cloth and says the words adapted from Isaiah 6:7: "This has touched my lips, and the Lord takes away all my iniquities and cleanses my sins." This statement is also profound not only for the priest but for each person who receives Holy Communion. We touch the Divine God, yet we are not destroyed. Somehow God allows us to do the incredible—to touch Him. He offers a miracle to us as He comes into us. This should be a renewed start for us each time we receive Holy Communion. We are cleansed and perfected, and we are supposed to live in a new way—in a way that honors the Gift we've received.

The Final Preparation of the Holy Eucharist

> And I saw the holy city, new Jerusalem, coming down out of heaven from God, prepared as a bride adorned for her husband.
>
> —Revelation 21:2

In the early centuries of the Church, the faithful used to commune in a similar way as the clergy. They approached and had the Body of Christ placed in their hands, and then they would drink from the chalice. In other words, they would receive the Body and Blood of Christ as separate elements. (This is still done when the Divine Liturgy of St. James is served, which is customary only on his feast day, October 23.) The way we receive the Eucharist today, with the Body and Blood of Christ on the spoon together, originated in the seventh century.

Because we now receive the Body and Blood of Christ together, they must be combined in the holy chalice. Thus, after receiving Holy Communion but before distributing it to the faithful, the priest carefully lifts the pieces of the Body of Christ from the diskos and places them into the chalice. Since Holy Communion is a foreshadowing of our personal resurrection in Christ, as the priest is doing this, he recites prayers and hymns from the feast of the Resurrection:

> Having beheld the Resurrection of Christ, let us worship the holy Lord Jesus, the only sinless one. Your Cross, O Christ, we venerate, and Your holy Resurrection we praise and glorify. For You are our God; apart from You we know no other; we call upon Your name. Come, all faithful, let us venerate the holy Resurrection of Christ; for behold, through the Cross, joy has come to the whole world. Ever blessing the Lord, let us praise His Resurrection; for having endured the Cross for us, He destroyed death by death.
>
> Shine, shine, O New Jerusalem, for the glory of the Lord has dawned upon you. Dance now and be glad, Zion, and you, O pure Theotokos, rejoice in the Resurrection of your Son.
>
> O voice divine, beloved and most sweet! For you, O Christ, have promised in truth to be with us unto the close of the age, and we faithful rejoice, having this anchor of hope.
>
> O Christ, our Pascha, most sacred and great: wisdom, Word, and power of God. Grant unto us to partake of You more profoundly in the unending day of Your Kingdom.

Also present on the diskos are particles of bread representing the Virgin Mary, the saints, the Church Militant, and the Church Triumphant. These are *not* the Body of Christ. When you receive Holy Communion, it is from only the Body of Christ. As a priest, I can tell which pieces are for the Virgin Mary and the saints, because they are triangular. The crumbs, the particles for the living and the dead, sink to the bottom of the chalice. And what is left are the four (unless there is more than one chalice used) pieces of the Body of Christ that float to the top.[45]

When the priest places the particles of the living and the dead into the chalice, whether he does it before the distribution of Holy Communion or after, he prays the following words:

> Wash away, Lord, by Your Holy Blood, the sins of Your servants here remembered through the intercessions of the Theotokos and all Your saints. Amen.

This beautiful prayer reminds us of two things: the Blood of Christ washes away our sins, and second, we are all one through the Holy Eucharist. You may recall from the reflection about the preparation of the Gifts that on the diskos (paten) is the place where my family stands together, even though my parents have joined the Church Triumphant and the rest of my family lives in another state. In this moment of transferring all the particles into the chalice, we again affirm that we are all one in the Body and Blood of Christ—those who are present, those who are absent, those who are alive, and those who have passed away. We are all one.

The priest uses a sponge to sweep all the particles off the diskos into the chalice. Undoubtedly in this process some crumbs will fall onto the antimension, the cloth that is placed under the Gifts in large part for this purpose. The priest will clean the antimension. Many of us flip over the diskos and run it over the antimension to clean up the loose crumbs and then wipe those into the chalice. This process is very meticulous because this is the Body of Christ, which must be handled

---

45 Remember that the Body was broken into four pieces after the priest intoned, "The Holy Gifts for the holy people of God."

with great reverence and care. Many priests also put the spoon in the chalice and break up the large pieces of the Body of Christ into smaller particles for easier distribution, which also takes more time.

Once in a while, someone will opine (or complain), "Why does it take so long for the priest to prepare Holy Communion to distribute it to the faithful?" My answer to this question is something I once heard from another priest: "You can tell a lot about a priest by how he handles the Holy Eucharist." I try to always be careful with the Gifts. I'd rather be reverent than efficient.

After preparing the Gifts and as I am about to distribute them, I always offer two more prayers. The first prayer is a personal prayer to the Lord to hold my hands steady as I am distributing Holy Communion. On a Sunday, distributing Communion to the faithful can take thirty minutes or longer. Thus, the prayer for stamina. And the second prayer is the prayer of St. Simeon, which he offered over the Lord when Jesus was presented in the temple on his fortieth day. Saint Simeon offered this prayer because God had promised him that he wouldn't die until he saw the Christ. This prayer was for his peaceful death and entrance into the Kingdom of heaven. It is part of every Vespers service, and I offer it at each Divine Liturgy, reflecting on my own life and asking the Lord that if I am going to be called back to Him before I celebrate the Divine Liturgy again, that my departure be in peace.

> Lord, now lettest thou thy servant depart in peace, according to thy word; for mine eyes have seen thy salvation which thou hast prepared in the presence of all peoples, a light for revelation to the Gentiles, and for glory to thy people Israel. (Luke 2:29–32)

When I was ordained, the bishop told me to celebrate each Divine Liturgy as if it were my first and my last: with the joy of the first and the purposefulness of the last. I encourage each of us to worship in the same way, as if this is our first and last Divine Liturgy, with both joy and with purpose. And with this, we turn now to our personal encounter with Christ in the receiving of Holy Communion. The most important moment of the Divine Liturgy is upon us!

Come Receive the Light: A Personal Invitation from Christ

With the fear of God, faith, and love, draw near.

> So faith, hope, love abide, these three; but the greatest of these is love.
>
> —1 Corinthians 13:13

The long journey of the Divine Liturgy has now reached its climax. The people are invited to receive Holy Communion with the words, "With the fear of God, faith, and love, draw near." A hierarch of the Church told me at the beginning of my ministry that when I intone this line of invitation to the people, I should hold the chalice in front of my face so that the people will hear the words without seeing me. Why? Because this invitation to draw near and partake is to be heard as an invitation from God Himself, coming only through the mouth of the priest.

Have you ever paused to consider the meaning of these words of invitation? "With the fear of God." What does that mean? In Greek, the word is *fovo,* which means "fear" in most instances. It can also mean "sense of awe," "reverence," or "respect." In approaching for Holy Communion, our hearts should experience this sense of fear, awe, reverence, and respect. This is why I always correct people when they say they are going to "take" Holy Communion. We receive a gift, but we take something with a sense of entitlement. No one is ever worthy to receive Holy Communion. Certainly no one should come into church with the idea that they are going to *take* it. We must approach the chalice with a great sense of reverence and humility. It is only by God's grace that we can touch Him.

Think about this for a moment. In approaching Holy Communion, we are preparing to touch God, and God is about to touch us. As one of my seminary professors used to say, "We are going to have an intimate encounter with the living God." This is so profound it is hard to wrap our minds around the concept. How can I, entangled in my sins, dare to approach—to touch the living God? My mouth sometimes spews gossip or foul language or argues with people. How can I open that same mouth to have Christ placed in it? These questions are profound and scary. If we truly ponder them, we will experience some fear.

But the invitation doesn't tell us only to come with fear—that invitation would probably go unanswered. We are invited also to come in faith. It is faith in God's mercies that allows us to open our filthy mouths to be filled with Christ. We believe in the mercies of God to allow us to partake of Him, the mercies and grace that have the power to save our souls for eternal life and to grant them strength in this life. Fear is counterbalanced with faith.

Receiving Holy Communion is also an act of love. In encountering Christ in the Holy Eucharist, we affirm His love for us and our love for Him. In 1 Corinthians 11:26, St. Paul tells us, "For as often as you eat this bread and drink the cup, you proclaim the Lord's death until He comes." In approaching Holy Communion, we affirm the love of Christ for us, which led Him to die on the Cross for our sins. In approaching Holy Communion, we recommit our love for Him.

Saint Paul does issue a warning about our approach for Holy Communion in 1 Corinthians 11:27–30:

> Whoever, therefore, eats the bread or drinks the cup of the Lord in an unworthy manner will be guilty of profaning the Body and Blood of the Lord. Let a man examine himself, and so eat of the bread and drink of the cup. For anyone who eats and drinks without discerning the Body eats and drinks judgment upon himself. This is why many of you are weak and ill, and some have died.

Saint Paul tells us that Holy Communion is a serious matter indeed, which leads many to wonder, *How can I accept this invitation to partake?* Saint Paul provides the answer: we must undergo an examination of our life and conscience. Of course, an examination of conscience can still leave us paralyzed in fear, so the Church offers to us the Sacrament of Confession as a way to cleanse our souls and prepare them to accept Christ's invitation.

Remember that Christ wants us to approach often to receive Him. To embrace this invitation, we sometimes need to unlearn old ideas. When I was a child, we didn't receive Holy Communion often. We received on Christmas, Pascha, the Dormition of the Virgin Mary, and our name days. Yet the invitation is without qualification. The Liturgy does not say, "With the fear of God, with faith and love draw near, if it is your name day." Or on Pascha, "With the fear of God, with faith and love draw near, everyone, because it's Pascha." The invitation to receive is a personal invitation to each of us, each time it is offered.

Should people receive every time they hear the invitation? As we've discussed earlier, this is an important question. Receiving the Holy Eucharist is a matter of conscience, which should be discussed with your spiritual father. My thought is that we should approach as often as we are prepared—as often as we are making an effort to grow in our faith. If this effort is constant, then we should receive often. But someone who gives absolutely no effort should consider abstaining. There are some who argue that the faithful should receive Holy Communion every time it is offered, and some who still argue that we should only approach a few times a year. The answer lies somewhere in between, though I believe that the intention of Christ was for us to receive often, as St. Paul confirms in his letter to the Corinthians.

One way to understand this is to think about what happens when a friend invites you to go somewhere. If the friend is someone you really like, you want to say yes to every invitation—you are not only going to accept two out of fifty invitations. But you probably won't be able to accept fifty out of fifty invitations. Christ offers you the invitation to receive Holy Communion at every Divine Liturgy. So, if you only accept the invitation a few times a year, what does that say about the strength of your relationship with Christ?

Knowing that the invitation is coming, ask yourself, "How can I accept this invitation?" And then ask yourself, "How can I *not* accept this invitation? It is so important, how can I stay away?" And if you are staying away habitually from Holy Communion, ask yourself, "Why am I not accepting this invitation?"

> Direct my steps according to Your word and may no wickedness conquer me. Free me from the slanders of men that I might keep Your commandments. Let Your face shine upon Your servant, and teach me Your statutes. Let my mouth be filled with Your praise, O Lord, that I may sing Your glory and honor Your magnificence all day long. Amen.[46]

46 From the First Hour, *The Services for Holy Week and Easter*, trans. Nomikos Michael Vaporis (Brookline, MA: Holy Cross Orthodox Press, 1993), 174.

The servant of God *[Name]* partakes of the Body and Blood of Christ, for the remission of sins and life eternal. Amen.

> When Jesus had spoken these words, he lifted up his eyes to heaven and said, "Father, the hour has come; glorify thy Son that the Son may glorify thee, since thou hast given him power over all flesh, to give eternal life to all whom thou hast given him. And this is eternal life, that they know thee the only true God, and Jesus Christ whom thou hast sent.
>
> —John 17:1–3

We've discussed many times why we receive Holy Communion. In this reflection, we will discuss *how* to receive Holy Communion, both from a practical and spiritual perspective. First, the spiritual decision to receive should be made well in advance of the priest's call to come forward. Second, the decision to receive Holy Communion is a choice that we make with careful consideration. We are not supposed to hear the words of invitation to Holy Communion and just go without thought. The call is not a surprise, so we should prepare to receive well in advance of the Divine Liturgy.

In many communities, the Communion line on Sundays is long. While waiting in line, recite the prayer of the penitent thief, which is also the last line of the Holy Communion prayers: "Lord, remember me when You come into Your kingdom" (Luke 23:42). Holy Communion is not only preparation for God's Kingdom; it is a foretaste of it. In receiving the Eucharist, we become one with God for a finite moment. In heaven, we will be united with God for eternity.

What else can one do during the long wait in line? If you have already received, you can pray the prayers of thanksgiving after Holy Communion. (We will discuss those in a future reflection.) You also can pray for those who are receiving, either by name or in general terms. Everyone who comes forward has a different need: some are hopeful, others need hope, some are lost, some need forgiveness, some need strength, and so on. In praying for those who are receiving, we are showing love for our neighbor. In receiving ourselves, we are showing love for the Lord. This time of Holy Communion, which can be half an hour or longer in some parishes, can be used as a time of personal retreat, to pray to the Lord on our own behalf as well as for others. In doing this, we fulfill the two great commandments, to love God and to love one another.

Many people complain about how long it takes for everyone to receive Holy Communion. By using this time prayerfully, the wait will make it more meaningful.

During Holy Communion, the choir usually chants the last of the Holy Communion prayers:

> O Son of God, receive me today as a partaker of Your mystical supper. For I will not speak of the mystery to Your enemies, nor will I give You a kiss, as did Judas. But like the thief, I confess to You: Remember me, Lord, in Your Kingdom.

Sometimes, they also sing a psalm, like this adaptation of Psalm 135/136:

> O give thanks unto the Lord, for He is good. Alleluia. For His mercy endureth forever. Alleluia.

The verses continue in this way, with everyone singing the refrain. You can sing along with the choir as well to make the time more prayerful.

As a priest, when I distribute Holy Communion I try to not be so rushed that the person receiving can't hear the prayer I am offering for them. In the past I spoke more quickly, until someone pointed out how much they anticipated the Eucharist each week and what a special moment it is. This caused me to slow down a little to try to create space for each person to receive.

As I am distributing Holy Communion, I also think about safety. The Eucharist is the Body and the Blood of Christ, and it needs to be treated with great reverence.

When the person before you is receiving, make the sign of the cross. You shouldn't make the sign of the cross at the chalice for fear of hitting it by accident. When you approach to receive, take the cloth and put it under your chin, or allow the altar server assisting the priest to do that. The purpose of the cloth is to catch any particle of Holy Communion that might fall off the spoon, so that it does not land on the floor. So, make sure there is no gap by holding the cloth under your chin.

Say your Orthodox name even if the priest knows it. The reason for this is twofold. First, baptism was your entrance into the life of Christ, and Holy Communion is your sustenance in that life. You present yourself to the Lord at Holy Communion by using your baptismal name.

The second reason is a practical one. Priests forget names, especially when someone's legal name and Orthodox Christian name are not the same. Also, priests have minds that wander. I remember many years ago, a parishioner was suffering from cancer. He came up and received Holy Communion and said to me immediately after receiving, "The doctor says I have only days to live. Please come see me this week." People aren't supposed to make comments to the priest at Holy Communion, and his comment stunned me, as I was hoping he would live a little longer. We were friends, and I started thinking about what he said and what he meant to me. I started crying, and I couldn't think about much else in that moment. I've had other days where a parishioner died early on a Sunday morning, and I was wrapped up in the emotion of that. On behalf of my brother priests, please say your name, even if we know it. It is your presentation of yourself to the Lord and also a practical help for us.

Open your mouth wide and allow the priest to put the spoon in your mouth. Close your mouth on the spoon. Here is where some people get a little nervous. Can't disease be communicated through Holy Communion? The answer is no. This is the Body and Blood of Christ. There is no evidence of anyone getting sick from receiving Communion. After the Divine Liturgy, every priest or deacon consumes the remainder of the Holy Communion. That means that after putting the spoon in the chalice multiple times on a Sunday, the a member of the clergy consumes everything that's left over. If hundreds of people have received Holy Communion, the odds are very high that someone present was sick. If Communion could spread disease, all the priests would be sick all the time.

After you receive Holy Communion, wipe your mouth with the cloth and make the sign of the cross as you walk away from the chalice. Take a piece of antidoron (blessed bread) and eat it. The purpose of the antidoron is to "break your fast" with a bit of food and also to make sure none of the Eucharist remains in your mouth. If you receive Holy Communion and then sneeze, perhaps a particle would come out of your mouth. Consuming a piece of the antidoron assures that none of the Holy Communion is left in your mouth.

The formula that the priest uses as he distributes Holy Communion is the same for each person who receives.

The servant/handmaid of God. We are all identified in the same way, as servants of God. (*Your name.*) The only thing that distinguishes us from one another in receiving Holy Communion is our names. The priest doesn't offer any other qualification or distinction. He doesn't say, "Eleni the mom," or "Thomas the doctor," or "George the college graduate." Only our name. The only exception occurs when a priest receives from another priest. The priest distributing Holy Communion says, "George the priest." When the priest receives on his own, he says, "Unto me, *[Name]*, the unworthy presbyter, is imparted the precious and all-holy Body of our Lord and God and Savior, Jesus Christ, for the remission of my sins and life eternal." When Holy Communion is offered to the priest's wife, whom we honor with a title (Presbytera for the Greeks, Matushka for the Russians, Khouria for the Antiochians, etc.), the priest will say, "The servant of God, Elizabeth, *[Title]*, partakes of the Body and Blood of Christ."

For remission of sins and life eternal. The purpose for receiving Holy Communion is twofold. We receive as part of our continual repentance of our sins. Christ, through His Body and Blood, wipes out our sins. Holy Communion is also supposed to help us prepare for eternal life. Again, these two concepts are very hard to grasp. So, first we "do" church by learning the appropriate mechanics of receiving and also worshiping at the Divine Liturgy. As we grow, eventually we learn to "be" the church, living a life in Christ of continual repentance and continual looking toward our salvation. Holy Communion is the chief aid to these practices in our Christian life.

After receiving Holy Communion, as the priest finishes, "for remission of sins and life eternal," this prayer ends as all prayers do, with the word "Amen." And even though the priest usually says this word, all those who receive should say it, because "Amen" means "Let it be so." If the priest has prayed for you to have "remission of sins and life eternal," you should respond with an "Amen," praying to God for this to be so.

> May Your holy Body, O Lord Jesus Christ, our God, be to me for life eternal, and Your precious Blood for remission of sins. And may this Eucharist be to me for joy, health, and gladness. And at Your awesome Second Coming, deem me, the sinner, worthy to stand at the right hand of Your glory,

through the intercessions of You all-pure Mother and all Your saints. Amen.[47]

Save, O God, Your people and bless Your inheritance.

> On that day the LORD their God will save them for they are the flock of his people; for like jewels of a crown they shall shine on his land.
>
> —Zechariah 9:16

Having prayed for each person to be granted "remission of sins and eternal life," the priest covers the holy chalice and collectively blesses the congregation, asking God to save all His people and bless all those who have inherited the Faith. He then returns to the altar table and sets down the chalice. If he didn't transfer the particles of bread for the Virgin Mary, the saints, the Church Militant, and the Church Triumphant before distributing Holy Communion, he does so at this point.

This prayer, "Save, O God, Your people" should be heard with great joy. Through the Eucharist, we are blessed in this life and move one step closer to being saved for eternal life.

What do I mean "one step closer"? Are we not already saved? In many churches, people are taught that we have already been saved by the death and Resurrection of Christ. If this is so, then what is the work of the Church? Why participate in the life of the Church if salvation has already been achieved?

47 From the thanksgiving prayers after Holy Communion.

In the Orthodox Church, we believe that our salvation is possible because of the death and Resurrection of Christ. Without His saving work, no one can attain salvation. However, salvation is a gift that is given by the Lord to those whom He deems worthy, based on their faith and works and ultimately His grace. Jesus says, "But he who endures to the end will be saved" (Matt. 10:22; Mark 13:13), and in Matthew 16:27, "For the Son of man is to come with his angels in the glory of his Father, and then he will repay every man for what he has done."

Thus, salvation is a process, not something that happens in one moment in time, and it is a combination of faith (what we believe), works (how we act on our belief), and grace (a gift from God). It is then correct to say, *I have the potential to be saved, and I am working my way toward salvation each day*. It is a continuous action.

One practical way to think of salvation is to relate it to marriage. If someone asks me, "Are you married?" the answer is yes. However, marriage is a continuous action. I was married on a specific day, I am married today, and I hope to be married tomorrow. And because I hope to be married tomorrow, I am working on my marriage today in an ever-growing and deepening relationship with my wife.

In terms of our salvation, we have the potential to be saved because of the death and Resurrection of Christ. We begin our journey the day we are baptized. We work on salvation today. And we hope to be saved for eternal life. And because we hope to be saved for eternity, we work on our salvation today, obeying Christ's commandments and knowing Him more deeply.

A second practical way to look at our salvation is to use a cup, some rocks, and water to illustrate the process of faith, works, and grace that we need to inherit eternal life. The cup represents faith—what we believe. An empty cup, while providing a vessel in which to hold something, is just an empty cup and has little value.

The rocks represent works. If we have works without faith, it is like spilling out rocks on a table. They have no order to them. A cup filled with rocks represents the life of faith, manifested in good works.

Now, if you try this experiment at home, fill a cup with rocks, and you will see that the cup is not full. There are still empty spaces. Pour water into the cup and fill it to the top, and then the cup is truly full; there is no more room. The water represents God's grace, poured out a spoonful at a time in Holy Communion. The goal of our life is to have our cup filled when we go before the awesome judgment seat of Christ. So, we need a strong faith, a good cup. And we need lots of good works, or rocks, to fill the cup. But no matter how strong our faith or how filled our cup is, we need the water of God's grace. We don't receive grace in one shot for our whole life. Because if I receive all the grace I'm going to receive in my life today, what happens a year from now when I am spiritually infirm and incomplete? We need grace continually, and through Holy Communion we can be filled on an ongoing basis so that at the end of life, we find our cup filled and running over with God's love and grace, prepared to be with Him for eternal life.

> O Master Christ, our God, King of the ages and creator of all, I thank You for all the good things You have granted me and for the Communion of Your pure and life-giving Mysteries. I beseech, You, therefore, O Good One who loves mankind, keep me under Your protection and in the shadow of Your wings; and grant that, with a clear conscience and until my final breath, I may worthily partake of Your Holy Gifts for the remission of my sins and for life eternal. For You are the bread of life, the well-spring of holiness, and the giver of all that is good, and to You we ascribe glory, with the Father

and the Holy Spirit, now and forever, and to the ages of ages. Amen. (Prayer of St. Basil the Great, from the thanksgiving after Holy Communion.)

We have seen the true Light; we have received the heavenly Spirit; we have found the true faith, worshiping the undivided Trinity, for the Trinity has saved us.

> Then they told what had happened on the road, and how he was known to them in the breaking of the bread.
>
> —Luke 24:35

If receiving Holy Communion is the high point of the Divine Liturgy, then one might think of the remainder of the service as a quiet epilogue to this main event. In modern parishes, where a long line for Holy Communion disrupts the flow of the service, the end of the Divine Liturgy feels almost like a gasp of relief.[48]

The better way to see the ending of the service is to compare it to the end of a fireworks show. Fireworks shows start with a bang and then ebb and flow in energy until the grand finale, where many fireworks are shot off in rapid succession, filling the sky with color until their sudden yet triumphal ending. I try to remember this when celebrating the end of the Divine Liturgy. We are, in fact, still celebrating, not just slinking to the finish line.

48 I'm not criticizing the length of the Communion line. I'm just making the point that an energetic service filled with prayerful exclamations by the priest and joyful responses by the choir and the people can be transformed into what seems to be an endless wait for the distribution of Holy Communion.

The epilogue to the service begins with the hymn of triumph above. Read the words a couple of times: "We have seen the true Light; we have received the heavenly Spirit; we have found the true faith, worshiping the undivided Trinity, for the Trinity has saved us." We should sing this hymn with the same excitement we would have in saying, "I just got promoted!" or "I'm getting married!" or "I just won the lottery!" The words should be *exclaimed*.

Read each statement that follows, slowly and with conviction:

- We have just received Holy Communion; we have beheld with our own eyes the Body and Blood of Christ!
- We have touched God!
- God has come into us!
- We have received the Holy Spirit! We have again received grace and mercy and an infusion of all His Gifts.
- We have found the true Faith! This means that our life not only has focus, but it has purpose and meaning. We are one step closer to the Kingdom of heaven!
- We have worshipped the Trinity! We have relived the journey to salvation. We have worshipped the Uncreated God. We have prayed for the entirety of God's creation.
- We have acknowledged sins and shortcomings, the consequences of the Fall.
- We have relived the life of Christ, heard from the Scripture, reaffirmed faith in the Creed, and partaken both of the Last Supper and Pentecost.
- The Holy Trinity, individually and collectively, has blessed us and has led us one step closer to our salvation.

The biblical quote above refers to the experience of two disciples, one named Cleopas and the other unnamed, who were on the road to Emmaus on the afternoon after the Resurrection. This story is told in Luke 24:13–35. The two disciples were talking about all the things that had happened. Jesus approached them, but they didn't recognize Him. The disciples were sad as they talked about Jesus, their friend, who had died. Jesus played ignorant, asking them questions about what happened. After the disciples explained their confusion in understanding the meaning of the empty Tomb, Jesus "interpreted to them in all the scriptures the things concerning himself" (24:27).

The two disciples, still not knowing that the stranger was Jesus, asked Him to stay the evening with them. "When he was at table with them, he took the bread and blessed, and broke it, and gave it to them. And their eyes were opened and they recognized him; and he vanished out of their sight" (24:30–31). Then they returned to Jerusalem and told the other disciples that they had seen the Lord and "how he was known to them in the breaking of the bread" (24:35).

By the grace of the Holy Spirit, we also come to know Christ in a deeper way in "the breaking of the bread"—Holy Communion. In receiving Holy Communion, we see the true light, we receive again the grace of the Holy Spirit, and we deepen our faith. Our eyes are opened, and hopefully our hearts as well, not only to a deeper understanding of the Faith but a deeper commitment to living the Faith. This is yet another reason to receive Holy Communion.

During the Divine Liturgy, after a long wait for Holy Communion on Sundays, this hymn is sometimes not sung with the proper joy and gusto. It can sound worn and tired, like "We have just stood through a long line for Holy Communion and are relieved that it's over." But this hymn, perhaps above all others, should be almost shouted with joy for the great gift that God has given us.

> O Christ, the true light which illumines and sanctifies every man who comes into the world, let the light of Your

countenance be shown upon us, that in it we may behold the Light ineffable; and guide our footsteps aright, to the keeping of Your commandments; through the intercessions of Your all pure Mother and of all Your saints. Amen. (Prayer of the First Hour)[49]

Always, now and forever and to the ages of ages.

> Now the eleven disciples went to Galilee, to the mountain to which Jesus had directed them. And when they saw him they worshipped him; but some doubted. And Jesus came and said to them "All authority in heaven and on earth has been given to me. Go therefore and make disciples of all nations, baptizing them in the name of the Father and of the Son and of the Holy Spirit, teaching them to observe all that I have commanded you; and lo, I am with you always, to the close of the age."
>
> —Matthew 28:16–20

As the people sing, "We have seen the true Light," the priest, carrying the chalice, reenters the altar and sets it down on the altar table. If he hasn't already transferred the particles of the Virgin Mary, saints, Church Militant, and Church Triumphant into the chalice before distributing Holy Communion, he will do so at this point. He then takes up the censer and censes the Gifts, offering the words of Psalm 56/57:5, "Be exalted, O God above the heavens! Let Your glory be over all the earth!" He offers this prayer three times.

49 From *Greek Orthodox Holy Week and Easter Services*, trans. Fr. George Papadeas (South Daytona, FL: Patmos Press, 1996).

This verse of Scripture makes for a beautiful prayer in itself. Imagine offering this prayer each morning several times—before a meeting or before driving:

- *Be exalted, O God, above the heavens. Let Your glory be over all my day.*
- *Be exalted, O God, above the heavens. Let Your glory be over my commute to work.*
- *Be exalted, O God, above the heavens. Let Your glory be over my marriage.*
- *Be exalted, O God, above the heavens. Let Your glory be over my children.*
- *Be exalted, O God, above the heavens. Let Your glory be over this meeting.*

The possibilities are many.

The priest next offers the words that begin each service (aside from the Divine Liturgy), "Blessed is our God, always, now and forever, and to the ages of ages." However, we are nearing the end of the service, so the emphasis here will be on the last half of this phrase. "Blessed is our God" is offered silently, and the priest then turns toward the people, and holding the chalice aloft exclaims, "Always, now and forever and to the ages of ages."

There are two meanings to raising the chalice. The first is that it represents the Ascension of Christ. Holy Communion is our preparation for our personal resurrection in Christ, so before we leave the church we, like the disciples, experience a "post-Resurrection" appearance of Christ—this final viewing of the Holy Gifts, representing the Resurrection. As we approach the Divine Liturgy's end, we are nearing the end of our re-creation of the life of Christ, and we will be commissioned again to go out into the world and spread the Gospel. And so we hear the last verse of the Great Commission from Matthew 28:16–20, that Christ is with us always, to the close of the age.

The second meaning of the raised chalice is in the words "Always, now and forever." The climax of our lives should be receiving Holy Communion. After all, what could bring greater joy? Now that we have received Holy Communion, we are faced with the prospect of reentering the stressful world. Our experience of entering heaven in worship is about to end. That's kind of a depressing thought.

But the Church doesn't want us to leave the service sad, any more than Christ wanted the disciples to mourn after His Ascension. Jesus reassured His disciples that He would be with them always, even to the close of the age. In the Divine Liturgy, we hear these words as well. Christ is with us not only in the church, not only in receiving Holy Communion, but now that we have been fortified by worship and the Eucharist, He will go with us as we exit the church. He will be with us at work, on the road, in our families, in our relationships, in our triumphs, and in our struggles. He is with us always.

Imagine for a moment this image. You stand in front of a door. Christ is on the other side of the door, knocking on it.[50] The door has only has one knob, and it is on your side. Christ is *always* present, knocking on the door of our hearts, wanting to come in. He does not, however, force His way in. It is up to us to invite Him. As I think of this line, "Always, now and forever," I recall that Christ is ever present with me. And then I have to assess honestly, *Am I always present with Him?* These words should serve both as an affirmation that Christ is always with us and a statement of recommitment on our

50 There are multiple versions of this painting, including the most popular "Christ at the Heart's Door" by Warner Sallman (1892–1968).

part, that we will strive to walk with Him, that we will invite Him into our hearts, "always, now and forever," beginning with this day.

> Let our mouths be filled with Your praise, O Lord, that we may sing of Your glory, because You have made us worthy to partake of Your Holy Mysteries. Keep us in Your sanctification, that all day long we may meditate upon Your righteousness. Alleluia. Alleluia. Alleluia.[51]

51 This hymn is sung in certain parishes and monasteries following the exclamation "Always, now and forever."

The Dismissal

Arise! Having partaken of the divine, holy, pure, immortal, heavenly, life-creating, and awesome Mysteries of Christ, let us worthily give thanks to the Lord.

> His divine power has granted to us all things that pertain to life and godliness, through the knowledge of him who called us to his own glory and excellence, by which he has granted to us his precious and very great promises, that through these you may escape from the corruption that is in the world because of passion, and become partakers of the divine nature. For this very reason make every effort to supplement your faith with virtue, and virtue with knowledge, and knowledge with self-control, and self-control with steadfastness, and steadfastness with godliness, and godliness with brotherly affection, and brotherly affection with love.
>
> —2 Peter 1:3–7

As I've written previously, certain lines of the Divine Liturgy light the afterburners of my soul, and this line is one of them. After distributing Holy Communion for a long time on Sundays, as a priest I face the temptation to fly through this petition and the ones that follow. The congregation probably is tempted also to tune out these petitions. Both are mistakes. These words are *very* important.

In fact, the petition begins with a command unlike the others in any service. First we are reminded, "Arise," which means, "Pay attention; something very important is following."

We have partaken of Holy Communion, which is "divine, holy, pure, immortal, heavenly, life-creating, and awesome." How amazing is that? That in one moment we have touched the Divine Christ Himself! That we have received a measure of holiness! That we have received a dose of purity! That we have been allowed to experience a foretaste of the heavenly Kingdom! That by partaking of Christ in this life, we are more prepared for the eternal life because Communion is "life-creating."

Having done all of this, what should be our response? We are called to give thanks in a manner that is "worthy" of the Gifts we have just received. Are we going to go back to business as usual after the service? Will we be forgiving, or will we hold grudges? Will we try for spiritual growth or be complacent? Will we be filled with joy and hope or negativity and cynicism? Having partaken of the Divine Christ, will we offer thanks worthy of this great gift?

This petition is a powerful reminder. It reminds us that receiving Holy Communion is not an ending but a new beginning. We worship on Sunday, the first day of the week, to make a new beginning with Christ in the new week. Before Christ's Resurrection, the day of worship was the Sabbath, or Saturday. It was the practice of the Jews to work all week and then rest and worship. But after Jesus rose from the dead, the day for worship became the day of the Resurrection, the first day of the week. In America, we call this day Sunday. In Greek, the word is *Kyriaki,* which means "the day of the Lord." So, we are to begin (rather than end) each week with a day dedicated to the Lord, to set in proper motion the rest of the week.

Holy Communion is an opportunity not only to partake in the future but to recenter and refocus ourselves in the present. This petition reminds us that as we are about to exit the church—on Sunday or any other day when the Divine Liturgy is offered—Holy Communion has provided us an opportunity for a new beginning.

This petition also reminds us that when we receive a gift, there is an implicit requirement of a response. We say "Thank you" to the giver of the gift. And not only do we give thanks, we honor the giver of the gift. We don't accept a gift from someone and then go and insult them or harm them.

Having received this gift from God, as we finish the journey of the Divine Liturgy, we need to evaluate how we are going to honor God in thanksgiving. Fill in the rest of this sentence:

> *Having partaken of the divine, holy, pure, immortal, heavenly, life-creating, and awesome Mysteries of Christ, I will worthily give thanks by* ____________________.

Now, if our answer is "Nothing" or "I'm not going to change anything" or "I already have plans to do something ungodly this afternoon or this week," we are not offering "worthy thanks" to the Lord.

Every time we receive Holy Communion, we should plan to glorify and thank God in some way, as this petition reminds us. After receiving the "divine, holy, pure, immortal, heavenly, life-creating, and awesome Mysteries of Christ," let us plan each time for something that constitutes worthy thanks.

Help us, save us, have mercy on us, and protect us, O God, by Your grace.

> Do thou, O Lord, protect us, guard us ever from this generation.
>
> —Psalm 12:7

If you filled in the blank as I suggested in the last reflection on how you plan to give worthy thanks to the Lord, you will need more than just words. You'll need some inner resolve. And you will need some help from God.

I once heard a story about a monastery located just outside a large city. One of the monks asked his abbot if he could go into the city for a day in order to find some demons. His abbot gave him leave. So the monk went into the city and looked everywhere, trying to find a demon. He searched the streets, the stores, and the crowds of people. He couldn't find even one. Finally he saw one demon sleeping under a tree in the park.

So the monk walked back to the monastery. As he neared the monastery entrance, he saw hundreds of demons climbing up the walls, into the windows, and on the gates. He said to the abbot, "I went all over the large city and found but one demon, and he was sleeping under a tree. Then I came back to our small monastery, where we are a few monks praying together, and the demons are all over here." The abbot replied, "In the big city, where the people are distracted and there is so much to do, the demons have no work to do. But here, in the small monastery, where we try to live a life of prayer, they attack us relentlessly."

As for us, after we have "partaken of the divine, holy, pure, immortal, heavenly, life-creating, and awesome Mysteries of Christ," we don't encounter an army of angels waiting outside the church to celebrate with us or to be happy for us. Quite the opposite. It is the devil who is not happy that we came to church, who does not want us to give thanks to God, and who doesn't want the experience of worship to change us for the good. He lurks outside in subtle ways, ever seeking to distract and disturb our hearts and our lives.

Therefore, immediately after calling on us to "worthily give thanks to the Lord," the very next line of the Divine Liturgy calls upon the Lord to "Help us, save us, have mercy on us, and protect us" by the grace that comes only from Him. The Church knows—and God knows—that it is hard to be a Christian. It is hard to maintain the momentum and good feelings that we get from worship. So, we offer a petition that we have already offered several times in the service. And now following Holy Communion, having received His grace and the gift of the Holy Spirit, we ask for God's protection and help to maintain what we have prayed for and received until we gather again.

From a practical perspective, as you hear this petition again for God to "help us, save us, and have mercy on us," don't gloss over it or tune it out because it is repetitive. After making your plan to "worthily give thanks to the Lord," ask God to help, safeguard, and protect your work toward this plan. Additionally, now that we have received His mercies, we can pray this throughout the week, long after the service has ended. Because we are in a continuous state of preparing for Holy Communion or thanking God for this gift, we should be continuously asking for His help, safekeeping, mercy, and protection to preserve our faith and to grow it.

> Lord, Master, the Father of mercies and God of every consolation, bless, sanctify, guard, fortify, and strengthen those who have bowed their heads to You. Distance them from every evil deed. Lead them to every good work and make them worthy to partake without condemnation of these, Your most pure and life-giving Mysteries, for the forgiveness of sins and for the communion of the Holy Spirit. By the grace, mercy, and love for us of Your only begotten Son, with whom You are blessed, together with Your all holy, good, and life-giving Spirit, now and forever and to the ages of ages. Amen. (From the *Divine Liturgy of St. Basil the Great*)

Having prayed for a perfect, holy, peaceful, and sinless day, let us commend ourselves, and one another, and our whole life to Christ our God. To You, O Lord.

> Then [Jesus'] mother and his brothers came to him, but they could not reach him for the crowd. And he was told "Your mother and your brothers are standing outside, desiring to see you." But he said to them, "My mother and my brothers are those who hear the word of God and do it."
>
> —Luke 8:19–21

We have journeyed through the Divine Liturgy and partaken of Holy Communion, and now we end with petitions that tell us what to do once the service has finished. Being an Orthodox Christian is not something that we compartmentalize into an hour or so on Sundays and a few other days at the Divine Liturgy. Rather, the Divine Liturgy serves to reeducate and remind us what the Christian life is all about. It reconciles us to God and to one another. It encourages and comforts us. And as it is about to end, it calls us to action: "to commend ourselves, and one another, and our whole life to Christ our God." We have heard this phrase multiple times in the Liturgy, and this is the final repetition. Its repeated use reminds us that the Orthodox Christian life is indeed a part of our everyday experience. It is not enough to commend ourselves and one another and "one hour on Sundays" to Christ our God. Instead, we commend our whole life—every day—to loving Him and to loving and serving one another.

This last petition is a challenge for us to go and be what we've been praying for: to be a peacemaker, to make decisions based on what is good for our soul and on what promotes peace in the world, to love one another, to give thanks to the Lord, to live our life in peace and repentance, and so much more.

When we compartmentalize our Christian faith to the one hour of the Divine Liturgy on Sunday, our participation in the life of the Church is a formal, check-the-box type of activity. When we limit our prayer life to the service and our study of Scripture to the Sunday Gospel, we are compartmentalizing them as well. Prayer and reading of Scripture should be daily habits. Living the Christian life of loving God and loving neighbor should happen on a daily basis as well.

The verse of Scripture quoted above reminds us that it is not enough merely to hear the Word of God. We are supposed to do something with what we've heard. We're supposed to love, to forgive, to help, to learn, to serve, and so many other things. And we are to encourage one another to be committed Christians. In loving our neighbor, we look out not only for the welfare of our neighbor but for our neighbor's Christian life as well.

> I thank You, O Lord my God, for You have not rejected me, a sinner, but have deemed me worthy to be a partaker of Your Holy Gifts. I thank You that You deemed me worthy, unworthy as I am, to partake of Your pure and heavenly Gifts. O Master, who loves mankind, who for us both died and arose and who granted us these, Your dread and life-creating Mysteries, for the benefit and sanctification of our souls and bodies: Grant that these may be to me for the healing of both soul and body, for the averting of everything hostile, for the enlightenment of the eyes of my heart, for the peace of the powers of my soul, for faith unashamed, for love unfeigned, for the fullness of wisdom, for the observance of Your commandments, for an increase of your divine grace, and for abiding in Your Kingdom; that being kept by them in Your holiness I may ever be mindful of Your grace, and no longer live for myself but for You, our Master and benefactor. And thus, when from

this life I have passed in the hope of life eternal, may I attain to everlasting rest, where the sound of those who celebrate is unceasing, and unending is the delight of those who behold the ineffable beauty of Your Countenance. For You are, indeed, the true object of our desire and the inexpressible gladness of those who love You, O Christ our God, and all creation praises You unto the ages. Amen.[52]

Thanksgiving Prayers for the Divine Thanksgiving

We give thanks to You, Master who loves mankind, benefactor of our souls, that even on this very day You have made us worthy of Your heavenly and immortal Mysteries. Make straight our path, fortify us in Your fear, guard our life, make secure our steps, through the prayers and supplications of the glorious Theotokos and ever-virgin Mary and of all Your saints.

Thanks be to God for his inexpressible Gift!

—2 Corinthians 9:15

Several reflections ago, we discussed prayers that are to be offered prior to receiving Holy Communion. Some of these prayers appear in virtually every edition of the Divine Liturgy in print. Many people, however, are unaware of the prayers of thanksgiving after Holy Communion. That is because they are not always printed in the Divine Liturgy books, and in some instances they are placed in

52 From the thanksgiving prayers after Holy Communion.

the back, after the main text. The other reason people are unaware of their existence is that no specific time is set aside in the Liturgy for offering these prayers.[53]

One of the prayers of thanksgiving after Holy Communion is offered by the priest inaudibly during the petitions that follow. In many churches where the priest serves alone, he may offer this prayer after he has received Holy Communion.

In parishes where the line for Holy Communion is long, if you are one of the first to receive, try going back to your pew and offering the prayers of thanksgiving. If not at that point, offer them while you are waiting for antidoron. Or purchase a copy of the Divine Liturgy book and offer the prayers in front of your icons when you arrive home.

Because the encounter with Christ in Holy Communion is a personal one experienced in a community context, the thanksgiving to Christ following Holy Communion should be a personal one as well. Offering these prayers among other parishioners is fine, and offering them after church is fine as well. But regardless of when or where, we should pause to thank God personally for the gift of the Holy Eucharist.

The prayers of thanksgiving after Holy Communion not only thank God, but they also ask Him, through the aid of the Holy Eucharist, to direct our lives, to keep us on the right path, and to guard our hearts. Through these prayers, the experience of receiving Holy Communion stays in our minds and hearts long after the service is over. If you have any questions about offering prayers before or after receiving the Eucharist, this is something to ask your parish priest, who can point out where to find these prayers and the proper time in which they can be offered.

---

53 In some parishes, these are offered aloud after the conclusion of the Divine Liturgy, as people venerate the cross and receive antidoron.

> We thank You, Lord our God, for the Communion of Your holy, most pure, immortal, and heavenly Mysteries which You have granted us for the benefit, sanctification, and healing of our souls and bodies. Grant, Master of all, that the Communion of the Holy Body and Blood of Your Christ become for us faith unashamed, love unfeigned, fullness of wisdom, healing of soul and body, repelling of every hostile adversary, observance of Your commandments, and an acceptable defense at the dread judgement seat of Your Christ. (From the *Divine Liturgy of St. Basil the Great*)

For You are our sanctification, and to You we give glory, to the Father and to the Son and to the Holy Spirit, now and forever and to the ages of ages. Amen.

> When you were slaves of sin, you were free in regard to righteousness. . . . But now that you have been set free from sin and have become slaves of God, the return you get is sanctification and its end, eternal life. For the wages of sin is death, but the free Gift of God is eternal life in Christ Jesus our Lord.
>
> —Romans 6:20, 22–23

The Blessing of the Waters (*Agiasmos* in Greek) in the Orthodox Church is a special service on the Feast of Theophany (January 6) and at the beginning of events. Water is fundamental to human life. It is the basic building block of the human body, and most of our planet is covered with water. And so we bless it and sprinkle it on ourselves and on our spaces—summer camp, Sunday school classes, and over the whole world at Theophany—as a way to set apart ourselves and places, dedicating them to God.

For example, at the beginning of summer camp, we bless the campers, the cabins, the lake, and all the areas of the camp in a Blessing of the Waters service, claiming (or reclaiming) them for God. This service occurs at the beginning of each session, blessing a new group of campers and blessing again the camp space. We do this to set apart the camp and the campers from worldly things in order to focus on godly things. By sanctifying them, we make a declaration that we wish to be holy, both the participating people and the space we are using.

The Divine Liturgy also reinforces the concept of sanctification as we near the conclusion of the service and prepare to step back into the world. We have consecrated the Gifts and have received them, resanctifying ourselves in the process. Just as we sanctify the summer camp each week, blessing the same place and asking God to descend on it, we are being sanctified each time we receive Holy Communion in the Divine Liturgy. Worship isn't just a weekly routine or some kind of superstition, as if we need to start off the week with a ritual just to make it through. This line in the service is a statement of repurposing ourselves each week as children of God, committed to loving Him and one another.

Saint Paul reminds us in Romans 6:19–23 that although we once yielded ourselves to impurity and iniquity, we should now yield to righteousness in order to be sanctified, because the end point of a life of iniquity and impurity is death. But the end point of a life of sanctification is eternal life. Sanctification is part of the means to that end. The Divine Liturgy reminds us of the end—eternal life—and gives us the means—sanctification through the Holy Eucharist. This exclamation emphasizes, "For You (God) are our sanctification," meaning that *You*, the Lord, are the means to our end as well as our end itself.

It is important for us as Christians to evaluate both our end and our means to it—to reflect on our purpose. If we understand our goal to be everlasting life, then we will set up our lives accordingly. What is our means to achieve that goal? If sanctification is our means, who is it that sanctifies us? Consider the statement, "For ______ are our sanctification." The exclamation of the Liturgy states, "For You (God) are our sanctification," If we are not filling that blank with "God," what are we filling it with? And if we understand that the Lord is our sanctification, then how does our daily life reflect that?

The Church has packed a lot of meaning in these last lines of the Divine Liturgy, reminding us of our purpose, our end, and the means to get there. The Liturgy is not the sole means to everlasting life; we worship in concert with prayer, Scripture reading, evangelism, and charity. But the Divine Liturgy is a regular opportunity for resanctification. And just as we wouldn't begin a week of summer camp without sanctifying ourselves and our space, we should begin each week by resanctifying ourselves through the Divine Liturgy and the receiving of the Holy Eucharist.

In 1 Peter 1:14–16, we read, "As obedient children, do not be conformed to the passions of your former ignorance, but as he who called you is holy, be holy yourselves in all your conduct; since it is written, 'You shall be holy, for I am holy.' The Divine Liturgy is a vital means by which we become holy.

> O Christ, our God, accept from those who call upon You with all their heart this spiritual sacrifice without the shedding of blood as a sacrifice of praise and true worship. You are the Lamb and Son of God who bears the sins of the world; the blameless calf who does not accept the yoke of sin and who freely sacrificed Yourself for us. You are broken but not divided. You are consumed but never spent. You sanctify those who partake of you.

In remembrance of Your voluntary passion and life-giving Resurrection on the third day, You have made us partakers of Your ineffable and heavenly and awesome mysteries of Your holy Body and precious Blood. Preserve us, Your servants, those who minister, our leaders, the armed forces, and the people present here, in Your holiness. Grant that we may meditate upon Your righteousness at all times and in every season. Guide us and our actions so that we may do what is pleasing to You, and may You find us worthy to stand at Your right hand when You return to judge the living and the dead.

Deliver our brothers and sisters who are in captivity, visit those who are sick, protect those who are in danger at sea, and give rest to the souls of all those who have fallen asleep in the hope of the eternal life where the light of Your face shines. Hear the petitions of all those who beseech You for Your help. For You are the giver of all good things, and to You we give glory, together with Your eternal Father and Your all holy, good, and life-giving Spirit, now and forever and to the ages of ages.[54]

Let us go forth in peace. Let us pray to the Lord.

Peace I leave with you; my peace I give to you.

—John 14:27

The journey of the Divine Liturgy is about to come to a close. Only two prayers remain. As we are about to offer the penultimate prayer, we are invited not only with the customary words "Let us pray to the Lord" but with a command, "Let us go forth in peace."

54 From the prayer of the Ambon, offered on January 1 in the *Divine Liturgy of St. Basil the Great,*

Peace is an ongoing theme in the Divine Liturgy. The very first petition calls us to gather in peace to pray to the Lord. The second petition asks "for the peace from above"—for God's peace to descend on us. And the third petition asks "for peace in the whole world," calling on us to be peaceful toward one another.

Peace is so important that three sets of petitions begin with the exclamation "Again and again in peace let us pray to the Lord." We've asked for "a perfect, holy, peaceful, and sinless day" and "for an angel of peace" in our petitions. Before the reading of the Gospel, reciting the Creed, and receiving Holy Communion, we have been blessed with the words "peace be with all," a reminder that we cannot understand Scripture, be people of faith, or become one with Christ if we have no peace.

And so now, as we are about to reenter the world, we are not only reminded but also commanded to "go forth in peace." In fact, in the ancient Divine Liturgy of St. James (which is celebrated now only on his feast day of October 23), the service ends with the words "Go in peace."

The Divine Liturgy and our identity as Christians are not supposed to fit into a compartment on Sunday mornings or feast days. The Divine Liturgy reminds us how to live our lives continually. As we head back into the world, we are to carry peace with us, to return to the world and its stresses with hearts that, by God's grace, are now more at peace than when we entered the church.

The Liturgy reminds us not only to carry peace within our own hearts and souls back into the world but to spread peace to others as well. We are called upon to be peacemakers. Remember the hymn of the angels, heard at the Nativity, which the priest offers prior to the beginning of the Divine Liturgy: "Glory to God in the highest, and on earth peace among men with whom He is pleased!" (Luke 2:14). The hymn says that peace is not something that comes to everyone; it is a gift that God bestows on people "with whom He is pleased." As we go forth from church, we pray that God will bestow this gift on us and that our hearts will be ready to receive His peace throughout the week.

Finally, peace is not an idea but an action. The Divine Liturgy isn't some kind of production that we watch but a work that we participate in, a work of the people—the literal meaning of "Liturgy"—both in church and long after the service is over. Like the call to give "worthy thanks" to the Lord, we are also called upon to be workers for peace. Peace should be part of our everyday lives until the end of our days.

For Every Good and Perfect Gift Is from Above

> O save thy people, and bless thy heritage; / be thou their shepherd, and carry them forever.
>
> —Psalm 27/28:9

> O Lord, I love the habitation of thy house, / and the place where thy glory dwells.
>
> —Psalm 25/26:8

> Every good endowment and every perfect gift is from above, coming down from the Father of lights with whom there is no variation or shadow due to change.
>
> —James 1:17

O Lord, who blesses those who bless You and sanctifies those who put their trust in You, save Your people and bless Your inheritance. Protect the whole body of Your Church. Sanctify those who love the beauty of Your house. Glorify them in return by Your divine power, and forsake us not who have set our hope in You. Grant peace to Your world, to Your churches, to the clergy, to our civic leaders, to the armed forces, and to all Your people. For every good and perfect Gift is from above, coming down from You, the Father of lights. To You we give glory, thanksgiving, and worship, to the Father and to the Son and to the Holy Spirit, now and forever and to the ages of ages. Amen.

Many outside of the Orthodox world criticize our practice of the Faith as being based more in tradition than in Scripture. I hope that these reflections on the Divine Liturgy help readers recognize that virtually every line of the service has some connection to Scripture. What St. Basil and St. John Chrysostom have done is to take pieces of Scripture from both the Old and New Testaments and weave them into a beautiful service whose centerpiece is the Holy Eucharist. The Scriptures are timeless in the sense that the Bible hasn't been changed or added to since it was codified in the fourth century. Similarly, because the Divine Liturgy of St. John Chrysostom leans so much on Scripture, it also has not changed since it was written in the fourth century.

The prayer we are examining today is a beautiful example of liturgical material that is scripturally based. In current practice, the priest offers this prayer before the icon of Christ.

As we are concluding the Divine Liturgy, our thoughts and prayers begin to transition back to the life we will resume once the service has ended. The prayer begins by asking the Lord to bless those who have gathered for the service to praise Him.

It is interesting to note that the word *trust* is used only twice in the Divine Liturgy: here, and very early in the service in an inaudible prayer that quotes the first half of this prayer. Those who put their trust and their faith in the Lord are sanctified; they are made holy. The path to holiness begins with trust and faith. And without trust, we cannot be sanctified.

As we are about to depart from the church, we pray that all God's people be saved and blessed—not only those present but all those we will encounter this week, after the service is over. We pray that the whole body of the Church be protected.

The prayer then becomes more specific, asking for sanctification for those who love the beauty of God's house. Here is a challenge for each of us. Do we love God's house? Will we be back for the next Divine Liturgy? And how will we prepare between now and then?

We ask that they may be glorified by God's divine power. We ask that God remember, and not forsake, all those who came to the service, who have put at least a measure of their hope in Him.

The prayer then returns to the wider society, asking for peace for the whole world, for the churches, for the clergy, for those who serve and protect us, and for everyone.

I have come to believe that if anything is not good, it's not from God. "For every good and perfect Gift is from Above." And if something is good, then it comes from God, because He is the author of everything that is good.

The evil in the world has a human cause; bad things are caused by our own bad decisions and the bad the decisions of others. "Natural" disasters are, in fact, not natural. God didn't create the world to have floods and earthquakes. They are part of our fallen nature. How ironic that when something bad happens, we are quick to blame Him, but when something good happens, we are slow to glorify Him.

God is the author of all that is good, and everyone partakes daily of something good. This is why we continually give Him glory, thanksgiving, and worship.

After offering this prayer, as the people sing the hymn that is the topic of the next reflection, the priest goes to the prothesis, where the chalice and diskos (paten) have been returned, and offers the prayer below. The whole purpose of the Divine Liturgy has now been fulfilled. We came to separate from the world, to praise God, to recommit ourselves, to remember what He did for us, and to commune with Him in the Holy Eucharist. All has now been fulfilled.

> Christ our God, You are the fulfillment of the Law and the Prophets. You have fulfilled the Father's entire plan of salvation. Fill our hearts with joy and gladness always, now and forever and to the ages of ages. Amen.

Blessed be the name of the Lord, from this time forth and to the ages.

> Blessed be the name of the Lord / from this time forth and for evermore!
>
> —Psalm 112/113:2

Today's reflection is yet another example of words that are borrowed directly from the Scriptures, as this last hymn of the Divine Liturgy is a psalm verse. Having offered a prayer to God for thanksgiving and protection, as the priest goes back into the altar the people sing a song of praise to God.

Remember how we began this journey? It began with the words, "Blessed is the Kingdom of the Father and the Son and the Holy Spirit, now and forever and to the ages of ages. Amen." The opening line of the Divine Liturgy is an invitation to participate in the

Kingdom of God revealed not at the Second Coming of Christ, or only after death, but in the here and now. We are invited to enter the Kingdom today.

This last hymn recognizes that the Divine Liturgy is ending. We are about to leave God's Kingdom on earth and return to our normal lives. However, we are to carry the name of the Lord with us. We are to bless and give glory to Him throughout the week until we return again to the Kingdom in the Divine Liturgy. Our goal is to give God glory each and every day, to bless His name as we work our way through this life to everlasting life. The purpose of the Divine Liturgy is to allow us to enter into His Kingdom as often as we attend and to be one with Him in Holy Communion.

This phrase "Blessed is the name of the Lord" is a good yardstick by which to measure ourselves. As we go through our daily activities and make our daily decisions, we should continually ask ourselves, "Is the name of the Lord blessed in what I am doing?"

This hymn is sung three times, and the last time, the word order is changed to "The name of the Lord is blessed, from this time forth and to the ages." It is not an instructional "Blessed be the name of the Lord" but an emphatic "The name of the Lord *is* blessed," as if to say that regardless of how much we might fail or how bad the news might be this week, the name of the Lord will be blessed from this time forward.

Today's prayer comes from the Divine Liturgy of St. Basil the Great. It is the prayer that the priest offers before the prothesis during this hymn. As with the prayer in the last reflection, it speaks to the completion of our work. It mentions the mystery of what Christ did for us and how we have offered the Divine Liturgy in the best way that we can, recognizing that none of our worship can approach the perfection of Christ. And we pray now that He will go with us, now and forever—meaning this week, until the next Divine Liturgy, and until we are perfected in His Kingdom.

> The mystery of Your dispensation, O Christ our God, has been accomplished and perfected as far as it is in our power. We have had the memorial of Your death. We have seen the *typos* of Your Resurrection. We have been filled with Your unending life. We have enjoyed Your inexhaustible delight which in the world to come be well pleased to give to us all, through the grace of Your holy and good and life-giving Spirit, now and forever and to the ages of ages. (From the *Divine Liturgy of St. Basil the Great*)

Let us pray to the Lord.

Lord, have mercy. Father give the blessing.

May the blessing of the Lord and His mercy come upon you through His divine grace and love for mankind, now and forever and to the ages of ages. Amen.

> The LORD bless you and keep you: The LORD make his face to shine upon you, and be gracious to you: The LORD lift up his countenance upon you, and give you peace.
>
> —Numbers 6:24–26

The next part of the Divine Liturgy is called the Dismissal, but I would like to note that any extra services—a memorial service, the Blessing of the Five Loaves, the procession of the Holy Cross, the procession of the icons on Sunday of Orthodoxy, and other services—take place at this point of the Divine Liturgy. They are not part of the Divine Liturgy, but when appropriate, they are appended to the service at the end. And when there is no such service, the Divine Liturgy continues.

As we end the service with a blessing, recall that the Divine Liturgy began with the words "Blessed is the Kingdom . . . now and forever." The intention of the Liturgy is to bring us into the Kingdom of God in the here and now, allowing us a break from our stressful lives in order to experience His Kingdom. With the service now drawing to a close and with the worshippers now preparing to leave the Kingdom and reenter the world, the priest prays that the Lord's blessings will come upon the people who have offered the service. And not only blessings but also mercy, a type of healing that comes from God, giving to us blessings we do not deserve.

God's blessings come upon us in many ways. This line reminds us of two of them. We receive God's grace and mercies through the love that God had when He created the world, when He sent Jesus Christ to die for our sins and to redeem the world from its fallen state. And we receive His grace when He sends the Holy Spirit to us each time we call upon Him to consecrate the Gifts we have offered.

Not only is the Kingdom of God blessed, both now and forever, but also we who have entered the Kingdom by coming to the Divine Liturgy receive a blessing. We carry that blessing out into the world and into our daily lives.

Many people, in my opinion, underuse the word "blessed." When we look at life through a lens of negativity, we tend to think that others are blessed more than us. Have you ever paused to think, *I am truly blessed because I have been blessed by God?* I wonder how many of us think that, because I realize that I don't pause and think about this. Many times I compare my blessings to what I perceive to be the greater blessings of others, rather than thanking God for the unique blessings that He has given to me.

I am blessed to be alive. I am blessed to have a family. I am blessed to have a home. I am blessed to have friends, to have a job, to have a car to drive. Many times, we think that others have a better family or a better home or a better job or a better car. Rather than compare, I try to thank God for what I have, recognizing that every good thing or situation that I have is a blessing from Him.

Remembering the Church Triumphant as We Take Our Place in the Church Militant

Glory to You, O God, our hope, glory to You.

May *[He who rose from the dead]* Christ our true God, through the intercessions of His all-pure and all-immaculate holy Mother; the power of the precious and life-giving Cross; the protection of the honorable, bodiless powers of heaven; the supplications of the honorable, glorious prophet and forerunner John the Baptist; of the holy, glorious, and praiseworthy apostles; of the holy, glorious, and triumphant martyrs; of our righteous and God-bearing fathers; of *[name of the saint of the church]*; of our father among the saints John Chrysostom, archbishop of Constantinople; of the holy and righteous ancestors of God Joachim and Anna; of *[saint of the day]*, whose memory we celebrate today; and of all the saints; have mercy on us and save us, for He is good and loves mankind.

> And he who searches the hearts of men knows what is the mind of the Spirit, because the Spirit intercedes for the saints according to the will of God.
>
> —Romans 8:27

We have spoken throughout these reflections about the connection between the Church Militant and the Church Triumphant. In fact, one of the reasons that we gather to worship in a church sanctuary is to be reminded through the icons on the walls that we are worshiping together with the saints and the angels. As we are about to leave the church, we are reminded that we do not head back into the world alone. The saints and the angels are continually interceding for us.

This part of the Divine Liturgy is called the Dismissal or, in Greek, *Apolysis,* which is a part of every divine service in the Orthodox Church. It is given for the same purpose: for us to know that we are not alone.

The Dismissal prayer at the end of the Divine Liturgy begins with the words "May Christ our true God." On Sundays and during the paschal season, the phrase "who rose from the dead" is added. On major feast days, other phrases are used instead, such as "who was born in a cave and lay in a manger for our salvation" (at the Nativity) or "who was transfigured in glory on Mount Tabor in the presence of His disciples and apostles for our salvation" (at the Transfiguration) or "who was baptized by John in the Jordan River for our salvation" (at Theophany).

Next, the intercessions of the Virgin Mary are always invoked, as she is the mother of our Lord, our Church, and all of us. She is always interceding for us. We mention the "power of the precious and life-giving Cross," which is our guide and our hope throughout our lives. The sacrifice of Christ on the Cross guides us to the meaning of love, sacrifice, forgiveness, and faith. The Cross leads to the Resurrection, which opens again the door to Paradise, our ultimate destination and hope. We ask for the protection of the angels when we mention "the honorable, bodiless powers of heaven." Next we ask for the intercession of the saints, beginning with St. John the Baptist and including the apostles, the martyrs, and the ascetic fathers. We also invoke the intercessions of Joachim and Anna, the parents of the Virgin Mary, as well as the patron saint of the parish where we are worshiping.

When the Divine Liturgy is celebrated, we always commemorate St. John Chrysostom, St. Basil the Great, or St. James, the authors of the Divine Liturgies. We also commemorate the saint whose feast is celebrated on the particular day that the service is being offered. For instance, on January 17, we would add, "of the Venerable Anthony the Great, whose memory we commemorate today." And the last phrase is "and of all the saints," emphasizing that we will receive the intercessions of thousands upon thousands of known saints and the untold number of unknown saints.

It is amazing to think that a person can enter one church and be surrounded by an infinite expression of holiness through the intercessions of holy people. And equally as amazing is that all these holy people can make intercessions for a single person—that we, in our lowly and sinful state, are still blessed by the intercessions of God's saints.

Before Holy Communion we are reminded of "the Holy Gifts for the holy people of God." The Apolysis reminds us one last time that our purpose in life is to be numbered among these holy people, to find our salvation in God's Kingdom, and to prepare for this by living holy lives, following the example of the saints we are commemorating.

Lord, protect for many years the one who blesses and sanctifies us.

> Pray at all times in the Spirit, with all prayer and supplication. To that end keep alert with all perseverance, making supplication for all the saints, and also for me, that utterance may be given me in opening my mouth boldly to proclaim the mystery

of the gospel, for which I am an ambassador in chains; that I may declare it boldly, as I ought to speak.

—Ephesians 6:18–20

In his letter to the Ephesians, St. Paul asked for this early church community to pray for him. He was in prison at the time. Yet he still made the effort to write and to lead. He didn't ask for prayers for deliverance, or health, or joy. Rather, he asked for prayers to be a good ambassador for Christ, to be able to proclaim the mystery of the gospel in a way that would edify the people.

Throughout the course of the Divine Liturgy, the priest has offered prayers on behalf of the people in the congregation. His role is as the celebrant of the service. Or perhaps more accurately stated, he serves as God's vessel to offer the service of which Christ Himself is the celebrant.

As the priest offers the Dismissal prayer of the Divine Liturgy, in some parishes the people of the congregation sing a brief hymn, asking the Lord to grant long life to the one who has offered the Divine Liturgy.

Allow me to share a few personal thoughts as I reflect on why this prayer in the Divine Liturgy is important. Someone once asked me to describe the priesthood to them. I said that the priesthood is at the same time one of my life's greatest blessings and its greatest struggle. It has offered to me some of the highest highs in life and some of the lowest lows imaginable, and sometimes both occur on the same day.

There can't be too many joys in the world greater than holding the Light of Christ on Pascha and singing "Come, receive the Light." Kneeling before the holy altar and consecrating the Gifts, offering with my own mouth the sacred prayers of the Divine Liturgy, celebrating the wedding of two friends, conducting the funeral of my own father, hearing confessions and watching people be loosed of their burden of sin—these are blessings so great that it is nearly impossible to describe the feelings of ecstasy that accompany them.

On the other side, there are the difficult days, like burying children—something I have done far too many times. People bring tough problems to me—marriage struggles, loss of faith in God, lack of self-confidence, life setbacks, divorce, job loss, serious medical issues, and spiritual sicknesses. Seeing many people in their greatest sorrows and trying to bring meaning to their difficult circumstances is hard, humbling, and impossible to describe adequately.

Perhaps the worst experiences as a priest are the feelings of betrayal. When parishioners, friends, and even fellow clergy turn on me, when they gossip and criticize seemingly without ceasing, when I have to make a choice between helping someone and hurting someone, sometimes it all gets to be too much. I just can't please everyone.

The other feeling that I never considered before I was ordained was the profound sense of loneliness that a priest feels at times. I remember a funeral I celebrated with nearly one thousand people in attendance, many of them close friends. The deceased was a good friend, as were all the members of her family. Despite being surrounded by friends and the emotions they brought to the service, I still felt a profound sense of loneliness as the only priest. I remember looking down the aisle as the front door of the church opened. Instantly, the light from outside came in and backlit everyone who was at the door, making them into dark silhouettes. In the midst of all the dark shapes was a dark square—the end of the casket in which lay a good friend. And then I made the long walk down the center aisle to the back to greet that dark square and a grieving family. I've made this walk hundreds of times, and it always feels lonely and long. Because we were burying someone who had died at a young age, I remember asking a friend to make eye contact with me when I walked down the aisle so that I would not feel alone.

I'm not writing this reflection for any pity but to point out on behalf of my brother priests that we count on the prayers of the people. We need them. Many studies have shown that most priests suffer from depression and experience serious doubts in themselves, in the Church, and even in the Lord on a regular basis. Most clergy do not exercise regularly. Most struggle to balance work and family. And most suffer from feelings of loneliness.

Again, speaking on behalf of priests, please pray for us, and please encourage us. Many times we feel like we're selling a product, salvation, that no one wants to buy. People overlook mistakes that others make, but when a priest makes the same mistake, it becomes a big deal. Think about cursing for a minute. Almost everyone curses, and no one notices. But if the priest curses, people will remember. Many people drink too much on occasion, and no one remembers. If a priest does that, everyone remembers.

At most Divine Liturgies, the hymn at the beginning of this reflection is sung only by the choir. How glorious it would be for a priest if everyone sang it! And then pray for us, encourage us, and ask those who say bad things about us to please stop.

I wouldn't trade my priesthood for anything. It is, as I said, one of God's greatest blessings in my life. It is also my life's greatest struggle. And many times, the people I am serving determine the difference between blessing and struggle. When I say "Peace be with all," I'm hoping you'll respond with "And with your spirit," because I want that peace also. When I ask for forgiveness before I receive Holy Communion, I'm hoping you are looking up and offering it because I need forgiveness too. And when I pray at the Great Entrance for the Lord our God to remember all of you in His Kingdom, I really mean that. I hope that by His grace and mercy we will all find our way there. I pray that my ministry and my writings, however lacking they may be at times, will help you in your journey to His Kingdom.

Through the prayers of our holy fathers, Lord Jesus Christ, our God, have mercy on us and save us. Amen.

> God also said to Moses, "Say this to the people of Israel, 'The Lord, the God of your fathers, the God of Abraham, the God of Isaac, and the God of Jacob, has sent me to you': this is my Name for ever, and thus I am to be remembered throughout all generations."
>
> —Exodus 3:15

We live in a world that is constantly changing. Technology is evolving so fast that if you own something that is three months old, a new and improved version is available, and what you have is already considered obsolete. Jobs are eliminated, and new jobs are created. The economy booms and busts. Governments rise and fall. Old worlds are explored, and new worlds are discovered. Think about all the changes that have happened in the world in the last decade, the last century, the last millennium. It's mind-boggling. People are alive today who remember a world without computers.

The Divine Liturgy that we use today was set in its current form by the end of the fourth century. The last line of the service was "Through the prayers of our holy fathers," as it is now.[55] This line affirms that this service is timeless, just as God is timeless. There is continuity to what we believe and how we practice what we believe.

---

55 One liturgical note here: during the paschal season, the service does not end with the words "Through the prayers of our Holy Fathers." Instead, it ends with the paschal hymn "Christ is risen from the dead, by death trampling down upon death, and to those in the tombs He has granted life."

The Orthodox Church and the Roman Catholic Church shared a common history until the year 1054, when the Roman pope and the archbishop of Constantinople excommunicated each other in what historically is referred to as the "Great Schism." The Protestant Reformation began in 1517, based on the "protest" of Martin Luther concerning abuses in the Catholic Church. And since then, tens of thousands of Christian denominations have come into existence based on "protest." Since the Reformation, when a group of people becomes unhappy in their denomination, they simply create another church.

To be sure, the Orthodox Church doesn't appeal to everyone. There are people who leave the Church, just as there are people who join it. However, the beautiful thing about the Church is that it doesn't change often. That doesn't mean that it never changes, only that the change is purposeful. There is continuity to our practice of the Faith. And this not only true from age to age but also from parish to parish.

The Divine Liturgy is celebrated in virtually the same way across the entire world. In Africa, Orthodox Christians incorporate liturgical dance, and in America, we sometimes use four-part harmonies. But wherever the Divine Liturgy is celebrated, it is celebrated by a priest or bishop, bread and wine are consecrated into the Body and Blood of Christ, and there is a Great Entrance, a reciting of the Creed, and offering of Holy Communion. The same lectionary of Scripture is read in every church the world over. As a priest, I can participate in the Divine Liturgy in any church, with any priest, and feel comfortable. I once attended a Divine Liturgy in Mexico that was conducted entirely in Spanish. While I could not understand the words, the actions were all the same. I didn't hear the priest say "Peace be with all," but when he turned around and offered a blessing from the altar, I knew that he was offering peace to me and everyone else.

This is continuity.

So, when we end the Divine Liturgy each Sunday and return to our daily routines, we are reminded that we are part of something that is bigger than ourselves. We are part of something that is bigger than our parish. We are part of something that is bigger than our times. In celebrating the Divine Liturgy, we are connected to every Orthodox Christian, in every Orthodox Church, in every century from the time of Pentecost onward.

Our purpose in life is also not just temporary, restricted to the year in which we live, the town in which we live, or the job we hold. Our unchanging purpose is to glorify God so that when our time on earth is over, we enter into everlasting life, and we go to live with Christ on a permanent and eternal basis.

The end of the Divine Liturgy reminds us that we are part of a continuum that began with the creation of the world and continues through its redemption through the saving work of Jesus Christ. The spreading of the Christian Faith through two thousand years since Christ walked the earth will also continue until His Second Coming. However, we don't need to wait for the Second Coming to experience the heavenly Kingdom. It is present "now and forever" in the celebration of the Divine Liturgy. And because we honor the saints and all the people who have been part of the Church in every service, we are connected to Christ, the saints, and to our loved ones who have departed until the day we see them again.

In a world where things are constantly changing, it is a comfort to know that Christ does not change, and our encounter with Him in the Divine Liturgy and the Holy Eucharist does not change either. The Divine Liturgy provides a constant source of joy, comfort, and purpose.

Afterword

Every line of the Divine Liturgy that is offered by the celebrant requires a response from the people. The first line of the Divine Liturgy is an invitation into the Kingdom with the response "Amen." In between the first line and the last line are many responses of "Lord, have mercy" and "Grant this, O Lord" to the petitions as well as to many hymns of praise and supplication. As the service comes to an end, the final statement by the people is "Amen," or "Let it be so": Let the prayers we have offered in this service be answered in God's way, in God's time. Let this miracle of the Divine Liturgy, which we have offered, indeed guide us through our lives into everlasting life.

As I mentioned in the opening reflection, the Divine Liturgy is the ultimate parable. To the untrained eye or the hardened soul, it is just a play starring a priest, a choir, chanters, and altar servers. But to the one with a soft heart and faithful soul, the Divine Liturgy is the Kingdom of heaven made present in the here and now.

I am neither a scholar nor a theologian. I do not have an advanced degree in liturgics. I'm just a simple parish priest who loves to celebrate the Divine Liturgy, and I wrote these reflections to give readers something to think about when attending this service.

Before the Liturgy begins, when the priest prepares the Holy Gifts at the service of the Proskomide, the first prayer he offers is a hymn from the feast of the Nativity. My last thought on the Divine Liturgy also comes from the Feast of the Nativity. In Luke 2:20 we read, "And the shepherds returned, glorifying and praising God for all they had heard and seen, as it had been told them." After seeing Christ with their own eyes and becoming the first human beings to behold our Savior, the shepherds resumed lives that were humdrum at best. Their encounter with Christ hadn't changed their social status. It hadn't changed their state of poverty or their lack of popularity. It changed *them*. It changed their hearts.

And this is what the Divine Liturgy can do for us. After we leave the service, we will return to the same jobs, the same families, the same challenges, and the same stresses. The Divine Liturgy doesn't change any of these things. But it changes *us*. When we attend often, when we are active in worship, and when we apply the words we pray to our everyday lives, we can change. The Liturgy can change you. It can change me.

I'm reminded of the story in Luke 17:11–19. Jesus encountered ten lepers who asked to be healed. He told them to go and show themselves to the priests. He didn't heal them in one quick moment. But they trusted in His words enough to make their way to the priests, and on their way they realized they had been healed. The Divine Liturgy, I believe, works in the same way over the course of our lives. We are not perfected in faith in one quick moment. We are not perfected at one Divine Liturgy. But over the course of our lives, the Divine Liturgy can, if celebrated properly before, during, and after the service, perfect us in faith. It is a wonderful aid on the journey to salvation.

As we exit the church, we come forward to receive a blessing from the priest as well as a piece of antidoron. (In the Slavic tradition, the faithful instead venerate a blessing cross, held by the priest.) The antidoron, or blessed bread, traditionally was given to those who did not partake of the Holy Gifts—hence the word *anti* ("instead of") *doron* ("the Gifts"). Receiving the blessed bread is also a sign of sharing fellowship by breaking bread together.

I remember as a child being taught to receive the antidoron and then walk to the door of the church. Right before exiting we were to turn around, face the altar one more time, and make the sign of the cross. We make the sign of the cross as we face the altar in honor of the Holy Communion, Christ Himself, that resides in the tabernacle on the back of the altar. This final gesture reminds us to remember what Christ did for us, what He does, and what He will do. It also reminds me of the words exchanged by the clergy when they offer the kiss of peace: "Christ is in our midst. He was, He is, and He ever shall be." As we exit the church and reenter the world, we do so with joy and with renewed purpose, remembering that Christ is with us always, "to the close of the age" (Matt. 28:20).

Jesus says in Matthew 5:14–16,

> You are the light of the world. A city set on a hill cannot be hid. Nor do men light a lamp and put it under a bushel, but on a stand, and it gives light to all in the house. Let your light so shine before men, that they may see your good works and give glory to your Father who is in heaven.

The Divine Liturgy makes our light burn brighter. If our lights already are burning strongly, they burn even brighter. And if our lights are going out, the Divine Liturgy rekindles them. The Divine Liturgy enables us to take our light back out into the world, brighter and brighter each time, so that we can share the light of Christ through our words and our actions—that through His grace, others can come to know Him through us.

Speaking personally, my life feels more in balance when I go to church on Sunday, and on the rare occasion that I don't, I find that I am truly missing something. I don't choose to miss the Divine Liturgy because of any sense of superstition or obligation. Rather, I don't like to miss out on the joy of the service. As my parish becomes larger and my responsibilities become greater, I feel the temptation to eliminate a few of the weekday Liturgies. However, I find that I am adding more of them. I realize how much *I* want and need to be at the Divine Liturgy.

In the early Church, the Divine Liturgy was celebrated on an almost daily basis. In modern times, it is celebrated each Sunday and on prescribed feast days. In a given year, I have the privilege of celebrating the Liturgy close to one hundred times—sometimes more. I try to celebrate each as if it were my first and my last, as a hierarch of the church once encouraged me.

I encourage you to attend the Divine Liturgy as often as possible, but not merely to attend, to worship, to work, to pray, to sing, to learn, and to commune. It is my fervent hope that each of you will allow yourselves to be moved by Christ in this divine service. And it is my hope that you will discover the joy and ecstasy of the Liturgy by reflecting more carefully on its timeless words. If nothing else, I hope this study on the Divine Liturgy has given you the opportunity to pause and to think more deeply about what we hear in the services and to realize that the Liturgy is not something to be taken lightly, or attended casually or infrequently. It is of infinite value. It is, in fact, the most precious thing we have in this life. For where can we, sinful human beings, look upon, touch, and become one with Christ Himself? In only two places: in heaven and in God's heavenly Kingdom brought to earth, the Divine Liturgy.

> Our God, the God who saves, You teach us justly to thank You for the good things which You have done and still do for us. You are our God who has accepted these Gifts. Cleanse us from every defilement of flesh and spirit, and teach us how to live in holiness by Your fear, so that receiving the portion of Your holy Gifts with a clear conscience we may be united with the holy Body and Blood of Your Christ.

Having received them worthily, may we have Christ dwelling in our hearts, and may we become the temple of Your Holy Spirit. Yes, our God, let none of us be guilty before these, Your awesome and heavenly Mysteries, nor be infirm in body and soul by partaking of them unworthily. But enable us, even up to our last breath, to receive a portion of Your holy Gifts worthily, as provision for eternal life and as an acceptable defense at the awesome judgment seat of Your Christ. So that we also, together with all the saints who through the ages have pleased You, may become partakers of Your eternal good things, which You, Lord, have prepared for those who love You. (From the *Divine Liturgy of St. Basil the Great*)

May the Holy Trinity protect all of you. (The final blessing of the Divine Liturgy.)

May the blessing and mercy of the Lord be with you. (The blessing at Antidoron.)

Thanks be to God for his inexpressible Gift! (2 Cor. 9:15)

To Him belong glory and dominion
for ever and ever. Amen.

—1 Peter 4:11

Bibliography

The Divine Liturgy. Translated by Holy Cross Seminary. Brookline, Massachusetts: Holy Cross Seminary Press, 1985.

The Divine Liturgy of Our Father among the Saints Basil the Great. Translated by Holy Cross Seminary. Brookline, Massachusetts: Holy Cross Seminary Press, 1988.

Greek Orthodox Holy Week and Easter Services. Translated by Fr. George Papadeas. South Daytona, Florida: Patmos Press, 1996.

The Liturgy of St. John Chrysostom. Translation approved by the Ecumenical Patriarchate. Brookline, Massachusetts: Holy Cross Orthodox Press, 2015.

The Order of the Divine and Holy Liturgy. Translated by Holy Cross Seminary. Brookline, Massachusetts: Holy Cross Orthodox Press, 1987.

The Services of Holy Week and Easter. Translated by Fr. Nomikos Michael Vaporis. Brookline, Massachusetts: Holy Cross Orthodox Press, 1993.

We hope you have enjoyed and benefited from this book. Your financial support makes it possible to continue our nonprofit ministry both in print and online. Because the proceeds from our book sales only partially cover the costs of operating **Ancient Faith Publishing** and **Ancient Faith Radio**, we greatly appreciate the generosity of our readers and listeners. Donations are tax deductible and can be made at **www.ancientfaith.com.**

To view our other publications,
please visit our wesite:
store.ancientfaith.com

Bringing you Orthodox Christian music, readings, prayers, teaching, and podcasts 24 hours a day since 2004 at
www.ancientfaith.com

www.ingramcontent.com/pod-product-compliance
Lightning Source LLC
Chambersburg PA
CBHW021701120626
46545CB00004B/1347

* 9 7 8 1 9 5 5 8 9 0 6 8 7 *